SQUASH
How to Play, How to Win

Laura Torbet
with Doug McLaggan

SQUASH
How to Play, How to Win

Interviews with: Victor Niederhoffer, Sharif Khan, Gretchen Spruance, Peter Briggs, Diehl Mateer, John Reese, Jay Nelson, Barbara Maltby, Charles Ufford, Gordon Anderson, Juan de Villafranca, Roland Oddy, Geoff Hunt, Mike Pierce, and Peter Bostwick.

Photography by Carl Roodman

Dolphin Books
Doubleday & Company, Inc.
Garden City, New York
1978

LINE DRAWINGS BY JO PRIBULA

Library of Congress Cataloging in Publication Data

Torbet, Laura.
Squash: How to play, how to win.

Bibliography: p. 205
1. Squash racquets (Game). I. McLaggan, Doug,
joint author. II. Title.
GV1004.T67   796.34'3
ISBN: 0-385-12556-9
Library of Congress Catalog Card Number 77–76284

Contents

Acknowledgments

I started out to write this book for a couple of very simple reasons. I am a writer, I wanted to write a sports book, and I was learning to play squash. As I was learning, I soon found that the game is much more complex than other simpler, more "linear" sports. Many more elements are involved than the predictable factors—how to execute the strokes, what shots are possible, how to score, etc. It became early apparent that squash is not only intricate in its physical demands, but also that its nature is to a great degree mental and psychological—that is, more intangible and harder to pin down than, say, skiing, or even golf. It became clear that to learn to play was one thing; to learn to win, another.

The people with the answers, then, were those who played to win—the top competitors and their teachers. It was to them I turned for information, and they were—every last one—helpful, gracious, and informative. And in the end, it was these people who provided the truly valuable and otherwise unavailable information in this book: the secret documents. I became the organizer, analyzer, interpreter—I assembled this book from their knowledge.

Who are these people? Many top players whom I interviewed directly and whom you will find liberally quoted in this book. Many others whom *they* quoted to me (people like George Cummings, Jack Barnaby, and Al Malloy). Many people whose advice I gathered from books and articles.

The Bancroft Sporting Goods Company helped me with photos that I could not get otherwise. The Century Company provided equipment to photograph.

Many other people helped in the production of this book. Leon Van Bellingham offered unlimited use of the facilities of the Manhattan

Squash Club. Tom Jones posed patiently for all the step-by-step pictures in the instructions section. Bob Lehman supplied some hard-to-locate photos and information. I had help from the associations and their leaders—Darwin Kingsley of the USSRA and George Morfitt of the Canadian association. Harry Saint, patron saint of public clubs in New York, offered his facilities to photograph several tournaments. I'm indebted to Roland Oddy for his advice and contacts, to Carl Roodman for his work on all the photography, to Jo Pribula for illustrations, and to Paul L. Hecht for typing at all hours from my chicken scrawl.

Finally, there is the teacher in this book— the person who is really showing you how to play and win this game. This is Doug McLaggan, the highly respected pro at New York's Racquet and Tennis Club. It is his method and his expertise that form the backbone of this book.

LAURA TORBET

N.B. I feel that an explanation is necessary for my use of the word "he" throughout the book in describing tactics, strategy, etc., especially since I hope that the book will have wide readership among the growing numbers of women players. But the English language is difficult on this point, and every other alternative is very unwieldy.

SQUASH
How to Play, How to Win

Introduction

This is a book about playing and winning at squash, a game that until recently was restricted in North America to the bowels of private men's clubs and colleges.

But times have changed. The game has gone both public and coed, and new players are taking to the game at a quite incredible rate. It's easy to understand why, for the game has much to recommend it to our fitness-conscious, sports-loving, and increasingly urbanized society.

Devotees are eloquent on its benefits and attributes: It's an enjoyable way to keep fit, it's exciting, it's always possible to improve, it's easy to learn, it keeps your weight down, it's a great tension releaser, it's fun for duffers and challenging for sportsmen, it's the best half-hour workout there is, it's good for character, it's economical, it's a year-round sport, etc.

Whatever your reasons for playing and to whatever level you aspire to play the game, there is something in this book for you. The intent is to give the beginner an understanding of and a feel for the game, and a foundation of sound strokes and shots, from which the player can move ahead into instruction and understanding of the sport at its higher, more complex and demanding levels.

This book is full of advice and commentary from (and pictures of) some of the top players in the game today. Almost all of them agree that it is very important to take a couple of lessons when you're first learning the game, to be sure that your grip, your strokes, and your basic grasp of the game are correct. But, with the game mushrooming as it is, good squash instruction is scarce, and new courts and players have put good teaching pros at a premium. So *they* will be your teachers. If you cannot get lessons (and even *with* lessons), we hope this book will go a long way to helping you learn to play the game better, to enhance your enjoyment of this exciting sport, and to make you a winner!

Manhattan Squash Club

About This Book

Squash is a multifaceted game. Once the beginner learns the rules and scoring of the game, the proper way to execute the basic strokes—forehand, backhand, volley, and serve—and a knowledge of possible shots, many other factors creep in. These more elusive qualities, which are the very heart of the game—mobility, deception, anticipation, strategy, gamesmanship, psychology, attitude, etc.—cannot be taught in a particular order, or in a linear "step by step" fashion. Our intent is to discuss these aspects of the game as we go, "building" them onto the total game in an integrated manner.

Constant analysis and refinement of the many components of the game are essential to playing the game at its higher levels, and the top players interviewed provide information and insights that would take years of experience to discover.

As you read the book you will find, at the end of each section or topic, quotes from these top players on the subject under discussion, giving different points of view (and oh, how they differ) and advice. You will also find pictures, some of them step-by-step demonstrations, some of them action shots illustrating the subject under discussion. The pictures and quotes are as important as the main text. Almost everyone I interviewed stressed the importance to them, during their early squash days, of learning by talking to, and watching, the experts at their game.

Well, many of the experts are here for you to listen to and to see. Just read on. . . .

1

•

Squash Today

The most commonly proffered story about the origins of squash is that it developed as an offshoot of "racquets," a game invented by the debtors of Fleet Street prison and played in their courtyard; and that at the Harrow School in England in the midnineteenth century, where there was but one racquets court in great demand (some things never change), the students developed a softer ball that they could use for practice in off-court areas and that literally made a squashy sound when it hit the walls.

Whether or not the story is true (and it hardly matters), it is certainly true that, like all sports, the idiosyncrasies of its rules, equipment, and court are a result of its circumstances of origin—the dimensions of the area, the equipment available, and the ingenuity of its founders. And it is also true that when the sport came to these shores in the late nine-

teenth century, we Americans, always wanting to put our own mark on things and to build a better mousetrap, managed to change the court size, the rules, and the equipment just enough so that today we have a substantially different game from that played everywhere outside North America—our "hard ball" game and the English, or international, "soft ball" game. (The term "international game" is increasingly used to refer to a possible compromise game currently under discussion, which would combine the hard-ball and soft-ball games so that competition would be truly international. So for reason of clarity we will refer to the soft-ball game as the English game.)

In this book we'll be dealing with the hard-ball game; a chapter on the English game will be found on page 153.

So what's the story on squash in North

America today? Well, it ain't what it used to be, for one thing. Long a passionate and privileged pursuit of men only at private clubs and schools, it's now played by men and women, young and old, at a burgeoning number of public courts and clubs. The United States Squash Racquets Association estimates that more than half a million Americans now play —double the number playing ten years ago— and the growth continues. There is now a slick magazine exclusively devoted to squash. Top players are turning professional to fill the instruction gap at the new clubs and to compete for the increasingly large prize money at the increasing number of tournaments. Colleges and universities now build squash courts as a matter of course, and well over a hundred colleges have *women's* teams registered with the national association. The surge of women to the game has done a great deal to popularize the sport.

Squash is an absorbing and thrilling game to watch, but the speed of the game and limited gallery areas have so far kept the game from a wide audience. However, things are happening. Glass backwall courts, and a portable, collapsible, all-glass court are already realities. Many new facilities are being built with TV in mind and with videotape installations. If you stop at the bar of the Uptown Squash Club in New York, you can see great closed-circuit TV replays of matches shot with cameras in the overhead gallery, behind the glass wall, and from the vantage point of the Plexiglas panel under the telltale. There's even talk of it becoming an Olympic sport, the impetus being the introduction of squash courts in the Soviet Union, where the next games will be held.

Ideally suited to fast-paced modern life, economical of time, space, and money, a game that is fun, sociable, healthy, and challenging, squash seems ideally suited for a prominent place in our sports-loving society.

But as of this writing, the "state of the game" is in flux as never before. Predictions on its future vary widely. Already, problems and controversy abound. The low-key squash world was caught flat-footed by the sudden stampede and is valiantly trying to keep up with and accommodate the hordes of new players—men who never belonged to a private club, and huge numbers of women players—while maintaining the integrity of the game.

The USSRA, the organization which for years has quietly been the governing body of the game—overseeing rules and procedure, eligibility, sanctioning tournaments, equipment, etc.—is likely to be challenged by a completely new association more geared toward the expansion of the game and toward the money involved. The professional organization (the North American Professional Squash Racquets Association, or NAPSRA) and the owners of the new public clubs are increasingly influential. The thrust of the NAPSRA itself is changing fast. Its membership, now predominantly composed of teacher/players, will soon be dominated by players who are turning professional to take advantage of tournament money and endorsements.

●

MIKE PIERCE: The powers that be right now are stunting the growth of the game. The pros are up in arms over the people running the game of squash. I think the old guard is slowly being eased out, but they've retarded the growth—not intentionally. But I think their way of thinking has held the game back the last few years.

●

The growth of the women's game has been astounding, and many feel that their participation has been a major factor in the game's growth. The women's association (the United States Women's Squash Racquets Association, or USWSRA), highly organized and active on national, state, and local levels, boasts an impressive tournament circuit.

Paper telltale? George Plimpton with Wendy
Zuharko. PHOTO: RAIMONDO BOREA.

●

JOHN REESE: One thing that will make squash more interesting is if the women participate more, as we've seen here in New York City and in other parts of the country. Particularly in New York, there's a tremendous ground-spread interest in the women's game. Up until a few years ago, a lot of women did not like the dangerous aspects of the game, the sweaty aspect of the game. Also, where could they play? But now, I think, they understand the game, they are able to go out and play by themselves. I think they feel that it is a sport that they can express themselves in. They have more license to be aggressive, and as a result I think they're finding it to be a popular approach, a very popular event for themselves, far more attractive and appealing to some extent than racquetball, but still, perhaps, not quite as exciting as tennis or paddle tennis. I

think that the women hold as many of the cards to the expansion of the game as do the so-called good players.

VICTOR NIEDERHOFFER: As for the key to squash's longevity, that's the women's game because wherever there's a commercial club there will have to be a lot of women to take up the afternoon and weekend play. It's absolutely essential that the women be encouraged to play on a high plateau. It adds a tremendous amount of excitement to have women involved in the same sport. It provides a certain sense of emotional rapport, an uplifting to both parties. I think almost every club that's done well in one way or another has opened itself to women. Heather McKay is as close to the men's level of play as women can come in almost any sport. Heather can, I'm told, come

Roger Corbett of Bancroft congratulates Heather McKay on her Bancroft Women's Open win.
PHOTO: BANCROFT SPORTING GOODS CO.

within about five or six points of the best male player. That's probably a lot more than any woman could do in tennis or handball or racquetball. It'd probably be interesting to quantify the difference between women and men. So we hope that the women's game is going to grow from its extremely low base rate and allow the male game to stand on the women's shoulders.

SHARIF KHAN: I love watching the women play. It's colorful, and I'm all for that. They should have been playing a long time ago . . . but there was no place to play. Now it's possible.

●

Squash was predominantly an amateur game until recently—albeit with a very active tournament and team circuit. It was a game for collegians and for businessmen. Now that there are numbers of professionals and lots more money tournaments, the question of "open" squash is hotly contested. Some people feel that there should be separation of amateur and professional circuits; others feel that all tournaments should be open. (The winnings of an amateur in an open tournament are donated to a school or association.) The present

feeling is that there will always be a place for the amateur circuit on the high school, college, club, and national team level (as in tennis), and there will always be a few "professional only" tournaments, but that open squash, where both amateurs and professionals who qualify are entitled to play, is the wave of the future.

●

CHARLES UFFORD: People tend to lose sight of the fact that in tennis there is an amateur game; there are a number of ranges of amateur tournaments. So to say, "Let's do away with the rules of eligibility" is misconceived. The rules of eligibility will always have a role. The point is, the major effort of support from the U. S. Association—financial, manpower time, administrative—will eventually go to the open game, as it should. But it has to go in an orderly fashion, in my view, over a period of time, commensurate with a degree of commercial sponsorship that's brought into the game and the number of tournaments that can accommodate open players. There are still going to be tournaments that don't want to convert to open play—and there is no reason they should be obliged to. If a private club wants to hold an invitational tournament, fine; it would be nice if they make it open, but I don't see that they should be obliged to. We're at a difficult transition period now for top players because they now feel, and quite correctly, that there are not enough tournament weekends for a professional to obtain top-flight competitive play; and that's true. But there are several new money tournaments this year that did not exist last year, and I hope that they will continue; and hopefully, there will be more. Pretty soon, there will be a fairly substantial circuit. We're not yet at the point where a professional can sustain himself on the tour as a sole source of livelihood. But it might not be too long before that comes to pass. The playing professionals are anxious to convert what is now the U. S. Amateur Nationals weekend into an open event, as they regard that as signifying the commitment of the National Association to open play. I still think the top tournament, unquestionably, is the North American Open. It draws the top caliber of players, and it is on a restricted basis . . . accepting only the top players. And I think from the point of view of spectators that that is the top tournament. But it doesn't have the same atmosphere as the Nationals does. This business of the team championships, this lends a whole different dimension to the whole weekend. And I think that it's increasingly difficult for the U. S. Association to hold that tournament; there are so many players competing for the team championships—they may have to split it up eventually. It might be nice to retain that. It might be possible to have the singles open and the team still under the so-called national rule—which would be interesting.

PETER BRIGGS: We don't have pros at the level of those guys (like Hunt) in the English game. I only turned pro as a goof. Sharif is a pro—a teaching pro. Hunt does not teach— he's a touring pro. He tours around, he gives exhibitions, plays tournaments, he's sponsored. That's his life; that's always been his life. He's the best at what he does, and that's the true professional. His outlook and approach are truly professional. Niederhoffer turned pro and I did, partly out of egoism, and plus, it's just part of the game . . . something you do. Sharif did it because that's his livelihood.

MIKE PIERCE: I think the game should be opened up. I think it's absurd that there's not more open squash. I think their approach should be the same as tennis: Keep it amateur at the intercollegiate level. If a kid is going to school and wants to drop out and play open squash for money, that's his choice. Sharif Khan has been giving me the hard sell to turn pro . . . because to quote Khan, "You two are the best doubles players. If you make the move, you're going to put pressure on the people that run doubles tournaments to open it

up." My comeback to him at this point is probably a copout: "There's just not enough money in it, and if I turn pro, I can only compete in two or three tournaments and maybe make $1,000–$1,500, and that puts me out of all the other tournaments I would compete in." That's what holds me back, and his comeback is: "If you don't do it, they'll never open up." You have to force their hand.

JOHN REESE: I'm an amateur, I'm president of the New York Association, and I am very much for open squash. But I am not for open squash at the expense of the total extinction of the amateur game. The amateur game has got to continue because obviously we get our wealth of players from college ranks. So there must be at least a satellite amateur effort going on. But I do think that the concept of open squash is valid. It's only through this that the public gets to see the best players.

●

Darwin Kingsley of the USSRA. PHOTO: BANCROFT SPORTING GOODS CO.

With more and more money at stake, the rules of the "gentleman's game" are facing a stiff challenge. They are difficult to define and enforce at best. Many longtime players fear for the future of their sport. Some feel that the rules must be gone over, clarified, and tightened wherever possible. Others stress the importance of teaching and maintaining high standards at the local level. But the test comes in match play, especially where the stakes are high—where a bad call by a referee, or a clever abuse of the rules by a player, could decide the fate of a game. The problem of training large numbers of qualified referees and judges to enforce these rules is a prime concern. Refereeing the game is very difficult and almost requires a playing knowledge of the game in addition to a consummate understanding of the rules and unflagging attention to everything that goes on in a match. In tennis the linesmen call "in" or "out" (and there are still questioned calls); squash calls for far more interpretation. So far, there have been no major problems. There are good player/referees and many older devotees who regularly referee as part of their duty to the game. But the day is coming when thousands of dollars will be riding on one appealed call.

●

CHARLES UFFORD: The greatest need we have now in the U. S. Association is to develop a cadre of referees who are experienced and who are granted recognition for their ability in the game; because it's going to take someone who has the respect of the players to be able to stand up there in 13- or 14-all in the fifth game to call that play, to call that let point. Yet, if you haven't got a group of people who will have sufficient respect from the players to do that, pressures will be tremendous; people will take advantage of the rules . . . and the game will disintegrate into a shambles.

MIKE PIERCE: The game needs better referees. The referees doing big matches these days are

Squash rituals: the wiping of the towel.

not always very qualified; they're amateurs. Some of the referees are older and have been around years and years. I don't think they can see as well, I don't think they know the players as well, and I don't think they understand the rules the way they're interpreted nowadays. And, of course, the concentration required to referee a squash match is tremendous. At top competitions, I think we should have the best referees available. Whether we do or not, I don't know. Hopefully we will because you could wind up out there with a problem, especially playing for a lot of money.

JAY NELSON: The refereeing in tennis is fairly cut and dry; in squash, it's much more difficult. There are some good ones; I think players make the best referees. In squash there's a lot more balls you call up or down, and there's the whole let problem. In general, I feel much better with players doing it; in fact, with a good player, there's almost no flak at all. And there are other guys who you just get scared to death with. It's just a flip of a coin, you know. Both players realize that on a given call and you're as likely to get the right one as the wrong one.

PETER BOSTWICK: I think there'll be more and more good referees. What happens now is that a lot of the players help out in the tournaments and do the refereeing, and most of the players seem to be pretty good sports on the courts, so they seem to be pretty fair when they're refereeing. But I'm sure as time goes on, like in tennis, there will be more competent referees who can really control particular situations in tough matches.

●

Squash rituals: the wiping of the wall.

Still other rule changes are under debate, some which liven or tighten up the game, some of which clarify fuzzy rules. For example:

At this time it is technically permissible to hit one's service off a bounced ball. A new ruling would prohibit this. There is also talk of cutting down to one serve. This would limit the advantage of the sheer power player who blasts his first serve in, knowing that if it goes out of bounds, he still has the safety of the lob on his second service. Another new rule would move the five-minute rest period from between the third and fourth games of a match to between the fourth and fifth games. This would move the rest to where it's really needed. Another difficult and often unfair situation comes up when a player calls his serve a fault after the point has been played out and lost. Revised rules would make it mandatory to ask for that fault immediately or forfeit the fault call.

●

VICTOR NIEDERHOFFER: Now as far as the rules on sportsmanship, I think the rules are fine, they've been working out over thirty or forty years, and I trust the evolution. They've come pretty close to optimum. No matter what the rules are, there's always going to be the opportunity for good and bad sportsmanship.

SHARIF KHAN: The game is getting tougher and rougher. With more money coming in, more incentive, more young guys are playing. The concept of the game as a gentleman's sport . . . that's changing. People are becoming more competitive, more money is coming in. They have to change the rules—that is, define the rules: what a let point is, whether you turn on the ball, etc. They're having troubles with the rules because everybody is getting more competitive; it means much more. Before, there was no need for it; now there is. It's good to see the way the game is taking off, the big boom in the game. More people have access to the game now because of all the public centers going up. Before, squash was a very, very private game, and now commercial centers are going up in Canada and in the States. It's allowing a lot more people to play.

JOHN REESE: This game, because of its origins, has always been considered somewhat of a "gentleman's game." It has a rather "WASP" background to it. Most of the prep schools used to play the game and the Ivy League schools and in the private-club environs of, let's say, New York City, Boston, and Philadelphia. When you have two players playing as close as they are to each other in a match there has to be an awareness of the proximity of that player as well as a judgment or willingness on the part of an opponent not to overstep his bounds because it is very easy—in fact, painfully easy—to strike someone with your racquet. Therefore, there must be mutual respect between yourself and your opponent. This has always been the case; rules as a result have been very gray—they are not black and white as to what you can do. There's always that sort of gentleman's clause in the rules that says you just don't go over and clobber your opponent on the head to win the match. What I'm afraid could happen is, as money comes into the sport, as open squash becomes more and more popular, you're going to get an individual who comes in, who's a real athlete, who sees that when ten thousand dollars is on the line, he's going to take it into his own hands to make sure that he wins that money. I think that to offset this you're going to have to develop far stricter rules, far more clear-cut rules, stronger refereeing to maintain or to compensate for the decline in the gentleman's clause, as I call it. There isn't a ball hit in the game that you couldn't call a let on. It's very important, or this game will just not get off the ground.

There are very intelligent people who play the game who use the let to their advantage. The let call must be clarified; the let-point call that is much more strident an argument must be clarified. The events leading up to a let-point call and where that call is justified must be clarified. Stronger definitions are needed, and disciplinary actions against players with default penalties for reckless action on the court. It comes down to an objectivity on the part of the players in recognizing that they're competing against another human being and that they must have respect for that individual.

BARBARA MALTBY: As the game grows and as you put more money into it, it's going to be even more difficult to referee because right now calling lets is all right, but it's not defined enough that someone couldn't take advantage of it if they really wanted to. The question becomes exactly how much or how little you can move and still have the other person not call a let, instead of getting out of the way so they can hit the ball. That's fairly important now, because you can get quite an advantage if you can make the other person hit a worse shot than they could have hit, by moving a little bit slowly, so they just can't get it as fast as they might. I think they're going to have to define a lot of things.

The first thing they can do is stop players from crossing in front of the ball—you know, when you aim down the wall and it comes back in the middle and you cross in front of it, which in essence prevents the other person from volleying the ball. I think the first thing you have to do is make that into an automatic let point—crossing in front of the ball. In the English game, if you're between your opponent and the front wall, it's their point. They should also get rid of "coming around." I've seen a lot of people just terrify their opponent. The ball will be coming down the wall and it'll come out just a little bit and they'll come around. There are some times when you have no choice, but I think that could be an automatic let. I think they could write it in the rules so you can get absolutely no advantage by coming around, by making it an automatic let. That will get rid of some of the problems of let. It's not that hard to tighten the rules;

all you have to do is give the opponent the point. Once you give the opponent the point, the person has got to give you more room because he'll lose the match right there.

GORDON ANDERSON: The enforcement of the "sportsmanship clause" is really, really bad. There are two systems again. The English system is about five to ten years ahead of our system. They have referee classes and degree, etc., so that I might be here and be paid by the referee's association or by Colgate to be a referee. Right now it's "Joe, can you referee this match?" and he's been having a beer, and then there's an argument. The referee system is poor here. It is good overseas. They're much more direct in their calls—there's no talking back. It's still very bush league here, as far as I'm concerned.

There are referee rules, but none of us have read them in the past ten years. That's what I'm saying—nobody forces you to read them. I'm a referee, but the reason I'm a referee is I know the rules from being a player. So I'm the one who's got good eyes, and I say up or down. But I haven't sat down in a class and gone over all the specific rules, and there are a few that I am sure we would query if the problem came up. Let's say that the ball bounced and then bounced out of the court if it were really hot; is it a let, or is it a point for the other guy? Now, the guy who is refereeing, he might just not know, and that should be explained to anybody who's refereeing in this tournament, especially when there's fifteen thousand dollars at stake.

The other problem is roughness on the court. It's not like tennis, where there's a net between the players. You can hate the other player and call him names. But when you play squash it's man against man. There are a couple of players in this tournament that you definitely have to watch out for because they will purposely swing by your head, and if you're the least bit nervous and haven't grown up to be a rough-guy sort, that will lose you a couple of points. And when five thousand dollars is on the line, look out. I've tried to referee matches where the referee is nervous and the two players are about to walk out, and there's about to be a fight, and that's because there is no control by the referee. You've got to teach that guy—an offensive player—and boot him out. It needs to be cleared up because the only thing that's improved in the past five years in squash is the number of courts and the number of players. But the officiating part has never been improved. They're very good, but they're all volunteers. A fellow like Darwin Kingsley, for example, for years has been a volunteer. And now, this year, he's being paid a nominal fee to be USSRA secretary, for the first time. One guy trying to run a whole country's worth of squash. It's still a little catchy.

●

After all is said, the most important consideration for the future is what kind of squash we'll be playing here in North America. We have managed to differentiate our game from that played everywhere else in the world just enough to make it difficult for players of either game to adapt to the other. They are like mutually semi-intelligible dialects of the same language. Soft-ball players must adapt to the fast pace and different strokes of our ball game, while our champions are not trained to the level of physical fitness and endurance demanded by the English game. Yet more and more soft-ball players are lured here by the big prize money, and our professionals are attracted by the larger circuit and money of the soft-ball game.

Currently there is much talk about a compromise game—a game played with a ball somewhere in speed between the English and American ball, and most likely with American scoring. (In the English game only the server can win the point; it makes for long games.) A compromise game would serve two purposes. It would have a "blending" influence on the skills of players of both games and permit a

Pedro Baccalao takes a shot off the backwall as opponents Meg and Rich Rowe (center) and partner Marion Clement look on. PHOTO: RAIMONDO BOREA

truly international circuit. And it would solve the long-standing problem of televising squash matches and thus of reaching a large audience. The slower ball would be easier to capture on film or tape, and the more predictable time factor resulting from our scoring system would better meet TV scheduling needs.

The compromise game is by no means a certainty and will probably be argued for some time to come. One major problem is the difference in court size and configuration (the English court is 2½ feet wider), although the game would conceivably be acceptable on both courts. Time will tell.

The most bounced-around question of all,

and one of the most important in determining the nature of the hard-ball game, is the ball itself: Which ball shall be the "official" ball for the North American game? As the ball changes, so does the game.

Some feel we should stick to "our game," a game that requires skill and reflexes but doesn't require the physical conditioning and training regimen of a prize fighter—that is, we should stick to our hard, fast ball.

But the tide is already turning. Some players feel that a softer ball will in itself make our game more compatible and competitive with the English game. Others note the greater ease of learning to play with a livelier ball—one

SQUASH HOW TO PLAY, HOW TO WIN

way to combat the increasing popularity of racquetball (which some feel is poor reason for changing, and diminishes the unique quality of the game). We've just come through a period where the West blue dot ball was in favor, with many players still lamenting the passing of the hard old Cragin ball. Just as this book goes to press comes word that the West 70+ dot ball (a likely "compromise" ball) has been approved, and will be the sanctioned ball for most upcoming tournament play.

●

SHARIF KHAN: It's very difficult to say what kind of changes are going to take place, what ball we'll be using. I think that the market will dictate. It's not going to come from officials; it is going to be dictated at the club level . . . what people like, what makes for a social game where you'll be able to get a workout. It's not going to be just someone issuing a decree that this ball is it.

VICTOR NIEDERHOFFER: There are about eight or nine entrepreneurs who've produced commercial clubs over the past two or three years. If these entrepreneurs make a good profit in the game—a good, fast profit—we could see a fast boom in the game. If they don't make a profit, then we'll see the death of squash in twenty-five years.

CHARLES UFFORD: It's very close to the point now where you could have a league of touring professionals. That's how tennis started out, with a couple of professionals touring. I think you could probably do it now except that you've got to increase the seating capacities. And for that you need collapsible courts in addition to a glass-back court.

There are still some problems in developing the TV technology to the high resolution needed for picking up the ball on the screen. But once you get television coverage, the game will take off. They recently made a film at Cal-

gary; you ought to look at it. As I understand it, they put one of the cameras under the tell-tale at the front of the court, looking back. This permits you to show one of the players dashing to the front wall to return the drop shot. . . . I mean, there it is . . . right in your face. The reactions, they're so immediate and so intense—so much of this natural intensity will come across to the TV camera . . . to the audience. . . .

Many people are concerned about the future of the game. As commercial sponsorship comes in and the game expands to people from all different sorts of backgrounds, pressures will develop on young players coming along to earn that prize money. Unless we people involved in the administration of the game are very careful, the game, as we know it, will just disintegrate and disappear, because if once you get to the point where any kind of physical contact, unintentional or of an unnecessary character, is condoned as a part of the game, then the game ceases to be the game as we know it—body checking, for example. Once

Victor and Gail Niederhoffer's daughter Galt gets the feel of the court. PHOTO: RAIMONDO BOREA.

that happens, the game is out, and I and a great many people who enjoy and relish the game will just walk away from it.

JOHN REESE: The future of the sport is unlimited provided it catches on in the next two or three years. And for it to catch on in the next two or three years I also think that you're going to have to shore up this problem of the rules. But the game is very exciting. It has all the characteristics that most people like: it's very quick, it's a great deal of exercise within a very short period of time, and it's very competitive. Squash is a great spectator sport, but not many get to see it. Because there are no facilities now capable of housing a lot of people and because of the speed of the ball, it has not been easily televised. Therefore, our champions are not household words, are not apt to be. There sort of has to be a grass-roots revolution or evolution to really create an expansion of the game. But I think it could happen.

The "compromise ball," which is more similar to the international ball and of a softer nature than the U.S. ball, is one route to take in popularizing the game. It is not as desirable for businessmen like myself because it will call for more stamina, for far more conditioning than stroking ability. But it is a way of bridging the gap. And I think the more international the game goes, I think yes, that has an effect on the popularity of it.

I doubt if it will ever have the same mystique and same glamor as tennis. Once again, it is an indoor sport. And there are very few indoor sports that have great appeal all-year round as tennis does. You should know that in England and Australia, squash is considered one of the great sports, one of the three or four leading sports, and their champions are revered and honored.

GORDON ANDERSON: The game is expanding now. Entrepreneurs like Harry Saint in New York, who built his clubs, had tournaments. He was very successful, he didn't need the association's help because he was making money

and it was his club. That's where the power is. That's who's going to take over. All you have to do is look and see what Australia has done . . . because they have thousands of courts in Sydney. Now they have a court owners' association, and that's the strongest association over there. They're the ones who run the tournaments; they're very strict . . . he's being paid, or you're not going to play. A lot of players here are members of the North American Professional Association, and many of them don't pay their fees. It's bush-league stuff.

There's going to be, from what I can see, a split in games. You're going to have the American game, in the United States mainly and Mexico; Canada is starting to turn quite quickly to the English-size court and the English ball. Racquetball, for example, is taking off as fast if not faster than squash in the States. The reason is that a beginner can come off the streets and play it and enjoy it. They don't care whether they're going to be a world champion or not. What the Americans are doing now is working on a lighter, fast ball, a lighter *American* ball, because you need the speed. The speed makes the American game. I think the game is going to grow considerably in the States; there's going to be more money; more money, and more public courts. As yet, there isn't any squash circuit as such. There is for a person like Geoff Hunt; there's maybe one person in North America who doesn't work except for professional teaching tournaments: That would be Sharif. And that's because he's winning and there is enough money as a winner, but he's the only guy who can make a living. One or two thousand dollars every couple of weeks is not enough, and that's *top* prize money. But I think it will come. If someone wanted to get together a circuit to start out, four to eight professionals could tour for about six months and make themselves some good money playing a round-robin type, but it would still be a small number. You couldn't do any bigger than that. As it is now, even at the best tournament, look how many people are going to be in the gallery. One hundred fifty? Two hundred? *Sports Illustrated* isn't going to break the doors down for two hundred people at the University of Pennsylvania. Even though it's a great game, they're not going to come.

They're working on a court with three glass sides so that the gallery can be much larger. That'll be beautiful. But people are not going to invest thousands and hundreds of thousands of dollars in it unless they have a reason. It's sort of a back-to-back argument that *Sports Illustrated* and TV are not going to come in until the sponsorship is up. And Colgate is not going to build a glass court for a hundred thousand dollars unless the TV is there. They would rather go with PGA golf . . . so time is going.

PETER BOSTWICK: There seems to be quite a bit of money coming into the game, not a great deal of money, but there is some money in it for the pro now. And these new squash centers. It looks to me as though the game has a good future. One of the unfortunate things is that it's awfully hard for a lot of people to see it. So it gets less exposure than most sports. A couple of my friends, like Frank Satterthwaite and Peter Briggs, have turned pro, and these are guys who have good jobs . . . they obviously must think there is a future in the game. And the more people who turn pro, the better off the game is going to be, because as the competition gets better, the money will improve.

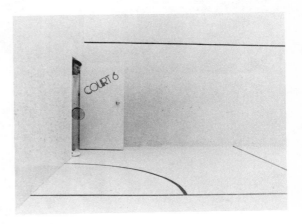

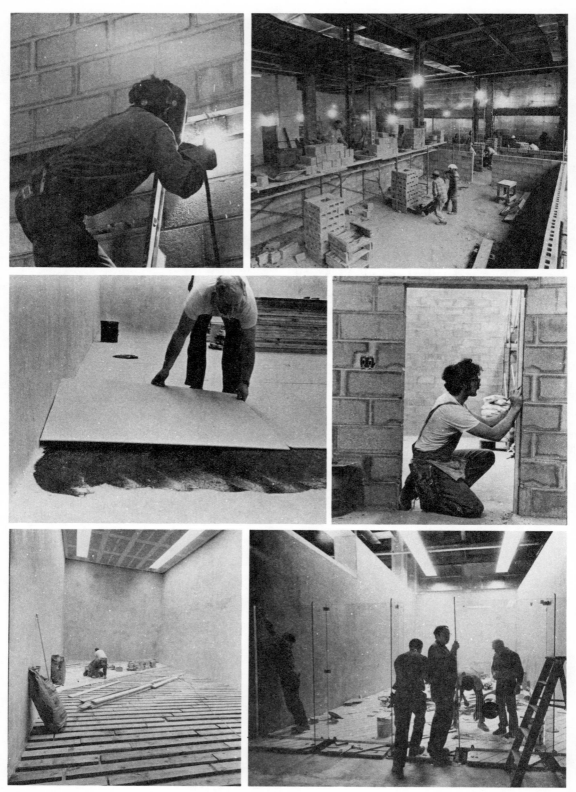

The making of a squash club. The Manhattan Squash club under construction in 1976. PHOTOS: RAIMONDO BOREA.

2

•

How the Game
Is Played

THE COURT

A regulation squash court is 32 feet long and 18½ feet wide. It is 16 feet high on the front wall and along the sidewalls to the point above the floor service line, where it dips to 12 feet. It is 6½ feet high along the backwall. With the exception of the area below the 17-inch-high telltale, which runs across the front wall, and the limited areas designated for service, this is the playable area of the court.

Until labor and material costs became too prohibitive, courts were built of 1-inch maple strips sufficient to withstand the punishment of the hard fast ball. Today, the floors of most courts are still wood, but the walls are often plaster, fiberglass or cement, or any of a number of new durable surfaces being developed specifically for squash. And of course, shatterproof glass backwalls are becoming very com-

mon. Walls and (usually) floors are painted white, with No. 100 aluminum oxide grit added to the floor paint for proper traction. All court lines are red. In this compact little arena, with a ball that weighs less than an ounce and racquets weighing barely eight ounces, the battle is staged.

THE GAME

A fair shot must at some point hit the front wall. It may hit the sidewalls or backwall before (or after) it hits the front wall. For a return to be good, it must be hit before it has bounced twice; it may be hit in the air.

First service is determined by the spin of a racquet, and service is retained until the server

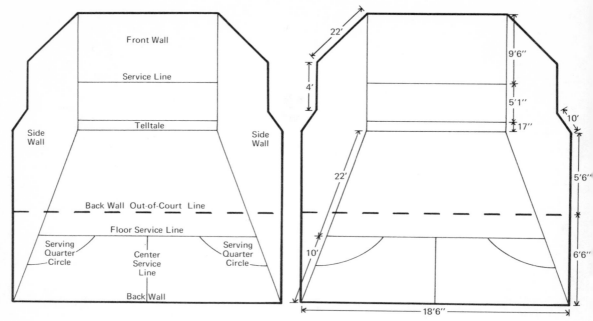

The court.

Front Wall

Service Line

Telltale

Side Wall

Side Wall

Back Wall Out-of-Court Line

Floor Service Line

Serving Quarter Circle

Center Service Line

Serving Quarter Circle

Back Wall

22'

4'

9'6"

5'1"

17"

10'

22'

5'6"

10'

6'6"

18'6"

loses a point. The server can take his first service from either the left or right service court; service then alternates from side to side until the serve changes, when again the choice of side for the first serve is given.

The server stands with one foot wholly inside the serving quarter circle (touching the line constitutes a foot fault). A legal serve must hit the front wall above the service line *first* and must land within the bounds of the opposite service court. The server is allowed two attempts; a double fault costs the point, and the serve goes to the other player. The rally continues with the players alternately hitting the ball until one player fails to make a fair return and loses the point. Either player may score, and the game is played to 15 points, with the two following exceptions:

If the game reaches 13–13, the player who has lost the tying point can elect to play "no set" (15 points), "set 3" (making the game 16 points), or "set 5" (18 points). Should the score reach 14–14 (without having first reached 13-all), the loser of the tying point can elect to play to either "no set" (15 points) or "set 3" (17 points).

A let, or replay of the point, is the rule when a player gets in the way of his opponent's stroke or his most direct route to the ball. If a player refrains from making his stroke to protect his opponent, a let is also called. Interfering with your opponent's potential winning shot is subject to a call of "let point," and the point is forfeited.

Circumstances dictate the call when a player is hit by a ball. If the ball would have hit the front wall first, the player who hit the ball wins the point. If the ball would have hit a sidewall first, the point is replayed. If the ball would not have been good (that is, not have hit the front wall above the tin), the player who hit the ball loses the point. A player hit by his own ball loses the point.

Let, let point, and other subtleties of the rules are discussed officially in the Appendixes, page 177. They are difficult to grasp until you have actually played the game enough to see the basic procedures and patterns of fairly sharing the court with your adversary. But a careful reading of the rules, even in the early stages of learning the game, will help eliminate the usual beginner's confusion.

Newman watches and waits on the T for McKay's forehand volley return.

3

•

The Nature
of the Game

Points are won in squash by making shots that your opponent cannot retrieve. Because the four-wall space in which the game takes place tends to keep the ball within bounds, the player who controls the center of the court (the T), from which most shots can be reached, has the better chance of retrieving the next shots. The player who can hit shots that keep his opponent away from the center of the court has the best chance of making shots that his out-of-position opponent can't reach. The idea then is to hold the center of the court and hit shots to where your opponent isn't. Of course, since you are both battling over the exact same territory with the same equipment, the winner is the one who can best accomplish this. It is also intrinsic to the game that you must fairly share the territory, and having made your shot, give your op-

ponent the opportunity to see it and to retrieve it by the most direct path.

The skills involved in playing this relatively simple game are complex: It is a physical, mental, and psychological game.

· Physical in its demand for strokes, shots, strength, fitness, stamina, quickness, mobility.

· Mental in its demand for tactics, strategy, analysis, selectivity, anticipation, deception.

· Psychological in its demand for competitiveness, concentration, resolve, patience, courtesy, calm in the face of adversity, desire to win, and the ability to endure exhaustion and pain.

Squash offers a great opportunity for self-expression. It is a game in which you use, in a highly integrated way, all your skills, abilities, and ingenuity. Observe and talk to good

33

players and you will find that, in the end, their individual personalities determine the game they play. Each player brings his own style, attitudes, and abilities to the game and uses them in the measure and combination that is optimum for him. You will see, from the wildly different opinions and approaches put forth in the book, how true this is. As Charles Ufford said, "[Squash is a game] dedicated to the proposition that no man is created equal." (And, one might add, in which it doesn't matter.) Squash champions have been large and small, young and old. There are players who win on sheer power, players who win on cleverly thought-out strategies or excellent racquetwork, others who win on sheer will and competitiveness. Squash champions are great athletes, great minds, and great psychologists, in very varying combinations.

●

ROLAND ODDY: I believe that squash is *the* outstanding game, not *an* outstanding game, because you can get a lot of exercise in a limited period of time and during that limited period have a great deal of enjoyment. I believe that squash can be played, with equal merit, for expertise, enjoyment, or exercise.

It is a very, very strong mental and psychological game. I think that it's a combat between two people . . . I'm referring to the mental aspect. Very often, to win, the match comes down very close and comes down in the final analysis to who is willing to punish himself, punish his body, a bit more to be able to win. First of all you do have to learn the game, obviously. It takes some time to learn it to a certain level, but if you're in good shape, and you can run, and you have good knowledge of strokes—not necessarily fabulous, but good knowledge of strokes—then it does come down to one aspect: It is desire, just the desire.

JAY NELSON: Because of the geometry of the court and the fact that it is relatively easy, compared to a lot of games, to keep the ball in

play, I guess the biggest success factor is persistence or stick-to-it-iveness. Also, there's a trade-off of self-control and the creative mode, and people come on different sides of that—there's almost a spectrum. Too, people play according to their personality. To a lot of people, patience is a big factor. On the creative side, there is an appreciation of the beauty of the game.

DIEHL MATEER: I'm a converted tennis player—I played tennis for eight years before I even saw a squash court. And the first time I played the game, I had fun. Granted, I could hit a moving object . . . but squash has the advantage over tennis. Tell people who are trying to learn tennis and are having a difficult time, tell them to take up squash. Because, really, the first time you go out, even if you're a duffer, the ball is always there, even if the point seems over. If you make contact with the ball, it will stay in play. And what's more important, *after* the point is over, the ball is within five feet. The first time you play tennis, all you do is pick up tennis balls, and it's a very boring experience.

I think Niederhoffer has proven that a person who has it upstairs—the brainpower—has a tremendous advantage over a person who doesn't. You can almost see Niederhoffer thinking on the court; you can almost hear the gears turning. I've played him doubles, but I'm certainly glad I haven't played him in singles. But certainly that is a key, and without it, you don't have much chance of winning a national championship. You've got to, of course, be quick in the game, but you don't have to be overly quick. One of the things that was a great help to me, I think, was the fact that I always knew where the ball was on the court. You watch—I would guess maybe one third of the players don't watch the ball.

VICTOR NIEDERHOFFER: Squash is a sport in which one's game constantly grows and evolves while utilizing all of the characteristics and abilities of the individual player. It's a game that can be likened to chess and boxing but has a three-dimensional element to it. It taxes the mind, body, and character. One is always learning something new in the game, constantly developing. The great players must, as a prerequisite, have good strokes and good conditioning. And once they have those two attributes, it's possible to refine and utilize every conceivable talent and achievement that a human being is capable of. But without stamina, there's no opportunity for anything else. Conversely, what a beautiful thing it is when someone is able to . . . think about the rest of squash without having to worry about his condition, for, to me, this is the utopian goal, to be able to completely forget about condition so that I can worry about shots, tactics, and everything else.

BARBARA MALTBY: I think there are a couple of important components of the game. First of all, you have to have a certain amount of stamina, whereas in tennis there is so much standing around and walking up for the ball or having someone else walk up for the ball; there's a lot of time when you're not doing anything. In squash, there is very little time when you're not doing anything. It's also very mental, because first of all it isn't exactly obvious what shots you should hit. In tennis, if the person is standing on the other side of the court, you know where to hit the ball, whereas

Barbara Maltby steps into the ball in perfect conformation.

in squash there are various shots that you can hit and still have the ball end up on the farthest point of the court; plus, in squash, how you move your opponent is very important.

CHARLES UFFORD: Even for the game to take place there must be an understanding and a willingness to play with utmost fairness. It's unique and really marvelous. It puts a kind of pressure on character that is just good for the human soul. It's not as difficult a game to play as tennis. Tennis is harder because in tennis you're playing a game that is much more difficult than the human psyche and constitution was designed to accommodate. This business of so hard and no harder is so difficult. We're just not intended to be able to do that. It's remarkable how well it is done. But in squash, you can hit the ball just as hard as you want, and you still haven't lost. You may not have made an effective shot, but you're not out of the point. The ball is going to come back, and you're still in the point. It makes it a much easier game. You can see this statistically because at top-flight play in squash, the number of errors per game on either side will be no more than three or four at the most. In tennis, at the center court at Forest Hills at the national championships, you'll see a final match in which 60 or 70 per cent of the points are errors: They go out of bounds; they get a good crack at the ball, but they miss it. You don't miss that way in this game. There are forced errors or there are winners or there are shots that go right in the nick, but very few outright errors. It's just not demanding in that respect. But it's demanding far more on your character as a person.

It's a game played by people of all shapes and sizes. It's really dedicated to the proposition that no man is created equal. Take the great confrontation of the fifties between Diehl Mateer and Henri Salaun. When those two guys were at their peak, they would each, in their own distinct and totally different styles, wipe out everyone else. There they would be, in the finals, year after year, head-to-head. It was fabulous stuff. Mateer would take control, power-hitting. Salaun would scamper around him and catch the reverse corners, and it would come down right to the fifth game or close points in the fourth, every year, and they traded the title back and forth pretty much. And I think it was the onus of defending it—it was too much of a psychological burden for a guy to win it two times straight. It's not just a level of physical ability that prevents the smarter or keener intelligence to win because you have so many different styles of play that you can have two people—hypothetically—with equal IQs, but because their styles are different, one may beat the other constantly.

Every person has qualities that could make him a great player. We are told that the great skill of Harry Cowles, who was the Harvard coach in the thirties, was that he could look at a given player, any physical specimen, and develop that player in his own style for which that player was best adapted, to the point where he could wipe out all the exponents of the other styles.

SHARIF KHAN: I've become more professional about the game. Up until seven or eight years ago, I was an amateur, and your mentality changes when you turn pro. I've tried to study the game, be a student of it . . . because you can never stop learning it: the angles, the strategies, etc. To me, it relates to life. It's not just going in there and banging the little ball, because if everybody could do it, they would all be champions. Any endeavor like this is character-building, and I try to relate all this to life. And I've been a better person for it, I think.

JOHN REESE: I think I would be wrong to say that anyone who picks up a racquet is going to be a good squash player. I suspect that there are a number of characteristics that each player should have, although different combinations may turn that person into a champion or just an average player. I think you do need good

strokes. If you do not have good strokes, I think that you have to compensate in some other area—either by being extremely fast or having good tactics. I think while good strokes are important, a knowledge of your opponent's weaknesses (and more important, your own weaknesses) often creates a successful squash player.

I think the mental side of it is a very important aspect of the game, and I think it's becoming more important. Years ago, when the game was strictly played in the bowels of private clubs, people went out there and just hit the ball around; they were great *strikers* of the ball. They could move to the ball well; they hit it perfectly. But the game has evolved from that point to a game of far more mental gyration on the part of given players. You can be very mathematical about your game; it is a game of angles; it is a game of inches. It can mean a lot of things to different people; it is much more of a cerebral game than a lot of people think of it as.

MIKE PIERCE: It's not only so much the physical conditioning or any of that aspect that makes a great player. It's his mental approach, how he thinks when he's out there on the court playing, how he prepares himself for a match mentally. I feel that preparation for a squash match, or to become a great player, is 80 to 85 per cent mental; I think that's the most important part of the game. And then, I would say the other 20 per cent is the physical conditioning.

PETER BRIGGS: I like individual sports, and I think I like squash especially because of the intensity of it. You can hear somebody breathing. It's a reflexive game—I mean, you can look at diagrams till your eyes fall out, but it's still reflexes that count. I don't think you can say what makes a top squash player. In an individual sport, you can never break it down into what makes a champion. Each person is able, in different ways, to summon up the resources to meet the situation. I mean, everything has structure, but I just don't agree with it in this game. . . . Sharif has the right attitude. I've played Sharif, and he's the most fun guy to play against. Niederhoffer is a chore to play against; I don't enjoy it. But that's what makes a market, when you have two sides.

Some people will almost play as they were schooled or educated or as they were brought up, which really freaks me out, because there's a side to me that is superconventional and there's a side that's really radical, and I know that's a product of my first two or three years at college—a very conventional college, but Harvard has a totally radical side. In '70 and '71 we were having bonfires in the Cambridge streets. Although that's a college student standpoint and I've left college behind, there are still certain things that stay with you; I know that I am very schizophrenic. I can see that playing these guys over in Europe, you can also see different influences. But boy, are they strong!

Mexican kids are very hot-blooded, they hit the ball very hard, they're very fast and naturally talented, but when they get into a really emotional pitch . . . they are totally irrational. And someone like Niederhoffer, as you know, is totally analytical. You can see that in how he goes about his business, how he goes about his life. And that's fine.

PETER BOSTWICK: It's very easy to get a lot of exercise in a short period of time. In tennis, to get a good workout, if you're young and in good shape and competing, it takes an hour and a half or two hours. In court tennis, it takes about the same length of time; in racquets, probably the same also. In squash, you can really get a good workout in forty-five minutes, and if you're playing a top player who is competitive with you, you have perhaps all the exercise you might need in an hour. If you're a weekend player, or a businessman who isn't in particularly good shape, in half an hour you can get a very good workout. I think that this is one of the good aspects of the game. An-

John Greco returning to Stu Goldstein.

other thing is, it's always fun to hit the ball a lot of times, and squash is a game where you get a lot of rallies. Even if you're not particularly good players, the ball stays in play a long time, even though you may be hitting the ball ten feet over the tin and it's sailing all around the walls. You still get exercise and fun by getting a chance to hit the ball a lot. I think it's a little easier to play than tennis, but to play at a top level, all sports take a lot of time and dedication and practice.

JUAN DE VILLAFRANCA: One of the best things about the game is that when you're learning, it's very easy to pick up the game—just to begin, have fun, and enjoy it. As you start working at the game and start to improve, the game is very difficult, and at top levels it's very complicated because it combines fitness with a lot of strategy, and you have to work a lot at the shots. Although it's a very easy game to play, it's difficult to become very good at it. It's also a great equalizer. Some people are very big, some are small, some are very powerful, some have a tough game: You don't have to be 6-feet-2 and 230 pounds to be a good squash player. This complicates the game: You cannot play the same against everybody.

The Nature of the Game

Khalid Mir appeals to referee Tom Jones in Metropolitan Open match against John Reese.
PHOTO: RAIMONDO BOREA.

4

•

Sportsmanship
The Gentleman's Game

Squash is often referred to as the gentleman's game. Applied to a sport that involves a pitched battle in a limited space that resembles nothing so much as a pit, it may at first seem an incongruous phrase. In fact, the game is *impossible to play* unless the strictest ethical code is observed. Sportsmanship is built into the structure of the game as deeply as the fight-to-the-finish spirit necessary for winning in squash.

It is the central paradox of the sport. When partisans call it a character-building sport, it is more than rhetoric. On the one hand, you are trying your hardest, using every possible trick, to control valuable territory from which you can force your opponent out of position and to hit irretrievable shots. On the other hand, you must be prepared to immediately and completely cede to him as much territory as he needs to make the shot that he hopes will pull

you out of position or that you will not be able to return.

The official rules of the game have been refined and rerefined to clarify the subtleties of this paradox. Referees and judges work to uphold these rules in match play. But when it's one-on-one, all alone down there in the pit, it is incumbent upon the players themselves to maintain a high standard of fair play.

Giving your opponent enough room to hit the ball means that he must be able to hit the ball to either side of the court near the front wall, must have direct access to the ball, and enough room to swing at it.

Since you are both playing by the same rules, it is an equal, if trying, arrangement. Different players sometimes have different ideas of what is fair; the rules are somehow open to creative interpretation. Players who abuse the rules, however, or who interpret

39

them differently for themselves than for their opponents, don't make it in the game. For one thing, people won't play with them—it's frustrating and dangerous. For another thing, it's not enough of an edge to win with.

As a beginner, you are bound to make mistakes that incur lets until you learn the patterns of court movement, and until you make a careful study of the rules (which you should do early on). Once you have done this, play fair. Don't crowd your partner to within an inch of the law. Don't ask for a let on a shot you couldn't get to anyway. Call second bounces down; don't make your opponent do it. If you are crowded, call a let. Don't chance hitting your opponent. And never question your opponent's calls. If you feel it is unfair, take it in stride. It could have been a mistake, and your judgment is not necessarily superior to his. If he repeatedly abuses the rules, don't play with him again. But don't argue on court. You don't need the point that badly. And you owe it to yourself, and to the game, to be a good sport.

●

VICTOR NIEDERHOFFER: I define sportsmanship in squash as trying to treat your opponent like a gentleman. It means applying the golden rule, never trying to win when your opponent isn't full strength, feeling very positive, setting a good example, maintaining a very high personal integrity, living with your own self, and taking your own values that are important to you and expressing them.

CHARLES UFFORD: You can't overestimate the importance of a high level of sportsmanship, because of the intensity and closeness of the players on the court. During a competition when you're playing at such a pace and your reaction becomes so instinctive in your movement—if you do not maintain this high degree of sportsmanship, this character of the game, it just isn't going to be recognizable. And for that reason, to the extent that

you can retain this character of the game, I think it's a marvelous educational experience. I mean, it's something I would wish more people in this country would subject themselves to; to put them under this kind of pressure—where you want to make that shot good and you don't let your opponent get it—*but* you've got to give him a fair chance to get it, and that means a fair chance for him to get it wherever he wants to play it, not where you think he should.

Once, against Henri Salaun in the nationals at 12-all, he appealed for a let; it was denied by the referee. Then he had another theory and appealed for a let point. He went through the rigamarole again, denying the let point, etc. Meanwhile, I'm walking around the court, wheezing and loving every minute of it. I just wished he could think up six more things to appeal; anything he wants to appeal—even if the decision goes against me, that's fine with me. I got just enough breath back to be able to run for a couple of more points and snuck out. I was very pleased with that. Poor Henri was upset about that because the call was not to his liking. I'm not saying that I've never called a let to gain time. It's the letter of the law—it's not the spirit of the law.

ROLAND ODDY: There's no question that squash can get out of hand if the certain "code of gentlemen" is not observed; you really have to play fair and consider your opponent's rights as well as your own. And most of the players do do this. Some of the rules though could be problems. For instance, it says in the rules that if you strike your opponent with the ball and he's going to the front wall, it's your point. It is foreseeable that some bright boy can come along and see that in the rules, and set out on a quest to strike his opponent with the ball as many times as possible on the way to the front wall. If that did happen, of course, it would get out of control. But I don't see that ever happening.

Also, there are a number of people in the game who have a completely different idea as

Tom Jones referees. PHOTO: RAIMONDO BOREA.

to what their opponent can get and what *they* can get. As far as they're concerned, they can get everything, and their opponent can't get anything. There's a big gap there.

MIKE PIERCE: I'll do anything legally to win a match. Knowing the rules as well as I should know them, just taking advantage of everything I can. I feel that my partner and I are absolute gentlemen on the court, but we will not give in. If a player is pushing us around, I think we'll come right back and either call a lot of lets against him or become as physical as they are. If it means hitting him with the ball if he's in the way, we might have to do that. I'd hate to resort to that, and I don't think I've ever hit anyone intentionally. My approach would be, if my opponent were not giv-

ing me the room I thought I deserved, rather than hit him with the ball, to call let after let after let. I feel I have enough patience to call four hundred lets if I have to. I feel, against some players, that if you call enough lets they're just going to get sick of it, and you'll wear them down psychologically. I don't call let unless it's really called for. Sometimes people are accused of calling lets and there really wasn't any need to; there's a fine line there.

PETER BOSTWICK: I've always felt that sportsmanship is a big part of all sports and that while you should play as hard as you can out there, you ought to give the guy a fair chance to get at the ball. And when you lose, you congratulate him. I think most of the players are pretty good sports in the squash world. But there are some guys who circumvent the rules and regulations and crowd you all the time; it makes it tough. In my experience of playing in some important competitions in squash, I've never really run into any real problems. I've had to call plenty of lets on guys sometimes, but I think most of the players want to abide by the rules and not sort of cheat on them. Occasionally, I'm sure, everybody oversteps their bounds in asking for lets, but you have a referee and a couple of judges, so this is very helpful.

PETER BRIGGS: I hate to play someone who keeps calling lets. I really can't be bothered with stuff like that; I get really annoyed when that happens. I played Hunt last week; there were never any lets. I won't get into that kind of a war, at least of my own volition. I still go with the idea that you can hurt somebody. I mean, I can go through an entire season, and if I'm playing guys like Sharif who know what they're doing, I'll never get hit once with the ball. But there's always that one time when it's possible to mishit the ball, and what happens if you pop someone's eye out? It's possible. I've got lots of friends who have been really hurt. For a quick very, very emotional moment when you get really frenzied and annoyed? It's not worth it.

Charles Ufford (center) officiates at the Bancroft Women's Open. Looking on (right) is Peter Wood, author of The Book of Squash.

DIEHL MATEER: I've seen horrendous examples of overdoing let calls in the amateurs here last year. Every point was a let, or let point, complete with big discussion. It was bad enough that I even spoke to a couple of the players saying, "There was some great squash in your match, but it was the most uninteresting squash I've ever seen." As a matter of fact, I walked out after the second game. Who wants to watch a match and hear nothing but discussion after each point? I said, "If every match were like that, you'd ruin the game." Something certainly should be done.

JAY NELSON: It's unfortunate to have to think of it that way, but there are possibilities for physical intimidation. Maybe you don't want to admit to yourself that sometimes you go out there and you know that if the other guy is careless or if he's surly or something, you know you can get bopped. It's a little bit in the back of your mind, and it makes you a little nervous, and it can affect your play. Probably the best thing to do is become fatalistic—you know, just say I have a lot of choices: I can say something to the guy, and he may react one way or the other, or I can remain nervous throughout the match or try to duck out of the way, or I can do something to him or I can just say to myself that there are times I'm going to play in situations that will be like this and unless it gets ridiculous, I'm just going to shrug it off and take my chances. I think that's probably the best way, unless you're the sort of guy who thrives on that sort of scene. But I'm afraid it would affect my playing; it would make me very self-conscious.

I didn't used to like temperamental players; they used to bother me (the guy who's making a big scene). Now I kind of actually hope it happens, because if it does it means he's sort of falling apart, and it just doesn't bother me that much. I don't like repeated lets. Some guys can look for and find repeated lets. That slows it up. They say, "Hey, he's getting in my way all the time!" There's a lot more opportunity for Nastase-like behavior in squash because of the let thing. There are a lot of opportunities for that. There are some rules that are not that well defined yet. Certain referees can maintain tight rules. I think I could do it. I could say, "Hey, I know what you're doing.

I'm gonna start not giving you the lets or calling points against you." Hopefully, I could find something in the rules, because if some guy talks back and says that's a legitimate let, I would hope that I could refute it. I once suggested this: Notwithstanding the let rule, *it is incumbent upon a player not to call a let when he has a good chance to hit the ball.* You know, you could write it better than that, but the idea would be that a little bit of uncomfortableness out there is just part of the ball game. Some guys use the let as a tactic; I'm sure they just decide, well, all right, I guess things aren't going so well, so I'll call lets whenever I can.

Khalid Mir.

5

·

Fitness and Conditioning

It is said that you can play squash to keep fit, but you must keep fit to play squash.

To many, the game's great appeal is the all-around fitness that is its natural by-product. Played on a regular basis, the game is a complete conditioning program, one that is enjoyable and that yields a high return for the little time invested.

A player may have to build up to the level of fitness required to play the game, but once this level is attained, regular playing should be all the exercise needed. Regular playing means at least two or three times a week. It's not a game that you can leave for several months and expect to come back to at the place you left, unless you've been keeping equally fit at something else.

The fast pace of play, the quick, twisty movements required, and the often cold courts make squash a potentially injury-prone sport if played when out of condition. A warm-up regimen should precede every playing period. The most common injuries (other than those that result from being hit by a racquet or ball) are pulled muscles and tendons, especially in the legs. The best way to avoid them is to be in good condition, to do some brief warm-up exercises, and to rally before playing. Exercises that stretch and limber the body are also excellent preventive measures.

And for the player who wants to improve, or to play competitively, there's more to do than just play. Very few top players are "naturals." They are disciplined competitors who work and refine their game through considerable time, attention, and sometimes boring and agonizing regimens. Read the following section, which gives suggestions for practice, drills, and conditioning. Then plan a program that meets your needs and goals.

45

•Spend time alone on court: a half hour every day, once a week, or once a month working on your specific problems—strokes, shots, running, whatever—will pay off handsomely. Specific drills for strokes and shots are given under the discussion of the pertinent topic. Repetition and just putting in the time are the keys. If you have a particular weakness or are trying to learn a new shot, drill it over and over until you get it right. In actual game situations you won't have the opportunity to practice one thing separately, nor can you chance things you're unsure of. This time spent alone will allow you to focus on the problem until you solve it.

•Always warm up: Before you start practicing with the ball, take the time to do a few simple exercises, enough so that your muscles are a bit relaxed: Toe touches, deep knee bends, running in place, and stretching your arms above your head will do the trick. Just two minutes of this is a great injury-prevention measure. Have an adequate practice rally with your partner before playing. If the courts are cold, wear a warm-up suit until you're limbered up.

•Running: Run distances for endurance, run sprints for speed and wind. Running up and down stairs is good for endurance, wind, and timing.

•Jumping rope is an excellent way to improve footwork, timing, and wind.

•Mobility: The following exercise is good for moving quickly off the T, changing directions quickly, and grooving the footwork needed to reach all parts of the court. Time yourself as you go through the following sequence:

Stand on the T in the ready position. Move to the front left corner and back to the T; to the front right corner and back to the T; to the back right corner and back to the T; to the left back corner and back to the T. Repeat the sequence in the opposite direction.

Touch (don't slam) the racquet to each corner as you reach it, and assume the ready position momentarily each time you return to the T.

Set yourself a time goal based on your recorded time. As you repeat this exercise, cut down the time.

•The following exercises are good for strength, limberness, and general conditioning:

> Sit-ups
> Leg lifts
> Push-ups
> Toe touches
> Jumping jacks
> Deep knee bends
> Full upper body rotations from the waist
> Full head rotations from the neck

•To build power in the racquet arm, some players do curls from the elbow with five- or ten-pound weights. Squeezing a hard rubber ball in the hand is also recommended.

Needless to say, good habits with regard to diet, drinking, smoking, rest, etc., all contribute to one's physical ability in the game. Don't eat a heavy meal or consume a lot of liquids before playing. If you take liquid during a match, do so sparingly.

●

ROLAND ODDY: Basically, I've never been a believer in a tremendous amount of conditioning; I've never really needed it, I think predominantly because I play a lot and I have a very slow pulsebeat, which helps, because you don't get as tired. So my conditioning has really been running around an indoor track, half a dozen times—wind sprints. But I believe very strongly in loosening up before you play. I push forward with my hands, so it loosens my shoulders and back, and then I touch my toes, and then bend my knees, and then jump up and down about twenty times. It depends. The older you get, the harder it is sometimes to get loose. And I can go in there sometimes, and I won't loosen up in three games. It's very rare to loosen up in the first game. I think peo-

46

ple lose the first game a lot of times because they're still tight. And some people, no matter what they do, they can go out and play five games, and come into the match, and they're still tight!

VICTOR NIEDERHOFFER: To stay in top form, what it would involve is about two hours of input each day . . . wind sprints, weights, stretching exercises, long-distance running, work on the court. But to some players conditioning is not as essential because they may be more gifted; that evolved through heredity. Better aptitude for constant starting and stopping, fast speeds; that is really the essence of squash. One assumes that during a squash match you'll have to take approximately four strokes to five strokes per player per point. And each of those strokes might involve about ten to fifteen feet running on average that we're talking about. Fifty feet of running per point, 28 points in a game, so we're talking about 420 feet a game, four games—oh well, broken down, a third of a mile of running. Again, in the top matches you could be running up and back three or four times, which would be 100 feet per point; you do that 28 times and you're talking about 12,000 feet per match plus constant stress. It's a fantastic amount of conditioning required. I think that players who are closer to the ground (most of the champions have been rather small), I think it's easier for them to maintain their condition; they don't have as much weight or as much bending to do on the court. I notice that most champions of the game have been average or below average in height—Hashim Khan, Henry Salaun, and Ralph Howe. I guess Sharif [Khan] and I are the only two big (tall) champions. Stamina is key; it's the one characteristic that enables you to think about everything else.

BARBARA MALTBY: To keep in shape I do different things. I do one thing for stamina, and that's running. And then for agility in court movement I do court sprints, "stars." I

Satterthwaite awaits Greenberg's recovery.

find those good for stamina (as wind sprints) and court agility. You can do sprints on a track, but you're running straight; you don't run straight on a squash court. You have to adjust to turning. I've also found that training long distances for stamina actually makes you slower on the court, so you have to sort of pace yourself for the tournament. And jumping rope I do a little bit of, just for basic foot quickness.

DIEHL MATEER: How did I *used* to prepare for matches? I did a lot of running; it wasn't a regular schedule, but I did get enough. When I was really competitive I ran enough that I felt I could go in the court and really go the distance. I think that partly came about from the first Open in which I played Hashim. I was twenty-six and he was twenty-six plus—but he was at that time supposed to be forty! We played in the semifinals, and I won the first two games; he won the next three, with part of that being on condition. I won't say it was 100 per cent condition; I was tired but not exhausted. But I think that helped me in the future to work a little harder. The important thing in a tough squash match is to know, have the confidence, that your legs are going to go the distance. If you have to think about getting through a five-game match at all, then you shouldn't be playing it.

Fitness and Conditioning

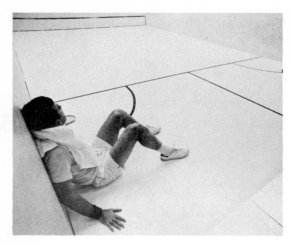
Niederhoffer takes a break.

I lost matches early in my career . . . in particular the 1952–53 Amateurs, where I lost the second match of the game because of a five-game match in the morning and a five-game match in the afternoon. I can even remember running in galoshes, in foot-high snow thinking: "This is ridiculous, but I'm going to do it." And it certainly was a help. I didn't jog; I ran. I tried to run more wind sprints than anything; I felt that was more important.

I think that instead of having drills, you might as well go in and play the game. If you love the game, as I do (and 90 per cent of the people who play it I'm sure love it, or are playing it because they enjoy it), if in practice you know you're not going to get to it, but at least you try to, what better practice could you get? I think having drills running up to the front of the court are meaningless in comparison to going after the ball.

JUAN DE VILLAFRANCA: I think each player has his own system of training. I don't have the facilities a lot of the people have such as gyms, where you can go and train, where they have special fitness programs. I don't have that, and usually what I do is take my car and I drive a little bit out of Mexico City and go up into the mountains; it's about eight hundred meters above sea level. I do some running. It helps my wind, but I have the disadvantage of not having top competition to play with. Basically, I work on my fitness. I go up and run, do some exercises, and I play a lot by myself.

GORDON ANDERSON: Maybe three years ago top squash didn't require the training to the degree it does now, because the game is getting more popular and there's more money. Therefore, everybody steps up a degree, so that you have people like Hunt coming over to compete here, etc. You know what kind of work he does, and you know the result on the court: If you don't work out, he's going to blow you off the court. He's in very good condition, so as a result we have to keep up. Top players can get a specific fitness program in a gym that is specifically designed to help your squash . . . like arm endurance, weight-lifting, etc. Not just sheer bulk weight-lifting, but more repetitious. . . . So most of us try to do that during the tournament season, and it helps. But four or five years ago, it was just the amount of time you could get out on the court and play.

CHARLES UFFORD: As far as training goes for me, it was always just a matter of playing intensively. I never did drills, calisthenics, exercises. I should have. I probably would have done better if I had taken a year off and trained. A lot of the players do that. Even though they didn't have the time, they made the time. They felt strongly enough about it to do that. But I got in very good shape . . . at least to the point where I felt I could play four- or five-game matches over two days and not be impaired after the fourth match. As long as I felt I could do that, O.K. But to do that today requires a far higher degree of physical fitness than it did the way the game was generally played.

Jack Barnaby was interested in teaching how to hit the ball properly. And it was up to you to get in shape. He said, "Look, we're not going to have organized calisthenics, running, and drills." I think they do some of that now.

I think the pressures of sports, of athletic competition in America is such over the past decade or so that there's increasing emphasis on physical fitness. You just have to have that additional degree of conditioning if you are going to be able to compete effectively. . . . It takes more time, that's all. Very few people can play three sports in college effectively.

PETER BRIGGS: I've learned all the strokes and stuff; I've played a lot of tennis. I've always been good with a racquet—I'm good at any racquet sport. I've never done any drills or exercises. I have this friend who has this treadmill, and I run on it. For this tournament I ran a lot.

GEOFF HUNT: On the court, I'll train with the ball, usually hit the ball. Off the court, I do some running and circuit-type training. [Jonah] Barrington is one of our players who is keen about on-the-court training. What he'll do is what he calls "movements in a minute." He'll stand in the middle of the T; then he'll run up and shadow-play a shot, and move back to the middle, and go somewhere else . . . he does it nonstop for about forty-five seconds, stops, and then breaks for fifteen seconds, and then does it again.

What I have done as well is running up and down the court. Where it's difficult to get outside sometimes and do some training, I do a few short court-spins, as they call them: run up and down, touch the wall, or touch the floor down on the back, and then up the other

way. It's very hard doing that type of work. Quite a few players have done that, as well as myself.

GRETCHEN SPRUANCE: I don't do any special exercises or drills or anything like that. I hate that sort of thing. That's what's so nice about squash; you can play an hour, and do a lot of running, and I'll feel so much better. I just love it for that, and to me having a tournament to work for makes me try harder. I try to play every day, and I've been going to the "Y" for about an hour every day and running, which I've never done in my life.

SHARIF KHAN: I stopped by to spend Christmas in Denver with my family. I was playing some exhibition tournaments on the West Coast and I stopped by and it was a good opportunity, because training at that altitude helped me with my breathing. I stayed there a month and I played with my brother and my father. At first, my legs were all like jelly, my wind was bad. You notice this, but after four or five days it's O.K.

There are different degrees of fitness. There's the international level of fitness, which is very strong and physical. Like this fellow [Mohibullah Khan] who plays an International game; he doesn't even get a sweat here. He could play a two-hour match here, like Geoff Hunt, and he doesn't even get a sweat. But there are different degrees of fitness. For the North American game, I feel I'm in good shape; that's about all.

6

•

Clothing and Equipment

As squash grows, so grows the array of clothing and equipment the player has to choose from when outfitting for the game. If you are lucky enough to play at a club with a pro shop, enlist your pro's guidance in choosing equipment. If you buy from a sporting goods or department store, seek out a salesperson with some knowledge of the game. Most choices boil down to personal preference, but here are a few guidelines:

Clothing should be comfortable, nonrestrictive, and unobtrusive. The tradition of white clothing is inevitably loosening up, and pastel-colored shirts and shorts are increasingly seen on the courts. But bright or dark colors, prints, etc., are still frowned upon. Watching that fast little ball bound around the court is hard enough without added distractions. Wearing suitable clothing is a courtesy. Too, many clubs have dress codes that must be observed.

The twisting, reaching, and running movements of squash dictate that your clothing must allow complete freedom of movement. Tight or binding clothing impairs free movement. Because of the fast motion required and the restricted playing area, even most women play in shorts rather than the dresses and skirts favored for tennis. Any but the most abbreviated or tailored skirts tend to get in the way.

So, for both men and women, the usual costume is shorts, T-shirt, and socks. For hot courts, wrist and head sweatbands are desirable. If you play on cold courts in the winter, you will almost certainly want a warm-up suit, or a sweater or sweatshirt. Playing squash on a cold court can cause serious muscle pulls if you're not properly warmed up.

Shoes are probably the most important article of clothing, as your feet take tremendous punishment in the game. A pair of comfort-

able, lightweight shoes is a most worthwhile investment. You can get by with regular tennis shoes; however, you may want a pair with better-gripping treads, especially if the court floors where you play don't have a proper grit mixture in the paint surface.

Your most important purchase is your racquet. As of this writing, there are a couple of dozen models available in prices ranging from about fourteen dollars to as high as fifty dollars, and new models are still arriving on the scene.

You should be able to get a perfectly serviceable racquet, including stringing, for twenty to thirty dollars. You have your choice of nylon, gut, or synthetic gut (which approximates the quality of gut) for the strings. Gut is reputedly livelier, and adds to touch, enabling you to hold the ball longer and put more spin on it. Nylon or synthetics are cheaper and longer-lasting. For all but the fussiest player, nylon or synthetic gut is absolutely adequate. Some

players swear that gut is superior; others swear they can't tell the difference. With the new 70+ ball, gut does have an advantage in that it seems to "grab" the rougher surface of the new ball better.

Then there's the argument about how tightly the racquet should be strung. As a general rule, tight stringing gives you power; looser stringing gives you control. A more loosely strung racquet allows you to hold the ball on the racquet just a fraction of a second longer; it allows the ball to go *into* the racquet so you can heave it out. Some of the pros who have great touch and control prefer the sensitivity of a tightly strung racquet. Generally, a more loosely strung racquet is recommended at the beginner-to-intermediate stage; you don't need power as much as you need control, for the time being. Weight and balance are the next factors. Until recently, the average weight of a strung squash racquet was 8 to 9½ ounces. However, the new 70+ ball has players

Left to right: The West 70+ ball, the West Blue Dot singles ball, the West doubles ball.

switching to lighter racquets—7¾–8½ ounces (manufacturers are rushing to develop the lighter models). The question of the ball aside, your choice is still between a heavier racquet for added power, or a lighter racquet for maneuverability and control. Some teachers recommend the heavier racquet for beginners and intermediate players, although "wieldability" of a light racquet is strongly in its favor. The important thing is that it feel good: You should have a sense of the racquet head, but it shouldn't be so heavy that it tends to drop.

The most crucial racquet characteristic is probably the grip. Racquet grips come in many shapes (oval, hexagonal, rectangular), sizes, and materials. The grip should feel absolutely secure and comfortable and should conform to your hand so that when you hold it, the racquet face is in a correct open plane. You shouldn't have to make your racquet conform to your grip. As to materials, the impor-

tant criterion is that the racquet shouldn't slip or turn in your hand. Synthetic leathers and plastics and very smooth grip surfaces tend to get slippery. Generally, well-made stitched and perforated natural-leather grips, or grips with replaceable terrycloth covers, are preferable.

The ball? The "official" squash ball changes so fast that it's impossible to say which one you'll want to use. Your choice also depends on the season (there is a "summer" ball), your personal preference, and the preference of the club or players where you play. The West 70+ white-dot ball—a ball that strikes a happy medium between the English and North American game—will probably be the one we stick with. It has recently been sanctioned for tournament play by several of the associations. Smaller and livelier than the old hard ball, easier to hit but harder to put away, it combines the characteristics of the American and English ball, and has met with wide approval from many of the top players.

Cartmel vs. Kurtz.

7

•

Learning the Game

While learning the game, it's important to understand *what* you're learning. You should know about the rules and scoring of the game before you ever go out on the court—it will help you to understand the objective of the strokes and shots and the patterns of the game. As you learn each new stroke and shot, you should learn as well why and when to use it. Take time to really read and understand the rules, especially the tricky let and let-point rules. A little knowledge can go a long way toward your grasping the subtleties of the game.

All teaching of strokes and shots presumes ideal conditions, and generalizations creep in. "Hit the wall first." "Squash is a wristy game." "Always face the sidewall." But if you learn everything the right way, and learn to build each new experience and scrap of information onto what you already know, you'll end up with a game greater than the sum of its parts.

Every time you learn a new stroke or a new shot or even a new tactic, practice it. Get out on the court and hit forehands from every position on the court, at every speed, paying attention to where the power comes from, what changes its direction, etc. Learn the footwork necessary to get into position; learn to hit closer and closer to the tin. Learn the difference between hitting on a hot court or on a cold court. If you've learned a new tactic or think you have a new insight into the game, try it out the next time you play. In short, get the full benefit of everything you learn, and make your knowledge work for you.

•

JOHN REESE: There are two ways of learning the game. One, obviously, is to watch it. What you develop in your own mind is the symmetry

Greenberg vs. Leavy.

of the court and players, and how they move in concert with each other and with the ball. Watching very closely and attentively, one can appreciate and understand the tactical nature of the game as well as the competitive nature. Obviously the other part of it is to go out there and try it yourself. The advantage of squash over tennis is that you can go out and play the game by yourself. There's nothing better, I think, than going out and attempting different types of shots and then forcing yourself to run up and get your own shots. Some of our great players practice a good deal by themselves. When I'm doing something poorly, then I will go out on a court myself. That's the only time that I'll have to analyze what's wrong, whether it's a hitch in my stroke, or poor footwork, or just not hitting the ball.

I think the first thing you have to do is attempt to show the novice, assuming the novice may have some knowledge of tennis or of some comparable sport, that the sport is done with the wrist. It is a wrist sport. It is not a full-arm swing. The stroke starts up around your shoulder and ends down around your waist. So I would first try to show the stroke. Then I would try to develop in the player the knowledge of the bounce of the ball off the

wall. The natural reaction is, for anyone who plays tennis, to go *to* the ball no matter where it is going. What often happens is that it bounces off the wall and hits them in the nose. . . . In this game you almost develop a contrary feeling about what's going to happen. You should have an impression in your mind that the ball will always come back to you; in fact, it normally does. And if you think of yourself as being the focal point and the ball rotating around you and your opponent rotating around you, you'll find that in fact that's what happens. It's much easier to learn the game thinking that the ball will come back to you than blasting ahead toward wherever the ball goes and bumping your head against the walls.

VICTOR NIEDERHOFFER: The best way to learn the game? Well, you might start by watching some good players hit, then by buying a good book (which is how I learned the game). Also, it's good to take a few lessons at the very beginning so that you have a few good shots and a good complement of shots right at the outset, and so that you don't learn bad habits.

The best way to learn the game is to play it with a positive attitude; try to work at the best of your own abilities. And try to sharpen mental and physical characteristics as well as emotional ones as you develop your game. Try to keep your racquet going very directly to the point of first contact that you wish to make with the ball; that's most important. The one beauty of the game of squash to me is that it's constantly growing; there's always something new to learn. I once used to keep a diary of my squash practice; each time I played I was able to get new concepts.

The best way to teach the game is to appreciate the individual differences in the students, and try to inculcate a sense of joy in the game.

BARBARA MALTBY: Learning the basic strokes at the beginning is good. First of all, you have to learn not to take a roundhouse swing, not to kill your opponent. At the beginning you have to just go in and play and see how the ball bounces off the wall. If you play billiards you'll understand it a lot better (knowing where the ball is going to end up), whereas people from playing tennis have no idea, and they'll run into the wall all the time.

In the beginning, a player should try just taking a position and hitting it at various spots on the front wall and seeing what happens. The first thing is that you just have to be able to hit the ball. But I think you should learn a few shots right at the start because first of all it makes the game a little more interesting than just bash, bash, bash, to see who misses the ball first. Also, if you start hitting the shots with people who aren't so good, this helps you develop your shots a little bit better . . . your shot-making ability, whereas if you have only a long game and you get to a certain level and *then* you try to develop shots, what you're doing is you're trying to play against good players with inferior shots, so you end up just getting creamed, and it's frustrating. So I think that when you start, learn shots. A lot of people don't do that. They just go in and learn to hit the ball very hard and they have two shots: a rail shot and a cross-court shot; these are all they use for a couple of years until they're so good at them, but they have nothing else. It's a lot harder like that. You should learn a few other shots so that you can try for a winner.

JUAN DE VILLAFRANCA: I think that you have to have competitive fire in your blood. You're a competitor, or you're not a competitor. The thing is when you're young and start to compete, I think that it's very important not just to play friendly matches but also to get into tournaments and get the feel of playing under pressure.

JAY NELSON: I'd certainly recommend taking lessons. I would try to teach power first—big, long, hard strokes. Then work backward to the softer strokes. You're in a congested area; the ability to make the proper stroke quickly is a big deal. Tactics would be last.

Points come as your game is developing when you suddenly feel that you do something right; you suddenly understand a certain stroke, or a certain shot, and that jumps your game another notch. Usually it's not in a match; usually it's formed on the court by myself. It happens all the time. I'll be hitting by myself, and I'll say, "Oh yeah, that's right!" I've been falling away from the ball, and now I'm hitting it better again—you know, for forgetting to hit sidespin on certain shots, or hitting too high. Well, you can find out you're hitting the ball a foot and a half over the tin, and you really have to hit it six inches over it. You make a note to yourself. Sometimes you learn something, and unless you really get it, it doesn't stick. I remember one of those things once where I had improved quite a bit one weekend and lost it. I mean, I was hitting the ball a certain way. I had this swinging down with an open face—I had that, I really did. I had a tournament the next weekend, and I can remember going up there early to Toronto, and I lost it. See, at the time, I wasn't analytical enough to know what I was doing. I lost it, and it was gone for like two years!

CHARLES UFFORD: In learning the game, the first thing you do is think about the stroke. You must be sure to get the information that

Caught in the corner, Khalid Mir flicks a backhand downcourt against John Reese.

the stroke is played with the wrist. I think tennis at the top level of play is played far more with the wrist than is acknowledged. The upper torso is positioned, yes, but there's no swing from the shoulder; it's all in the feel of the hand. It must be played from the wrist to achieve that quickness of reaction. I would certainly encourage beginners to play right from the start. And I would suggest they get in there and take lessons and practice just hitting the ball against the wall for a number of hours. The beauty of learning the game is that ball comes back . . . which is not the case with tennis.

As for tactics, the player is not going to have a feel for it until he's learned to sustain a rally. And here the key to sustaining a rally is to get over the apprehension about swinging at the ball when it's near the wall. You just have to get over that feeling—splinter time. At the point that you can sustain a rally you're probably ready for thinking about playing different shots in different situations. If you want to start a person who never played the game, start with an English ball, which will sit up and wait for you . . . it's lighter, and you can sustain a rally more quickly. It's so much easier with the English ball.

PETER BOSTWICK: I would think the best thing to do, like learning tennis, is that you start knocking the ball around the court and you try to go to a competent professional to give you a little guidance on the grip, which is terribly important. Occasionally you see someone with an unorthodox grip. But most of the guys who play squash all have pretty sound grips. I remember very few good squash players who had Western grips on the forehand. So therefore, I think it's pretty much like tennis or any other sport you go to a competent player or professional and get him to show you the proper way of doing it. I think everybody has his own natural stroke, so it's awful hard to say this is the only way for you to hit the ball, because everybody has a different natural way of swinging at it.

GORDON ANDERSON: Starting at an early age and being either lucky or fortunate enough to be taught by a leading coach or somebody you have trust in and knows how to teach is very important. You have to learn over a period of time. You can't teach a person everything he has to know in a month. I used to get one lesson a week over a period of two years. Slowly, it will sink into your head. I think everything in sport, or whatever else you might be involved in, goes in declines and inclines. When I started out, I was the worst person in the group. The second important thing would be tournament experience. I think that the most things the four or five of us now (at twenty-seven years old) remember is our tournament experiences as juniors; in driving to New York and Philadelphia from Toronto and never having done that before. So it's just getting it sunk into your head: Do you want to win, or do you not want to win? And you've come all that distance and your friends are out there and you're sitting here with your stomach in knots and all of a sudden you start to learn and sort of use it.

GEOFF HUNT: I think one of the best ways to improve is to play someone a little better than yourself all the time; there's nothing better than that. You've got to *play squash*; there's no alternative. You just can't go out and practice all the shots all by yourself, hit them, and then expect to win. You've got to play as many matches as you can, no matter what people may say. In a match you're more nervous. You can always hit better in practice; all of a sudden in a match the tension is there, and you change.

MIKE PIERCE: I don't do any exercises. I play a lot—six or seven days a week. That's how I keep my game in tune. I should do more training than I do. I don't go on to the squash court and do all those drills. I don't think you can integrate tactics and shots in practice when you're learning the game. I would say tactics come from experience and

58

playing matches. Learning shots, you can practice and practice; that's the best way.

I spent one year, four years ago, where I did something similar to what Niederhoffer has done—I didn't play squash with anybody; I practiced by myself every night for an hour, an hour and a half; just shots. I felt it was the best thing I'd ever done for my game. I primarily went out and hit reverse corners, drop shots—off the forehand and the backhand—and I think that it's the best thing that ever happened to my game. And as far as tactics and how to approach a match, how you're going to play somebody—that comes from experience, getting in there and playing practice matches.

You can take a million lessons, but you have to get in there by yourself.

SHARIF KHAN: How I teach the game depends on the caliber of the player. Obviously he is going to be influenced by my style, because that's the way I teach. People come to me to learn for many different reasons: Some come to learn, some come just to play me; some are overawed, some are not. The basic thing I would teach them is to be physically in good shape and to try to develop a good temperament for the game. You just have to keep cool. Inside, you've got to stay competitive, but outside, you've got to stay cool. I would teach them to try not to be too ambitious; try to recognize the confinements of their own game, the restrictions of their own game. If one guy has a weak backhand, I wouldn't say go and practice your forehand. I would say go and practice your weak shot. I would say that they should try to recognize where their strong points are, where their weak points are, and try to have a balanced game. It's no good having a heck of a strong serve but no other shot. A lot of people think that they can rely on one thing; the guy who succeeds is the one who has the most balanced game.

I try to teach something about tactics and positioning. A lot of people hit the ball straight to the back. I try to tell them to hit

the ball to a good length. That's where you keep the other guy from doing damage. If they're being pushed into the back of the court, they can't attack—they can't hit attacking shots. I try to teach a good, strong defensive game to start off with. No fancy tricks, not until they get the ball or racquet under control. Then, maybe, one or two winning shots. It's no good experimenting with new shots in a match. If you've practiced them and have enough repetition to throw them into a match, that's fine. But if you want to use the match as a guinea pig, then it's no good. For anything that you want to try, I think you should be prepared beforehand.

DIEHL MATEER: I've coached at Episcopal over the past three years on a part-time basis to help them out. But I'm taking boys who

David Linden crouches low to a half-volley return against Tom Page.

have played the game from anywhere between three and ten years, so I don't have the experience as far as teaching the game to beginners. I think that all I try to do is get them to look at the ball; to back up . . . to look at the ball when they're hitting it as well as when the other man is hitting it. And I've tried to teach them the fundamentals of getting under the ball. You can't really play good squash unless you are under the ball, to keep it down and keep it from coming off the back wall. Too many boys are hitting it flat or a little bit over the ball, and it just takes the ball up there late and takes it right down into the tin.

The key to making shots is to take a situation where you have an option of say, three shots, and teach them what those three shots are, and try to show them how they should be hit. That gives them a better option. It's surprising how the boys aren't aware of that.

●

THE FIRST TIME ON THE COURT

Unless you have played other four-wall sports, be prepared to be baffled the first time you go out on the squash court. That small, fast ball will make you feel very foolish. What you will learn very fast is that *it* is your enemy—not your opponent—and that as soon as you learn to deal with *it*, as soon as you learn how *it* behaves, you will have made a big step in understanding the game.

There are two things you can do right away (and keep on doing at every stage of learning) before you start worrying about strokes and shots or anything else, which will more than pay off.

1: Watch the game being played. Ideally, watch it being played well. At any stage of your learning it is good to watch the game; there's a certain kind of osmosis or transference that takes place between what you see

and what you then do that's invaluable. Right now, you're watching the game to see what the *ball* does: How fast does it travel? How far does it bounce? Secondarily, you're watching the players to see how they respond: How do they place themselves in relation to the ball? Which way do they run? and so forth.

2: Get out on the court, hopefully where no one can see you, and make a fool out of yourself. Hit the ball around. Watch what the ball does. See how it behaves. Hit it at different speeds from different parts of the court. You'll learn a few things right away. You'll see that most balls tend to come out toward the center of the court, so that if you understand which wall it's going to come off, and at what direction and speed, you don't really have to run very far. You'll learn to keep your body in the center of the court and use the reach of your arm, your racquet, and a few economical steps to get there. At this point, the most important thing, though, is not to learn what *you* should do. Learn what the ball does, and you're well on your way.

●

ROLAND ODDY: The big problem, and the hardest thing for the beginner to learn, is: What is the ball going to do? That's the hardest thing, because a ball can bounce two feet shorter or two feet longer, and it does something different in the way it hits the back-wall, in the angle and in the height. Everybody should hit the ball around by themselves, anyway, in the beginning. That's how you get familiar with it; there are little exercises you can do by hitting the ball up and down the wall.

BARBARA MALTBY: I've found that going on the court by yourself is essential—hitting the same shots ten, fifteen, twenty times. Hitting a shot well in a match really comes from confidence. If you don't have confidence in that shot at a critical point in the match, you're going to make an error. You're going to hit it a foot above the tin, and it's going to be a setup.

DIEHL MATEER: Practicing by yourself is essential. It's also one of the real niceties of the game. You can't do it on the tennis court—you can practice your serve and get a ball machine . . . but in squash you can go out and practice the same shot . . . go out and hit fifteen forehand rail shots, backhand rail shots. In doubles, I even take two balls on the doubles court because the roll corner is an important shot in the game, and it's very tough to practice that shot in a match. But if you take two balls on the doubles court, hit a roll corner, and take the other ball and hit a roll corner, you'll find that the other one that you've hit, when you've finished, has come back, right at your feet. You can keep the two going and just work . . . it's just perfect. So you hit a roll corner every fifteen seconds, or four a minute. And I've felt that has been a major help in a couple of the national doubles championships. You get a workout. I also practice hitting reverse corners and straight drops. You can really hit every shot by yourself in the singles or doubles court that is of any importance (99 per cent of them), mainly to develop that confidence.

GRETCHEN SPRUANCE: It's a funny feeling the first time you play, as I remember. It's a much easier game than tennis because you don't have to keep the ball in the court, and you can hit it as hard as you want. It's a great outlet, it really is; you go out there and slam the ball around, and you feel much better.

•

THE GRIP

The grip marks your first contact with a squash racquet, and it is crucially important. It's worth some attention to get it right, and it's disastrous to get it wrong.

The grip.

Because there is no time to change grip from forehand to backhand in squash—as is common in tennis—almost everyone favors the use of a single grip, one that is most easily comparable to the continental grip used commonly in tennis on the backhand. In squash, this grip serves to place the racquet in the hand so that the face is in the same plane as the palm of the hand and on contact with the ball will naturally impart vital underspin to it.

At the outset—before even grasping the racquet—keep in mind that your object is to have the racquet be an extension of your arm, not a foreign object that you are supposed to hang onto and stab at the ball with.

Try this image—again, before grasping the racquet. Picture a very bouncy ball no larger than a marble, which you must hit with your forefinger against the walls of the court. Picture the motion you must use to hit it on the

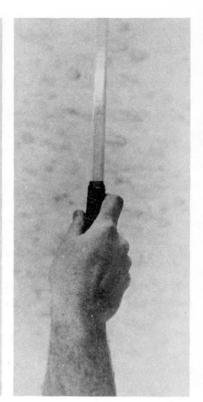

The Grip

Lisa Griffith, fully extended on a high backhand volley. Her shortened grip is no doubt a result of her teacher, Mohibulla Khan's, influence. The shorter grip allows more control but gives up reach and power.

pad of your finger on the backhand with the fingernail on your backhand. When you first grasp the racquet, pretend that the racquet is an extension of that fingernail.

The handle of a squash racquet is quite small, and is really held by your fingers rather than your whole hand. Specifically, it's held by your third, fourth, and fifth fingers, with an assist from your forefinger and thumb. Many people grab the racquet like a hammer—the analogy is used a lot (as is one that compares it to shaking hands), but they're both off base. The job of gripping the racquet belongs to those last three fingers: you should be able to wield the racquet with just that much of your grip. The "V" that's formed by your thumb and forefinger should not be riding tight on the racquet; there should be a little gap in there. The key finger is the middle finger, which runs up the center of your hand; it does most of the holding. It's your control finger, and you should learn to turn the face of the racquet with that middle finger. In actuality, all the fingers are used, the last three for strength and control, with the thumb and forefinger extended to control the plane of the racquet.

Your racquet face should end up in the same plane as the palm of your hand on your forehand, truly an extension of your hand, as though it had grown out from the base of your wrist.

Some beginners have a tendency to "choke up" on the handle a bit. Try not to do it. You need every bit of reach you can get; inches count.

THE READY POSITION

As its name implies, the ready position is the stance, both physical and mental, that you take *at all times* when you're not actually hitting or retrieving a ball.

It means always being on the balls of your feet, with your wrist cocked, in a crouch position, optimally on the T, facing the front wall, looking at your opponent and the ball, alert and ready immediately to maneuver into position for your next shot. When waiting on the T, the racquet head should never be lower than your own.

The importance of getting into this position on the T cannot be overstated. Only through experience will you learn the intricacies of footwork and patterns of movement that will bring you back to the T in the most economical way from all parts of the court, and in relationship to your shot and your opponent's position.

But do it. Make it a must, from the first time you walk into the squash court, to assume the ready position between every shot, even if you are just hitting by yourself. Make it a habit, an inviolable rule. Picture yourself there.

The ready position.

On the T, knees bent, on the balls of the feet, wrist cocked, watching your opponent.

Backhand volley by Stu Goldstein.

8

•

Stroke Basics

The dynamics of stroke execution involve the entire body. While there is no one perfect swing or stroke, there are several necessary ingredients of proper stroking. And good, "grooved" strokes are the foundations of a strong game and are prerequisites to shot-making ability.

Starting in the ready position is understood. The moment you see whether you are going to play a forehand or a backhand, pivot to face the appropriate sidewall, taking your racquet back in the same motion.

PREPARATION

Every shot should be prepared for in the same way, with a pivot to the appropriate sidewall and a full backswing. This way you are ready to hit any shot, and you leave your opponent guessing as to what shot that is until the last minute. The wrist is fully cocked at an angle to the forearm, and the elbow is fully bent—to a right angle at least. The arm is drawn back across the front of the body so that the racquet hand ends up level with your ear. If you get in that habit of always cocking your wrist first, you will always be able to put the wrist snap into your shot, no matter how little backswing you have time for.

ARC OF SWING

The arc of the swing is a full one, as in tennis, but it is contained; it makes a smaller circle. This saves time and conserves space. Every stroke makes full use of an arc that starts with a full backswing and ends with a follow-through in front of the body. Different shots use a different piece of the arc in their actual execution, the power drives using the entire forward portion of the arc and follow-through, the touch shots using shorter segments of the circle.

DOWNSWING

The downswing always leads with the wrist, so that at the point of impact the power of the shot can be put into the snap of the wrist. The cocked wrist and the wrist-first stroke production are all-important, so that no matter how little time you have, and how short a backswing you make, you still have the power of the wrist snap behind your stroke. The swing itself should make the full arc from full backswing position, but speed and power should not go into the stroke until it begins its forward motion. All power should be saved for going *forward*. If you try to build power from the top of the arc, you will lose the smooth, circular motion of the downswing.

POINT OF CONTACT

At the moment of contact your weight shifts from your back to your forward foot as your wrist snaps through the ball. The racquet face should be open, and contact should be made as the racquet comes down and through the ball, as though the racquet had no strings. Everything should be moving forward—the racquet and your body. On a power shot both your racquet and your body are moving fast. On a touch shot your racquet and your body are moving more slowly. But no matter what the shot, no matter what the speed, your whole body should race to meet the shot along with the racquet. The feet should be set at the moment of contact. As the wrist whips through the ball, the weight shifts to the front foot. The rear leg should end up fully extended, with the big toe still touching the floor. Pulling up on either foot will result in a

loss of power and direction. The body should be low to the ball to concentrate the power and to keep your eyes as close to the level of the ball as possible. Keep those knees bent through the shot.

FOLLOW-THROUGH

A complete follow-through is necessary to hold the ball on the racquet for precious fractions of a second. On a drive, the follow-through continues parallel to the floor out in front of the body. Even on a finesse shot or volley, the follow-through is important. If the racquet stops on point of contact, the ball will tend to bounce off the racquet, losing power, direction, and spin.

●

ROLAND ODDY: I teach, fervently, three things that I think are the basics of the game, three things that one must do if one wants to

Keep your head down through the follow-through. Doug McLaggan demonstrates.

be a good player. And they're so simple that most people don't do them. They are: You must always be on the balls of your feet so you can adjust to something unexpected that happens, like the ball changing directions quickly off the wall; second, you must always cock your wrist after you've hit the ball so that you're ready to hit the next ball—the squash ball comes back very quickly; third, and by far the most important, you must always face the sidewall when you hit the ball—try to keep away from facing the front wall and being back on your heels. If you face the sidewall, you naturally lean into the ball, which gives you the balance and helps in the timing for stroking it.

VICTOR NIEDERHOFFER: I constantly get a rise when someone talks about mental attitude being sufficiently important to warrant a win game. Frequently there *are* players so gifted and talented that if they could get their mind in order they could beat everyone. But this is a fallacy, like most of the other fallacies or theories of the game. Actually, without good strokes nothing else matters . . . like stamina. Some players have a weak backhand; for one reason or another they're too wristy, or they don't change their grip, or they take it up very high in back (this makes their backhands extremely erratic). It's just a question of time, with their weak strokes, before they must submit.

CHARLES UFFORD: Good strokes are very important. Most important is that you grow the game into your body in your formative years. It is very difficult to develop the natural, instinctive, reflexive strokes that will produce an effective shot if you take up the game in your late teens after you have achieved your full physical growth. You have a marvelous time with this game whenever you pick it up or at whatever level you play because all the shots are still there to learn and use. It's just the speed and the reflexes—the tempo of play—that make the difference.

Newman takes aim at a high backhand volley return against McKay.

SHARIF KHAN: It's good to have a good basic game and a solid knowledge of strokes, because ball control is so important. I would always say that you base your form on what makes you comfortable. Some guys, like in tennis, have the weirdest of serves, but that's how they're comfortable. So I wouldn't go so much by the textbook, so long as you are able to hit the ball cleanly, maintain good control, get good depth on the ball . . . as long as you can keep ball control.

JOHN REESE: Stroke production is very important, because that's what it really comes down to. It comes down to who can keep the ball closest to the wall at the proper length so that it doesn't come off the backwall or isn't too short. This is the big part of the game.

DIEHL MATEER: Shots are not critical to the game, not as important as the competitive aspect. And stroke production is just not impor-

Excellent form—a hallmark of young Lisa Griffith's game. Gail Ramsey on the T.

tant, because if you take four or five good squash players, none of them hit the ball in the same way. There must be more than one "right" way, because Niederhoffer and I never hit a forehand in the same way. He has his feet in a different position than I do; he holds the racquet differently. Peter Briggs does things footworkwise that are wrong theoretically, but he's so quick that apparently it doesn't seem to make any difference. If he changed things, it would be interesting to see if his game went up or down. He is probably so set that it would be difficult. Even Niederhoffer does that, always going in with the foot that's on the same side. If he's hitting a forehand, Briggs goes in with the left foot. And it should be the other way. [Briggs is left-handed.]

MIKE PIERCE: I think it helps tremendously if you have the proper strokes, hit the ball properly. I think that's a great advantage. A lot of people are able to overcome it. I would say Niederhoffer's stroke production is not the way it's taught, but he has, over the years, become a great player. He has learned to play his game, with his stroke. I really believe, he probably believes also, that the mental preparation for the game is the most important aspect of a good squash player.

OPEN, SQUARE, AND CLOSED STANCES

The stance with which you address the ball—the position of your feet in relation to the sidewall—influences the power and direction of your shot. In the closed stance, the leading foot is closer to the sidewall. This is the stance that yields the most power, as the weight of your entire body can be mustered behind the shot.

In the square stance the feet are parallel to the sidewall. Here you give up a bit of power but gain more flexibility in the direction of your ball, especially for cross-court shots, and especially from mid-court.

In the open stance, the rear foot is closer to the sidewall, so the player is facing somewhat toward the front wall. Volleys are usually

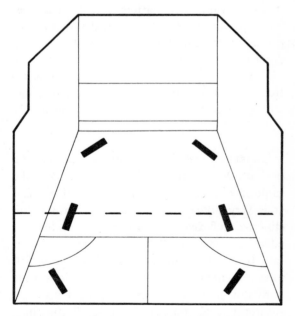

Deception and your stance. To keep your back to your opponent on the T, you would favor a closed stance in the backcourt, a square stance in mid-court, and an open stance in the forecourt.

SQUASH HOW TO PLAY, HOW TO WIN

Closed stance.

Open stance.

Square stance.

played in open stance. The open stance offers greatest flexibility in shot selection from the forecourt.

Your stance is also one of the weapons of deception. To keep your back to your opponent on the T, you would use a closed stance in the backcourt, a square stance in the vicinity of the service line, and a more open stance in the front of the court, using your legs to hide the ball from your opponent's view.

THE RACQUET FACE

The angle of the racquet face is described in terms of open, flat (or square), and closed.

An open racquet is angled toward the ceiling and makes contact a little below the center at the back of the ball.

A flat racquet face is in the same plane with the front wall and makes contact square on the back of the ball.

The open racquet.

A closed racquet is angled toward the floor and makes contact a little above center on the back of the ball.

For all intents and purposes, squash is played with an open racquet face, for it is the angle of the racquet coming under the ball that imparts underspin and keeps the ball down, bringing the first bounce more quickly to the floor. Putting underspin on the ball is of vital importance in keeping the ball from coming off the backwall on power shots, and dropping it at the front wall on finesse shots. It requires a developed sense of the degree of racquet angle and timing. Start playing with the face just slightly open, and as your timing improves, you will be able to use a more radical angle, using minute adjustments with your middle finger and wrist to turn the racquet under slightly as you hit the ball. The more open your racquet face, the more you can hit down on the ball. The open face makes it possible for you to have the ball on the strings

The flat racquet.

The closed racquet.

of your racquet a fraction of a second longer, and the spin keeps the ball above the tin.

SPIN

Spin is the turning of the ball on its own axis in flight, as a result of the speed, direction, and point of contact of the racquet with the ball. Only if the ball is hit squarely on the back and with an absolutely flat racquet face will it not spin.

Topspin.

Backspin (also underspin or cut).

In squash we are dealing almost exclusively with cut (or underspin) and slice (or sidespin).

Cut is the result of the ball being hit with an open-face racquet with a downward and forward motion slightly on the underside of the ball. The ball thus spins backward in its forward flight so that it comes down on contacting the wall; it's fighting the wall it hits. Underspin gives a drive "length"—it ensures that when it comes bounding off the front wall it stays down and barely bounces (and bounces low) behind the service line. Underspin causes a touch shot to drop abruptly after the wall takes the "starch" out of it.

Topspin, which occurs when the ball is contacted with a closed racquet face slightly over the ball, is used in squash only on the hard serve, where the racquet comes over the ball at the full extent of the arm, where the intent is to have the ball travel fast and on the fly all the way to the bottom of the backwall. In most other cases, topspin gets the opposite

effect from what you want. Sometimes you'll see converted tennis players with beautiful strokes whose games are less than wonderful because everything they hit has topspin and their shots come bounding up to meet their opponent.

Slice or sidespin is the result of contacting the ball with an open face on either side of the ball and drawing the racquet across the ball either toward or away from the body, causing the ball to make an awkward sideways bounce in the opposite direction after hitting the wall or floor. Used in combination with cut or underspin, the effect is to slow down the ball even more and to cause the ball to bounce low and erratically. It is only used on touch shots.

Using cut and slice require touch only acquired through practice. But cut is essential to the game. Contacting the ball with an open racquet face—which should be the natural re-

Ball contact. The place on the back of the ball where your racquet makes contact affects the direction of the shot. You would hit the center dot for the rail, the left for the angle, and right for a cross-court shot.

You would hit the top dot for topspin, the center dot for a flat shot, and the bottom dot (your usual target) for underspin.

sult of a proper grip and swing—will produce underspin. Controlling the amount of underspin and perfecting the timing that results in underspin or backspin without substantial loss of power must be learned. The angle of the racquet face can be changed by minute adjustments in turning the racquet with your middle finger or slight rotation of the wrist.

●

Direction of swing; The swing is parallel to the body, and the ball is struck on the center for the rail shot.

The swing for an angle shot starts close to the body and finishes away from the body, contacting the ball slightly on the inside.

The cross-court swing begins away from the body; the ball is contacted slightly on the outside and the swing finishes across the body.

JAY NELSON: Sure there's a correlation with billiards. I'm a pretty good billiards player . . . I've played an awful lot. Absolutely it's a factor. I have a pretty good three-wall shot. I've thought of this analogy several times. I know how to make balls accelerate off the sidewall, what kind of spin to make to hit them and make them take off, cause I've spent a lot of time hitting cueballs into sidewalls. So that's an edge I have with that particular shot; also, the roll corner; same thing. I am used to thinking in terms of hitting balls so they spin with sidespin.

I think people are analytical about it, studying the angles. But nothing has been written. Barnaby talks about the spin all the time. The roll corner—spin plays a big role in that. You don't hit that flat, and the same with the three-wall; it translates angular momentum. The sidespin adds to the speed so that it comes *off* faster than it comes *in.*

Sidespin is very useful in certain shots. Maybe guys don't talk about it or articulate it, but it's used. For example, if my opponent has hit a bad three-wall where I'm perched at the T, I will use sidespin, or sort of reverse sidespin, and hit it side/front—that kills it. I want to hit the kind of spin that will deaden it. It's hard to do. It requires timing and touch.

Stu Goldstein has told me that he tries to hit his drives with sidespin. If you hit the rail shot with sidespin, it really kills it. You give up your power, but it cuts the speed of the ball as it's coming off. Underspin, particularly on the rail shot—people get into trouble with that one. They don't know how to apply it properly. The idea is to come down on the *back* of the ball on it and take it down with an open face. It took a lot of years playing ineffectually to figure it out. I used to waste a lot of effort hitting the ball the wrong way. You give up a little power, but it's worth it. The idea is to come *down* on it, in back, as opposed to hitting level under the ball.

Putting spin on the ball, in my opinion, is to maintain contact with the ball for a longer period of time—a very subtle point, but a very important point. And maybe part of this thing of hitting it with sidespin is implicit. But the same holds true, I think. If I hit it with topspin, I also have a more accurate serve. Now we're getting down to how much time your hand has in contact, and I think if there's enough of a difference in your hand, if your hand is smart enough, if you've got a "smart" hand, that little extra contact, then you're more accurate. I think I stole that idea out of World Tennis a couple of years ago—a guy just mentioned it in passing. It's very important. You know, why do you put a little longer spin at the net in tennis doubles? Or in a volley? People have all kinds of reasons, but the main point is really it's just a by-product of a way to keep the ball and racquet together, it just happens to have underspin. It's a way that you kind of caress it a little bit.

I find that the sidespin will do it for me . . . keeping the ball on the racquet. Henri Salaun strung his racquet very loosely for that reason. He likes the ball to kind of go in. I find I have trouble putting it away now, if I have loose strings. I want the ball to go in and out quickly because I'm gonna swing hard enough that it's gonna go back; I don't need it going back like this and having a trampoline effect.

I've been hitting my serve a lot better than I used to. And I'm now hitting it with topspin. And I think I would recommend to everybody that they do this. I knew guys who were using it four or five years ago . . . Tom Poor. I said, "Jeez, what a great serve that guy's got," and I knew it was topspin. I guess I tried to duplicate it, but it never worked out till this year. I knew Sam Howe hit it with a little topspin. This is on the lob serve. It's one of these things where you just kind of brush it a little. The point is, if you think about the geometry, if you hit it with topspin, you're getting more height. The other way, the angle is not as abrupt. It really works!

JOHN REESE: I think that clearly the most sensible way to hit the ball is to give it a chop action, an action that imparts underspin on a ball, because, frankly, on a hot court, that is the only way for one to control the ball to any extent. Putting underspin on the ball means that when the ball hits the front wall and then comes off and hits the ground, it sort of has a breaking action on the ball. Therefore, you can hit the ball very hard, but it will not come quite as far off as if you hit it flat. If you hit the ball flat, the ball will just go straight forward and straight back, and you'll have trouble getting out of the way. Topspin? There's just no such thing. There are one or two players who try to hit that, but it's impractical; it's a short, compact swing.

GORDON ANDERSON: To learn the forehand drop, put your nose against the front wall and use your wrist; the only way you can learn to use your wrist is to play close to that front wall, because if you use your arm, the ball is going to go by you. That's the best way to get them to use their wrist. Tennis players always swing their arm like this . . . and they hit, but their wrist doesn't move because it's not supposed to move. But when you get to here [opposite your front foot], your wrist should be coming through.

For a beginner, it's excellent practice to hit from very close to the front wall, because you learn to chop it too. The only way to get above the red tin is not to hit flat; you've got to cut it. The best strokes, and it's proven, are the result of slicing the ball, or meeting the ball on an open face. In squash your hand should be just on top of the racquet when you grip it, because what you're going to do is open the face up; now the strong part of my hand is behind the racquet. With a lot of patience, you finally understand why you're doing that. If you don't do that, then your wrist turns. Your racquet is only going to do what your wrist does. It's just that movement, and that's very important in squash. There's a lot to teach that people don't understand.

●

FOREHAND

To plot the proper trajectory of your swing, picture a clock on the sidewall with twelve o'clock level with your head and six o'clock just below knee level. With your wrist cocked and your elbow bent, take the racquet back, almost in the same plane as the wall, with the face very open, so that your racquet hand is just about level with your ear—at about one o'clock. The swing then starts at one o'clock, comes around to six o'clock, and contacts the ball at seven-o'clock at a point in front of your left knee. The follow-through continues straight in front of your body at the level of the seven-o'clock point of contact. This is a bit of an oversimplification, but it helps to visualize the path of the swing.

O.K.: Now that we have plotted the path of the swing, let's see how to execute the shot. One of the crucial differences between tennis strokes and squash strokes is that tennis asks a stiff wrist—the entire arm makes the stroke. In squash, the wrist snaps at the moment of contact, and the racquet whips through the ball. It is somewhat like throwing a ball side-

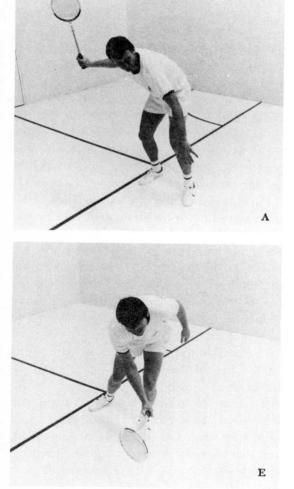

Forehand. Note that the wrist leads the way. The point of contact is opposite the left knee and the head stays down, watching the ball, until the follow-through is almost complete.

arm, a heaving motion with a wrist and hip action.

Your wrist is cocked and your elbow is bent at a right angle as you take the racquet back in the same plane as the wall. The ideal point of contact is opposite or slightly in front of your left knee. As you unwind into the swing with your wrist leading, step into the ball with your left leg, knee bent, so that you are low to the ball and your entire weight is transferred to your front foot and the power is transferred to the ball opposite that front foot at the moment of contact. The ball will sink into your racquet strings; heave it out of there in a whipping motion parallel to the floor.

If you follow the swing path described, you'll be coming down and under the ball at the point of contact to impart backspin. Although most hard-ball teachers advocate keeping the elbow tucked in close to the body, it's not really tactical. In actual play, you need the reach of your fully extended arm at the moment of contact.

By playing the ball at arm's length, you run less. In the English game the accent is on how much you can reach, not run. Americans go

C

D

G

H

Step into the ball. Always have your wrist cocked, and take your racquet back as you move to the ball. Your racquet should be fully cocked as you start the downswing. The weight of the body shifts to the front leg as contact is made opposite the left knee. Note left arm extended for balance.

into the corner to get the ball, so they've really gone an extra half step on every shot. Over the period of a match, it's a great distance, and each time they take themselves farther off the T than necessary. You don't always have time to go the full distance anyway, so learn to use that reach. By having your arm in close to your body, you can keep the ball hidden more, but you're losing a great deal of reach, which for most shots you'll need.

The follow-through is important. The longer the ball actually stays on your racquet, the more control you have over it. At the moment of contact, your back leg should be fully extended, with just the big toe touching the floor. It's important to keep your body low—there's more power in a low center of gravity—and your rear leg should not come off the floor until your follow-through is complete. Your power lies in transferring your weight into the ball. If you pull your rear leg around as you unwind your swing, or shift your front leg to a more open stance as you meet the ball, the

power is sometimes lost. Both feet should be planted, and stay that way, through the completion of the swing. If any foot-position change is made, it should go in the forward direction of the ball.

It goes without saying that in teaching the mechanics of strokes or shots or whatever, we're talking about ideal conditions—time to take a full backswing, get into proper position, to follow through, etc.—conditions that in actual play are often impossible.

But it's important to learn the *ideal* strokes, to groove them into your mind and body, and not get into bad habits. Practice the ideal stroke—no hitting off the back foot, or letting the ball get past your front leg, or not following through. The more often you do it right under practice conditions, the more often you'll do it right in actual play.

As you practice your strokes, you'll start noticing the different variables that change the direction, pace, and power of your shot: the position of your feet in relationship to the sidewall; the position of your shoulders; the trajectory and length of your backswing, swing, and follow-through; the spot and angle at which you make contact with the ball; the timing of your weight transfer; your position on the court. These are the things that turn strokes into *shots*, which will be discussed in the next chapter. Meanwhile, it's not too soon to take note of these things and see how they affect the behavior of the ball.

BACKHAND

Think of throwing a Frisbee, or flicking a towel in the locker room, and you have the image of the backhand motion and the reason why some consider it the "natural" stroke.

There are several basic differences in the execution of forehand and backhand. On the forehand, your rear arm is the racquet arm, and it must cross in front of your body to contact the ball at a point opposite your front leg.

On the backhand, your leading arm is wielding the racquet. In order to generate power, it's necessary to pivot your body more, from the hips up, so that you're actually turned toward the backwall. The toe of your rear foot should be pointing toward the back corner of the court. The racquet on the backswing still remains on a plane with the sidewall, but the upper body is in a position to uncoil so that additional power is built up by the time the ball is struck, ideally at a point about a foot in front of your leading leg.

Backhand. The body is pivoted on the backswing. The swing comes down and under the ball.

Contact is made at a point about a foot in front of the right knee.

Stroke Basics

Again, to plot the path of your swing, picture the clock on the sidewall. The swing starts at about eleven o'clock, and comes around and makes contact with the ball at about four or five o'clock, and the follow-through continues parallel to the floor at the level at which you make contact with the ball. Whereas the bottom of your swing on the forehand occurs at a point opposite your left (or front) foot, the bottom of your swing on the backhand occurs at a point in front of your leading (or right) foot.

VOLLEY

A volley is a shot hit, forehand or backhand, before the ball bounces. It is usually an attacking shot, one that prevents the ball from going to the backwall. And if you're preventing the ball from going to the backwall, you're speeding up the rally, giving your opponent less time to prepare his shot and get the ball back, and you are keeping him off balance.

From the T, and *with your wrist cocked*, you should be able to get off many volleys. If a ball is short, you can step up to get it. If it hits the sidewall, your shot should be timed to hit the ball just before or after it contacts the wall.

Volleying requires quick and deliberate action. You don't have to hit the ball hard, and, in the beginning, you don't have to worry about placement. You're trying to make contact with the ball at the earliest opportunity.

Usually, thoughts of proper footwork are thrown to the winds when volleying; there just isn't time to think about it. Ninety per cent of the time you're facing the front wall. If you're lucky, you may have time to pivot your body somewhat toward the sidewall. The important thing is to have your wrist cocked and take as much backswing as you have time for. The idea is to come from above, with a sort of chopping and punching motion, so that you make contact firmly, slightly under and behind the ball. (The forehand volley is like a punch-

ing motion; the backhand requires more of a chop.) The stroke should be made quickly and firmly, and you still must follow through. Most people are inclined to stop at the moment of contact and look at the front wall to see the result of the shot. But it's important to keep your racquet, and your eyes, on the ball as long as possible. This is where you get your control. It really has to do with your head—keeping your head still; don't move it abruptly as you hit the ball.

This is a good place to re-emphasize a point about racquet stringing. Generally, a tightly

A

D

strung racquet will give you power, but you often sacrifice control. Especially for the beginning and intermediate player, a more loosely strung racquet will enable you to keep the ball on the strings and thus under your control for a valuable fraction of a second longer—a meaningful length of time, especially on the volley.

The volley is an important weapon in squash, but is often neglected by beginners until they are well along in the game. Don't wait to start learning and practicing your volleys.

Build up your volleying along with your basic ground strokes. Start practicing by standing on the service line and hitting repeated forehand volleys. As you gain confidence, walk closer and closer to the front wall, shortening the time between shots. Then try the same thing on the backhand. The next step is to again stand on the service line and alternate forehand and backhand volleys. Just don't be intimidated by the speed with which the ball comes back, and don't try to do anything more than get the ball back to the front wall with a firm stroke.

B

C

E

F

Forehand volley. Take as much of a pivot and backswing as you have time for. Swing down on *the ball in a jabbing, chopping motion, and follow through.*

A

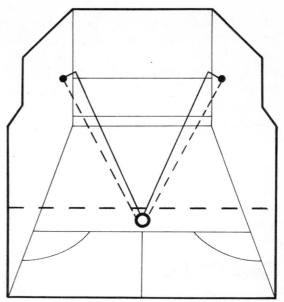

Volley practice.

B

Backhand volley. The racquet is taken back as you move to the ball, body erect to meet the ball high. The racquet chops at the ball as power is transferred through the shoulders and wrist snap. Follow through to the front wall.

C

D

Once you've gained confidence in your volley, it becomes a very versatile stroke. In many cases, you will have the chance to put the ball away on the volley; don't hesitate to do so when the opportunity arises. When your opponent is slightly in front of you, and you are slightly out of position, a volley can often move your opponent and give you the chance to reclaim the T.

And remember, the volley is not just a front-wall shot. With practice you can learn to direct and place a volley to make an angle shot, a reverse corner, etc. Learn to change the direction of the ball in mid-air—a matter of fine timing.

Variety on the volley can be developed through drills and exercises, such as standing on the service line and volleying to opposite sidewall corners.

HALF VOLLEY

A half volley is a shot hit on the forehand or backhand *immediately* after the ball bounces on the floor. When you make this shot you're saying, "I couldn't reach it in time to volley, but the half volley is the quickest thing."

On the half volley you're catching the ball just inches off the floor, again rushing your opponent, giving him little time to prepare his shot.

The half volley requires very fast reflexes, and you must get *down* to the ball. Since you're practically picking the ball up off the floor, there's not always time for much of a backswing. Your objective is to get the racquet behind and under the ball and flick it in a whipping motion to the wall.

E

F

Often the half volley is a defensive shot; it's coming right at your feet, and you know that if it passes you, you won't get another chance at it. But if you can play the half volley offensively, it's a powerful stroke. The term refers to any shot hit just after the bounce, but there are half-volley drops, half-volley angles, half-volley reverse corners, etc. These are not for the beginner, but all they require is practice and the recognition that they can be used to great advantage.

SERVICE

While the squash serve is not the potential killer shot that it is in tennis, its offensive and advantageous possibilities are often underrated.

The server has two chances to serve, and any ball is fair that hits first the front wall above the service line and makes its first bounce (or would) in the opposite service box. If the ball hits the backwall at any point during the serve, it must hit below the backwall line. Also, the server's foot must remain within the

service quarter circle until the ball has left the racquet.

LOB SERVE

The lob serve is often erroneously treated as merely a means of putting the ball in play while giving the server time to gain position of the T. In fact, with careful placement—which is just a matter of practice—the lob serve can be difficult to return with anything but a weak shot. It can even be unretrievable.

The lob serve is most effective on a high-ceiling court, when it can be angled to loop high and drop almost vertically into the back corners or glance off the sidewall at a point too high for the receiver to make a volley return.

Angle and placement are the keys; it is not a power shot. The server conserves his energy and maintains his balance while moving to the T to prepare for the receiver's return shot.

The lob serve is essentially a cross-court shot. In order to minimize the angle of cross-court and thus increase the chances of placing the serve in the corner or having it glance off

C

D

E

Half volley. Take as much of a pivot and backswing as you have time for. Get down very low and get under the ball, scooping it off the floor immediately after the bounce. Follow through.

the wall at the most minimal angle (in the strike zone shown on page 84), the server should maximize his reach from the service quarter circle out into the front and center of the court.

When serving from the left service box, your right foot is in the box as close to the red lines in the direction of center court as possible. Then take your left foot as far forward and toward the center as you can. Hold the ball ready for service toward the front wall as well, with the intent of hitting it at the full reach of your swing. Now you've got quite a start on the ball.

The stroke itself is a lifting motion, which starts very low and ends high. You drop the ball, and your racquet comes up under it with the face opened toward the lights and lifts it firmly. You don't have to put much spin on it; when it hits the wall at such an acute angle, the wall will put spin on it, and it will arc up over your opponent's head. If your opponent wants to volley, he's going to have to do it if and after it hits the sidewall.

Perfecting the lob serve is a matter of perfecting the angle of the stroke and its place-

Stroke Basics

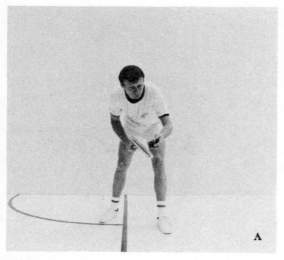

Lob serve. The ball should be dropped so that the racquet comes up under the ball in a lifting

motion. On the follow-through, take your first step back toward the T.

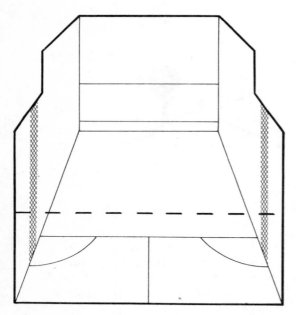

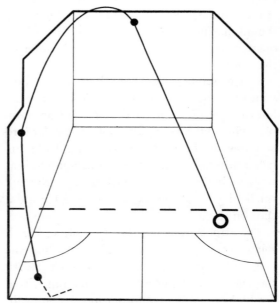

The strike zone. Lobs should strike the shaded area near the out-of-court line. Cross courts should strike close to the floor.

Lob serve.

ment on the front wall. The angle differs when you are serving from the left court (where your racquet arm is closer to the center) and the right court. But basically, the "spot" is high on the front wall just a little left or right of center toward the side to which you're serving.

Now, there are situations where you would want to vary the placement of the lob serve. If you're playing someone with a weak backhand and his backhand is in the center for receiving service, then occasionally play the lob down the center. You might do the same to someone who you know has a strong down-the-line volley return. Against that same person, you want to make sure the ball gets down to the floor before he's got a chance at it. With someone who has trouble backing or turning on the

Satterthwaite hits a lob serve.

HARD SERVE

The hard serve is an overhead shot, usually hit with some topspin, at the full extension of the arm and with as much power as you can muster.

The stroke is executed somewhat like a pared-down tennis serve. The right foot is in the service box; the left foot steps out a bit toward the center of the court. As the left hand tosses the ball to a point high above the left shoulder at arm's length, the right hand takes the racquet straight back over the right shoulder. The racquet should be cocked so that it is automatically dropped down the back somewhat. Watching the ball carefully, the racquet is thrown forward to catch the ball at the top of the toss at full arm's length. As you lean forward to contact the ball, the weight shifts to the left leg, putting the power of the whole upper body behind the shot at the moment of

ball, you would place it so that it hits the side-wall and backwall before he can get a good crack at it.

BACKHAND LOB SERVE

The backhand lob serve is a much-neglected shot, yet it can be very useful. Used from the right-hand service box, it can be utilized to maximize your reach into the front and center of the court so that you're cutting the cross-court angle down considerably—it's practically a rail shot. You're also facing the receiver rather than having your back to him, and you don't have to turn to move to the T when you execute the shot. There's really no reason why this serve isn't used more often; it doesn't require power, just the same direction and placement used for the forehand lob serve.

Backhand lob serve. This overlooked variation on the lob serve is useful from the right court. It brings your body closer to the T, and you are facing the court to make the serve.

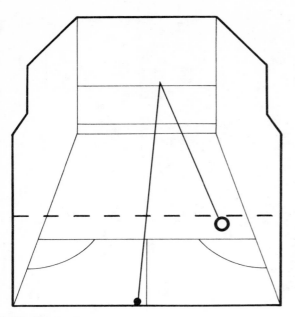

Hard serve to center.

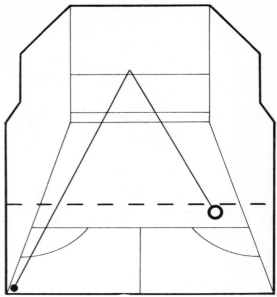

Hard serve (for nick).

impact. The wrist should snap at the point of contact, whipping through the ball in an outward and downward motion, as though the head of the racquet were being pitched at the wall. The follow-through is downward so that your racquet hand ends up close to your left knee. The ball should strike the front wall as close above the service line as possible.

Unless you already have a good tennis serve, it takes some practice to develop the combination of timing and power needed for a good hard service. And a weak hard service is an easy putaway for the receiver, especially since the server is usually off balance for a second as the result of his efforts.

Building a sound hard serve is a worthwhile endeavor, however. It can be used as a change of pace, when your opponent has gotten used to preparing for lob serves. It can be used to rush your opponent. It's also good to use it when the score is tied or when the score is in double figures—10-all or more—when you want to get the crucial point that breaks the game in your favor. When you use the hard serve, you're hoping it's going straight into the nick for a winner; that's what you're trying for.

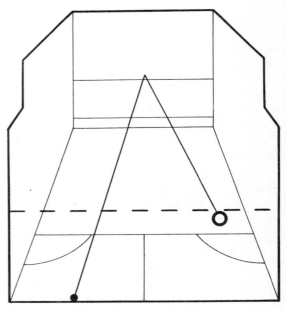

Hard serve at opponent.

But if you don't get that, you're hoping to throw your opponent off balance, to surprise him, baffle him, generally make him run around, and force a weak return.

Other than trying for the nick, one of the

Hard serve. Ball contact should be made over the ball at full arm's length, with a snap of the wrist, as though pitching the racquet head at the front wall.

Doug McLaggan demonstrates the hard-serve toss.

best places to aim is straight at your opponent. At high speed, it's very hard just to get out of the way of the ball. If he can't volley very quickly, he's going to have to go to the backwall, and then anything can happen. It may go into the nick, and it may rebound way down along the sidewall or back to the service line, where it will need to be chased after.

Some players can't return the fast serve at all, in which case just use it as often as possible. But it does take precious energy and it does leave you, the server, momentarily off balance. So in most cases it's advisable to save it for the important points. It's also important to keep in mind that it can backfire. If your opponent is ready for it, he may just score right off it. You've got to have confidence in the serve, which means it must be consistently powerful enough to make it to the bottom of the backwall on the fly. Until you can do this —and it just takes practice—it will be effective only against the weakest of opponents.

CUT (OR SLICE) SERVE

The cut serve requires touch and a firm stroke. The left hand tosses the ball up and to the

right, not as high as for the hard serve, as the cocked racquet is taken back to the side just above shoulder height. The racquet comes down with the face very open and strikes the ball between shoulder and waist height. The ball should be struck with some pace, on the underside and outside of the ball (from the forehand court), and the racquet should maintain contact with the ball as it is drawn under and across the ball toward the body. A follow-through across and out front of the body is essential. The ball should strike the front wall just above the service line, just left or right of center toward the court to which you're serving. The spin causes the ball to drop sharply into the nick just behind the service line, or very low on the wall behind the service line, and to die before reaching the backwall.

Again, this serve should only be used as a change of pace, especially to win a crucial point. Because the ball drops so fast and so sharply, your opponent will have a hard time stepping up to volley it. And once it hits, it should make little, if any, bounce. A failed slice serve is a disaster, however, so don't try it until you have mastered the timing that enables you to put the required spin and firmness on the ball.

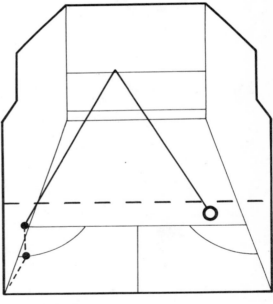

Cut (or slice) serve.

This is as good a time as any to restate the difference between cut and slice. Cut is up and down—coming under or over the ball. Slice is sideways motion—drawing the racquet *across* the ball—either toward or away from the body. This serve is often called the slice serve. In

Cut (or slice) serve.
Contact is made with a very open racquet face, and the racquet strings are drawn under and across the ball, toward the body. The follow-through is across the body.

fact, this serve requires at least as much underspin as slice. Unless the racquet comes well under the ball, all the slice in the world won't bring that ball *down*. The slicing or sideways motion requires even defter touch than just undercut, and much of the slice action is lost when the ball hits the front wall—much of the awkward bounce and sideways motion of the ball is lost by the time it gets back to the service line.

RETURN OF SERVE

Your first objective in returning the serve is to get the ball back: to make *a* return, which, for the beginner, means getting it above the tin. The next objective is to get it back and *not* return it to the middle of the court, so you can get to the T. The third objective is to make a calculated offensive shot.

Getting beyond the point where you're just worrying about getting the ball back, and

using the return of serve as a chance to get on the offensive, are big steps.

Every return of serve should be awaited in a position of readiness, just inside the center line of the receiving court, a few feet in from the backwall in a square or slightly open stance facing the sidewall. Your racquet should be cocked, you should be in a slight crouch on the balls of your feet, looking over your shoulder to see what the server is going to do. Knowing that you will be usually returning serve with a forehand in the right court, with a backhand from the left court, you must nevertheless be prepared for anything the server may try on you.

As soon as the server starts his delivery, you should be able to tell whether you're getting a lob, hard, or slice serve and be prepared mentally for the speed and type of movement required to return it. As soon as he swings, you should be able to judge its approximate path and prepare for the return, and immediately move to the ball. Remember that in most cases, the best return is a volley, because it cuts down your opponent's time and because once the ball bounces or caroms or gets to the backwall, you'll likely have a more difficult return and lose valuable time and court position. And sometimes the volley is the *only* chance you'll get before the ball dies.

Zachariah tries a cut serve on Barbara Maltby in the Bancroft Women's Open.

Barbara Maltby standing quite far into the center of the service court, but in perfect position for return of serve.

LOB SERVE RETURN

Once you see that you're getting a lob serve, you must judge at what point you will volley the ball, and move toward it. A good high lob serve may not be within reach until after it has hit the sidewall; in any case, you will probably be making a high volley just before or just after the ball hits the sidewall, so timing is critical. As you step up to the ball, take a short backswing. You should contact the ball out in front of your body. From your erect position

you won't be able to put much weight behind your shot; a short, firm stroke and wrist snap must generate the power. If you have confidence in either your forehand or backhand side, you should plan to make an aggressive return, especially if you're lucky enough to get a weak serve on that side.

If you've failed to volley the return and the ball doesn't die in the corner or nick, any number of things can happen.

You may have to scramble into the corner for a ball that's just barely coming off the sidewall and/or backwall. All you can reasonably hope to do is get under and behind the ball and flick or push it to the front wall, or blast it high and hard enough into the sidewall that it reaches the front. Crowded against the backwall, your backswing is severely limited and your shot must be timed to contact the ball during its brief travel between sidewall and backwall or backwall and floor. In this situation, it is helpful to almost face the backwall

for the stroke so that you start the swing parallel to the backwall.

A lob serve that's been overhit is going to carom off the side- and backwalls and come out toward the center of the court. There are two ways of handling this possibility:

Backing on the ball: This means literally backing away from the sidewall and moving toward the center of the court. The object is to get away from the caroming ball and into position to hit it at the place where you judge it will break out into the court. Needless to say, this must be done quickly. Now that you have placed yourself in the center of the court, you have forced the server to retreat even farther to the opposite sidewall. The best shot here is to hit a rail shot with good length. You, the receiver, are just about on the T at this point, and you have neatly backed up the server against the opposite wall. Even though he's likely to guess your intent, he'll have a hard time getting across the court in time.

Turning on the ball: This involves turning and pivoting toward the backwall as the ball passes you, and following it around as it caroms off the side- and backwalls so that you end up facing the *opposite* sidewall; where you were planning to hit a backhand, you're now on your forehand (or vice versa). When you do this about-face, you must so signify to your opponent by calling "coming around" or "turning," so he can readjust his position. His likely response is then to head toward the side you have turned away from, in which case your response is to hit a rail shot down the side toward which you've turned. Turning on the ball is a let-conducive situation, however. If you don't warn him in time, he may not get out of the way, or he may end up cowering against the sidewall in fear of getting hit by a wild ball.

Frank Satterthwaite has turned on the ball, but Victor Niederhoffer is still running to the opposite side of the court; a let (or let point) is likely. Note that Satterthwaite faces the backwall so he can take a full swing on his shot.

HARD SERVE RETURN

In volleying a hard serve return, time is of the essence. You will not be able to do much

Frank Satterthwaite hits his hard serve.
Niederhoffer is already on the move.

more than take a short backswing, get your
racquet behind the ball, and block it back;
with practice you'll be able to angle it in your
desired direction. The important thing is not
to be scared or flustered by it; just get your
racquet on it, and the speed of the serve will
carry it back to the front wall. Some hard
serves will be taken on the fly off the sidewall,
but many will be aimed right at you. Just
move quickly to the side and put your racquet
where *you* were.

A hard serve that isn't taken on the volley
will rebound fast and hard off the sidewall
and/or backwall, and you must be prepared to
quickly back off and chase it downcourt a considerable distance.

CUT (OR SLICE) SERVE RETURN

A half-volley return is just about the best
chance one has against the slice serve. As the
ball will drop not far behind the service line,
you must move up immediately, knees bent, to
prepare to make a low half-volley return. You
will likely be contacting the ball quite close to
the wall.

If you miss the half volley, the ball will hit
low on the sidewall or on the floor and make a
very low bounce, so you still have to move into
the ball and be in a crouch position for the
return.

Stroke Basics

Hitter too far away from the ball. By not stepping in close enough to make a good shot, the hitter loses the power generated by the

weight transfer and is forced to hit the ball on the end of his racquet.

Hitter too close to the ball. By stepping in too close to the ball, the hitter loses the power of a full swing and of the weight transfer. By not

being able to get down to the ball, he loses power and a good view of his shot.

Letting the ball get past. In not hitting the ball opposite or in front of your leading leg, you lose the power of a full swing and weight transfer.

Here the shoulders are practically facing the front wall; all power will have to be generated by the racquet arm.

Hitting off the wrong foot. When forced to hit off the back foot, pivot the upper body to the correct position, and arc the wrist snap for power.

Hitting the ball too far in front of the body. A good position for a lob, but by meeting the ball too far in front of the body, power is lost.

Stu Goldstein has Glenn Greenberg backed against the wall.

9

•

Court Coverage
and Control

Position is everything—or nearly everything—in squash, and the place to be is on the T. Good strokes and shots are all but useless unless combined with good court sense and the physical agility to use it. Good shots do, however, enable you to hold the T and to move your opponent away from it.

Court coverage is the art of moving to and from the T from anywhere on the court in the most economical manner, and without unlawfully interfering with your opponent's rightful use of the court.

Every shot you hit should be intended to move, and keep, your opponent off the T. This means hitting every shot into the area of the four corners of the court or within inches of the sidewall, and preferably into the corner that is the greatest distance from your opponent. Shots hit into the back corner give you the longest time to reclaim the T and give

your opponent small chance to hit a winner. But they also give him time to get set and give him the backwall as a second chance should the ball pass him. Shots into the front corners are harder to get to, don't offer the second chance of backwall shots, and are more likely to be winners. However, they require touch, and if mishit they will come out toward center court, giving your opponent a chance at a putaway and/or moving you off the T. Shots hit close to the sidewalls force a return requiring careful timing and usually force a weak return, because the ball cannot be hit in the center of the racquet, often resulting in the sound of wood hitting wall. Anytime you hear your opponent's racquet hitting the wall, you know you've made a pretty good shot.

Another important aspect of court control is *staying out in front*—of the court and of your opponent. This means volleying every chance

97

Yusuf Khan hits from behind Jay Nelson.

you get. It means not letting the ball past you if possible. It means moving up to the ball. It is easier to move back if you have to (because you often have a second chance at the ball) than to run the longer distance to the fore-court. It is harder for your opponent to hit a winner from behind you. The T is only in the middle of the court in relation to the side-walls; it is considerably farther from the front wall than the backwall. There's a far greater distance to go to reach a front-wall shot. Most players don't use enough short shots. You can put a lot of pressure on your opponent just making him get up there. Not every short shot has to be a winner. He's got to come a long way from center just to get it back, and no backwall behind him. If he doesn't make it, the rally is over.

In maintaining your position on the court, it helps to think not only of the T but also of the entire center area of the court in relation to the sidewalls. Picture a four-foot-wide car-pet going right down the middle, a red carpet. Then, no matter how far up or back you have to go to get a shot, make sure you always have one foot on the imaginary center carpet. Do this as you run to get shots in all parts of the court and you will be effectively maintaining your center position no matter how far up or back you go.

The T is an absolute territorial imperative; you should be there as often as possible. When not hitting the ball, you should be in the ready position, always in a crouch, on the balls of your feet, ready to spring.

Always watch the ball—not just your oppo-nent, not just the general area of the court, but the *ball*. Listening to your opponent's footsteps behind you is not enough. If he is behind you, look over your shoulder; if you feel overexposed, protect your face by holding the cocked racquet in such a way that you're looking through the strings. The sooner you know what that ball is going to do, the better. If you actually watch as your opponent ap-proaches his shot, you will get clues—from his balance, body position, speed, and swing—as to what he's going to do, and be prepared for his shot and plan your return. This is *antici-pation.* Every time you see your opponent's shot, by seeing him prepare for it, by under-standing the likely return in a given situation, you gain valuable time and insight to prepare for and move to your shot.

Watching your opponent actually strike the ball pinpoints further information you need to return it. Your first decision will be whether to take the shot on forehand or backhand. Imme-diately pivot to the appropriate sidewall, tak-ing your racquet back in the same motion. Then run like hell.

Running in squash has little to do with run-ning on a track or in a straight line, no matter how fast you do it. You're not talking about a player doing 100 yards in 9.6 seconds. You're talking about moving a few feet left or right, up and back. It is a matter of making a quick start in any direction, running, usually in a combination of long and short steps, even in a side-to-side shuffle, to the place where you want to meet the ball, in the fastest, most eco-nomical way, so that you arrive with your feet in the correct position, weight balanced, ready to step into the ball, and so that you can leave in a hurry.

Getting back to the T is as important as get-ting to your shots.

Correct and efficient footwork is important. Getting off on the right foot and knowing how many steps to take comes naturally to some. Others are always caught off balance or waste precious time getting into position. Only practice in running to all positions on the court, and then back to the T, will train you to know automatically what to do. Generally, you will take your first step off and back with your left foot to get to the left back corner, off and forward with your right foot, to get to the right forecourt corner, etc., and adjust to following steps in relation to your position for hitting the oncoming ball. To return to the T, take your first step in that direction, with the closest foot. In almost all cases, you want to hit the ball off your front foot. The exception to this might be in going for a forehand in the forecourt—the longest distance from the T. By ending with the right foot forward in the forecourt you're actually adding valuable inches to your reach, you're in good position to take your first step back toward the T with your left foot, and you're facing back toward the court as you make that first step back toward the T. Anytime you are in this situation of hitting off the right foot in the forecourt, keep your shoulders and upper body pivoted in the right direction to give power to your shot, so that you can still shift your weight forward, and also for the purpose of covering the shot.

To get to the ball, the rules entitle you, basically, to the most direct route. To go *from* the place where you hit the ball back to the T and to your next shot, you want the most direct route *that doesn't interfere with your opponent's rights to a fair shot.* Hopefully, you've made a shot that forces your opponent away from the T to make a return. Now you have an obligation not to get in the way. Until you understand the basic patterns of movement on the court, you will undoubtedly find yourself stepping across your opponent's path, bumping into your opponent, or plastering yourself defensively against the sidewalls in order to get out of the way. The sooner you get past this phase, the better. Players who run and swing wildly and unknowingly are dangerous; players who continually force let calls are boring to play with.

The interchanges of position between two players on the court are essentially rotations of position. Basically, you are circling each other and trading the T back and forth. If you hit a ball down the right wall, you move to the left, and your opponent moves right (and vice versa). If you are behind your opponent and the ball is deep in the right corner, you move left and then forward; he comes to the right and back. If you are in front, it's no problem. If you are in front of your opponent and the ball is short in the right corner, you move left and then back; your opponent moves right and forward. And so on. Study the accompanying diagrams of basic situations.

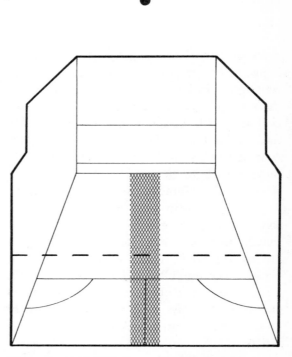

The red carpet. Picture a red carpet four feet wide running up the center of the court. No matter how far up or back you are on the court, use your reach and stretch so that you always keep one foot in the red-carpet zone.

Court Coverage and Control

99

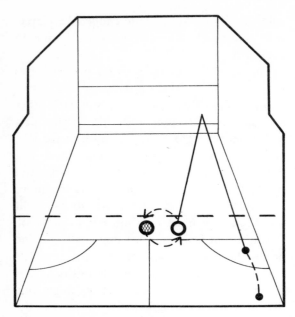

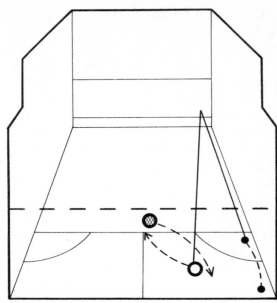

Hitter and receiver side by side. The hitter has made a deep rail shot. He must move forward and to the left as the receiver moves back and to the right.

Hitter in back of receiver. The hitter has made a deep rail shot. He must move left and then forward. The receiver moves diagonally right and back.

GEOFF HUNT: Always getting back to the T is just self-control. Part of my game is intercepting the ball, volleying with the ball. With the soft ball, you've got to get back into position in order to be able to do that, because for me, it's the shortest distance to any part of the court anyway, so it doesn't matter; I'm always moving back to the middle, and I'll try to dominate the middle of the game. The person, in our game, who stays in the middle the longest part of the game will probably win the match. And that's my objective: I'm going to try to get back there. Sometimes I can't, though, because I'll hit a bad shot and I'll have to keep out of the way. But as soon as the opponent plays, well, then, I'm off to try to recover . . . always back to that middle position.

DIEHL MATEER: I always knew where the ball was on the court. In this open tournament many players will not watch the ball 100 per cent of the time. They're quick and they want

to get out in front, and if their opponent is in back of them they might watch until he's ready to hit, but then they'll turn and be ready to go. But I wasn't fortunate enough to be quick, and I felt I had to see the ball leave the racquet. You're not going to see the ball that clearly, but you'll see the course that it takes, and you'll know from the motion of the racquet whether it's an arc, etc. You see the ball leave the racquet, with the blur of the ball, you know which quadrant—you can divide the court up into four quadrants: right front, left front, left rear . . . you should know at that instant in which quadrant of the court you're going to reply to that shot, and you can start to move for it. And in particular, if someone hits a straight drop, you can go with the ball, whereas if you are looking at the front wall, you've lost half the time that you really have. . . .

I think this is why Barnaby was such a great coach. He taught Charlie Ufford, Peter Briggs, taught them to wait on the ball and get their

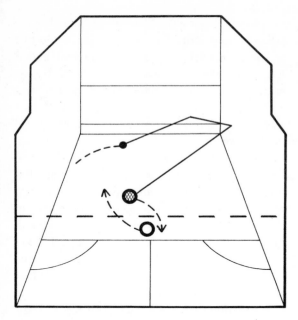

Hitter in front of receiver. The hitter has made a short reverse corner shot. He must move right and then back. The receiver moves diagonally left and forward.

JAY NELSON: There's a lot of misinstruction on watching the ball, or your opponent. Some guys tell you just to turn and watch the guy, and other people say that you have to do it all with peripheral vision. It's hard to do; I know I do it better than I used to, but I don't know what I do differently. Certainly you've got to look. Some people don't even look. At one time I was so bad at this, I thought, well, I'll try it without looking, maybe. But again, it comes down to this damn thing about your position on the T. I think I was so far forward—and again, maybe it's my own peripheral vision or my reaction time or something—that I had to turn my head so far around to catch anything that in the sweep of my head back to the front wall I was losing everything. I lost too much time. Now, if I'm hanging deeper the guy hits in the same place, I'm kind of looking at him *and* the front wall, and I don't have to jerk my head around; I can just sort of sweep it like that, almost just an eye motion.

BARBARA MALTBY: My anticipation is usually fairly good. If I've played or seen somebody play a few times, it's much better. Then I know their pet shots in certain situations. If

opponents to commit themselves, and they'd have the point go with them. Salaun, whom I played many times (and he'll probably disagree with this statement), but what I felt was that one of the two or three advantages I had over him was the fact that he didn't watch me hit the ball when I was in back of the court and he was out in front. I think he maybe had great ears . . . he actually relied on hearing the sound to tell him whether it was a short ball or a deep ball. That was the only thing I could figure, because very seldom did you fool him. I can't say he was 50 per cent faster, but he was at least 30 per cent faster than I. Of course, I could reach a little farther because of being taller, but I felt that if I had any advantage over most of my opponents, back twenty years ago, that was the most important advantage I had: always watching the ball. And in particular, in doubles. You go into doubles . . . there again the ball has to travel farther, and if you're late in seeing it, you've lost that much time.

John Reese hits from behind Khalid Mir, giving up as little of his center position as possible.

Court Coverage and Control

Always run with the racquet ready—as Carol Weymuller demonstrates.

to win—and George Cummings and I were talking about footwork. He had shown me two or three things. I was doing wrong that added five points to my game within a month. I went back and worked on one item in particular—and it just made all the difference; and that was basically in taking a step on the backhand or the forehand with the back foot before hitting the ball so that you've got your body in back of the ball ready to shift your weight forward. Then after our discussion on my footwork, George Cummings made this statement and said, "You can sum up the game of squash in one phrase." And I said, "George, I don't believe you. What's the phrase?" And he said, "The secret of the game of squash is 'Move your legs fast and your racquet slow.'"

Many times people come up to me and say, "You're never hurried on the court. You always seem to be moving sort of effortlessly and not racing to the ball." And I think this is for two reasons: No. 1, watching the ball, and No. 2, what George Cummings said, that you don't really have to move the racquet quickly. If you get your feet in position, then you've really got the whole day, in comparison, to hit the bloody ball.

they only have two or three favorite shots, that's good; then I can overplay those and make them hit something they can't hit as well. I think that's really important. I think my anticipation is getting better. You sort of know from a certain position they're only going to hit three or four certain shots, and sometimes something will tip you off so you can tell.

DIEHL MATEER: I've told this story to five hundred to a thousand people over the years (and it may even be five thousand). I think that it's the greatest statement about the game I ever heard—I wish I could take credit for it —but it came from George Cummings; he was pro at the University Club, I guess for forty years. I was playing doubles at the University Club and got into a long discussion after the finals of the tournament—which we happened

BARBARA MALTBY: It's very hard if you don't have the feeling, if you've never been in there relaxed, to know how much court you can cover in such little time. There's a great difference between being relaxed and being really tight and tense. Also, just in practicing covering the court, I've found on-court sprints to be very helpful because you can actually get to the ball and not even realize that you've actually started. You also learn how you can get to the ball, and how many steps it will take you to get from place to place. What I've been working on is trying to cover the court in fewer steps, maybe a few bigger steps.

As to being on the proper foot when you're hitting your forehand and backhand, actually I've never really figured that out yet. I wouldn't say you would have to; I think a lot of times you just don't have the time. If you want to volley, to quick-hit the ball, you just can't quite get the right foot in the right place. However, there are a lot of people who are kind of lazy and they want to leave one foot in the center of the court because they don't want to give up the T, so they sort of hit everything leaning backward. I was really interested to watch Geoff Hunt play last weekend; he was so fast that he could actually get in position and hit the ball really hard; he didn't do a lot of this stretching unless he really had to. He could hit a very effective shot every time because he was balanced.

JAY NELSON: Knowing how to move around on the court is important, but it's hard to teach that. You can see some guy and see that his first step is too big. It took me a while to learn that. I knew I was faster on a straight run than most guys I played but I didn't feel that quick on the court. You have to take a couple of small steps very rapidly to get up to speed. It's hard to say. I'd like to see films of myself so I could really be able to tell. But I know I run better than I used to, and yet I'm older. I know I run better now than when I was twenty-nine. I cover better on the court. I anticipate better. I watched Mo Kahn once from a gallery and I watched him just moving, and I improved just watching him. I got the message not to be frenetic. He would wait a fraction after the other guy hit the ball and then go. And you say, "Say, how the hell can you do that?" You're figuring the whole thing out, and somehow your brain is not only picking up the ball but it's also figuring how you're going to move to the ball. If you take off too soon you're going to wind up way out of balance, in weird positions. This way your brain is doing adjustments and figures it out, also figuring where the guy is. You're doing some "processing" before you start to run.

Footwork is very important; most people don't understand how important. Some guys have terrific footwork, and some guys penalize themselves. John Reese has excellent footwork; he's almost always leaning into the ball. Heth-erington has good footwork. I'm talking about moving from the T and ultimately the weight transfers into the ball. And the feet are the key to the whole thing.

Being on your forward foot on every shot from any position on the court is not crucial, but it beats the alternative. That is a very important factor. I now cheat back from the T and the whole reason is to have forward momentum, besides sideways. It's a trade-off, a gambit; you give up something up front. But then you can sweep forward. I think it's very important.

GORDON ANDERSON: There are good running exercises, like going from side to side, making sure that on this wall you end with your left foot forward; a lot of people can't do that. And run to the other side and as you step, you start with your right foot over, so that you're turning, then they finish the stroke above the ball and they run over here and step. I've had people trip into the wall and everything; and they're good athletes—soccer players, etc. So you say: "Work on that for a while."

Newman and McKay in a pas de deux.

Satterthwaite returns with a cross court.

10

•

Shots

Shots are strokes that are planned, paced, and placed. In this section we'll look at the standard shots of the game, and discuss the basics of choosing and executing the shots and their uses in the game.

Good, solid strokes are only the foundation of shots. Knowing when and how to use the various shots calls for some of the mental as well as the physical skills of the game: pace, power, touch, deception, quickness, anticipation, timing, and footwork.

One recurring problem in discussing or writing about squash is that of terminology. One man's rail is another man's alley; what's a Philadelphia to you is a Germantown to your opponent. A drop shot is usually thought of as a front-wall shot; in fact, any shot that drops near the front wall by virtue of underspin is a drop shot; gravity is gravity. So you can have a cross-court drop, a straight drop, a corner drop, etc. We'll try to keep it simple.

Some shots are considered the bread and butter of the game: the rails and cross courts with which you move your opponent around, tiring him, keeping him off balance and off the T. Others are touch and finesse shots—the shots that require deft timing and placement, some of them putaways that win the point once you've moved your opponent out of position with the setups.

The more shots you have in your bag of tricks, the more versatile a game you'll have and the more weapons you'll have to wage the battle. But you can only play the shots you know and have confidence in. Rails and cross courts present no special problem; they demand power more than anything. It's the finesse shots—drops and corners and boasts—

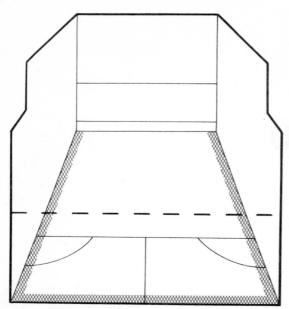

Most shots should finish in the shaded area, close to the sidewalls and backwall, in the corners of the court.

Hitting off the backwall. Niederhoffer waits on Stu Goldstein's shot. A ball coming out so far off the backwall is a setup. Goldstein is in perfect position—full backswing, eyes on the ball, weight ready to shift forward behind the ball as it heads downcourt.

that are error-prone. It's a fact that any shot that hits a sidewall first is more tricky; if misjudged it will come out into center court for an easy return.

One mistake that many beginners make is to rely solely on the rails and cross courts and leave the more difficult shots for "later." But these are the shots that take time to master, and in putting off learning them, the player loses valuable time. Most players tend to shortchange the sidewall shots. They feel comfortable on their drives and play the front wall almost exclusively. They're intent on getting that ball to the front wall, hacking away at it. It's unfortunate, because if you can make use of the sidewalls—the nicks and slow angles— you've often got a chance to score. It's worth working on these finesse shots; they're weapons that few players have and few know how to handle.

The short shots also make use of the length of the court to run your opponent around. If all your shots are deep, you may be running him from side to side. It's a lot harder and a

lot farther to run forward and back. Don't underestimate the value of those corners and drops in wearing your opponent down.

You should practice the touch shots along with your reliable rails and cross courts. You don't have to use them in actual play until you have confidence in them. It's not necessary to be able to play every shot, but every time you master and understand another one well enough to play it on the court, you've made another addition to your arsenal.

As you learned and practiced your strokes, you noticed what variables determined their power and direction—the length, path, and direction of the swing, the angle of the racquet face and the point on the ball with which it made contact, your stance, the angle of your shoulders, the shift of weight, the wrist snap, the follow-through, your position on the court, etc.

These are the things that concern us in executing shots.

But execution of the shot is only half of shotmaking. Choosing the right shot at the right time is the other half. The variables here are different: Where is your opponent on the court? What kind of player is he? Where am I on the court, and where do I want to be? What's my strength from here? Am I tired? Off balance? Is the pace too slow? Too fast? Is it time to hit the "winner"?

Learning what shot to hit when is as important as learning how to hit it. We could give you hundreds of diagrams showing various positions, various relationships of hitter to receiver, and giving possible shot choices. But in actual play, there are many variables, and your relationship to your opponent is only one. Diagrams assume a very static situation—one in which your opponent is without the brains and reflexes to get to the ball. Your opponent's mobility, weaknesses, and strengths, and the temperature of the court are all factors to consider. Every situation demands a unique response.

All we can do is give you the basics of execution and some guidelines as to their use. The discussion of strategies and tactics that follow in later chapters will go farther into the subtleties of deception, anticipation, game analysis, and flexibility, which will help hone your control and selection of shots.

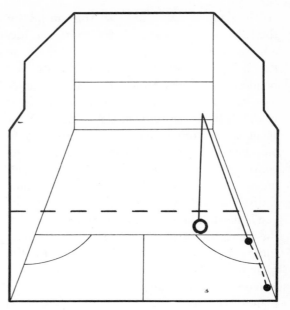

Rail shot.

RAIL SHOTS

One of the two bread-and-butter power shots of the game, rail shots are drives that hit the front wall first and rebound straight down the wall you are facing. A well-hit rail shot stays low and very close to the sidewall and has "length"—that is, it makes its second bounce near the bottom of the backwall.

The shot forces your opponent off the T and into the back corners of the court. If the ball is hugging the sidewall, he will have to make a careful return, most likely a weak angle shot that forces him to hit into the sidewall to scoop the ball away. In any case, he'll have to hit the ball near the end of the racquet. If the ball reaches the backwall at all, it won't come out far enough for him to get much of a swing at it. While he is making his return, you are reclaiming the T and awaiting what will hopefully be a weak return or a return that finds him hopelessly out of position.

How hard to hit the ball and how high above the tin it should strike the front wall depend on how far from the front wall you

Knees bent, racquet back, feet set in closed stance, body in perfect S formation, Victor Niederhoffer begins his downswing.

are, how much power and spin you can put on the ball, the temperature of the court, etc. Ideally, you're hitting just inches above the tin, so the ball rebounds low and makes its first bounce behind the service line. If you don't have the power to do this or if the court is cold, you'll have to set your sights higher. Your accuracy is another factor. It's much easier to aim low when you're hitting from the forecourt. The ball has a long way to travel coming from the backcourt, so you have to allow yourself as wide a margin of error as you feel you'll need. The execution of the shot makes the demands of any power shot: full swing, square to closed stance, body low to the ground with knees bent, snap of the wrist, and weight shift from the back to front leg at point of contact.

Rail shots and cross courts that keep your opponent off the T, out of position, off balance, and tired are standard tactics of squash. Eventually you will tire him or maneuver him so out of position that you can go for the winner.

Practice the rail shot from the backcourt, the service line, and the forecourt on both forehand and backhand. Try to increase your power so that you can keep the ball low and still have it make its first bounce near the serv-

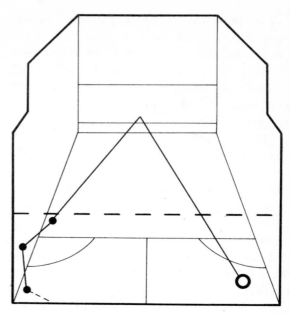

Cross court. All cross courts should hit the strike zone shown in Diagram 25.

ice line. Underspin is also important; a drive that sails straight to the backwall or that bounces hard against the backwall will come back downcourt and put the receiver in good court position. As you gain accuracy, you'll be able to hit the ball with confidence closer and closer to the tin.

CROSS COURTS

The cross court is a power drive that travels a V-shaped path from one side of the court to the center of the front wall and rebounds to the opposite sidewall behind the service line. This and the rail shot are the backbone shots of the game, the shots by which you move your opponent out of position until you see the opening for the kill.

In a way this shot is easier than the rail because you don't have to cross paths with your opponent in going back to the T.

Almost every cross court should hit the sidewall within the strike zone indicated on page

Khalid Mir sends the ball down the alley against Frank Satterthwaite in the Metropolitan Open.

SQUASH HOW TO PLAY, HOW TO WIN

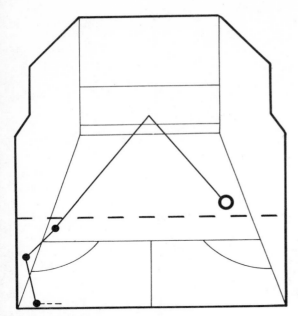

The same shot from mid-court.

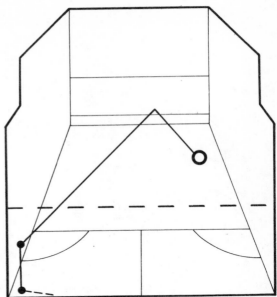

This cross court strikes the sidewall near the floor at the back of the service box and drops to the floor in the corner.

84, an area eighteen inches wide running up the sidewalls, from halfway back in the service quarter circle. Ideally, it should hit those sidewalls within eighteen inches of the floor. The ball should strike the front wall just above the tin with enough backspin so that it stays down. You need all the requirements of any power shot, as described for the rail.

The angle of the shot and the power with which it is hit depend on where you are on the court. To give direction to the shot, your stance would normally be square to slightly open. To combine deception with the shot, you would assume the square to closed stance of a straight drive and change the path of your swing, bringing it out and around the ball, contacting it slightly on the outside and continuing the swing in the direction in which you want it to go.

While you would hit a rail shot when your opponent was on the opposite side of the court, you would choose a cross court if he was on the same side—the longest distance.

Practice the cross court, both forehand and

backhand, from all court positions to see what angle is necessary in each case to hit the target zone. Lean a second racquet up against the wall with the butt of the handle on the floor within the strike zone on one side of the court. Hit cross courts from the opposite side until you knock the racquet over. Then switch sides.

Your basic game depends on being able to hit sound rails and cross courts from any position on the court and being able to return to the T efficiently and without danger of let calls. You should never make errors on these shots. They are your power shots. You are dependent on them to give you an opportunity for the finesse shots that win points.

ANGLES

Angle shots differ from rails and cross courts in that they hit the sidewall and then the front wall. Into this broad category of shots fall corners, reverse corners, corner and reverse corner drops, etc.

Shots

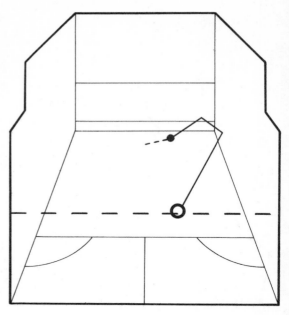

Corner.

Frank Satterthwaite prepares to hit a slow-angle shot against Khalid Mir. Note that Mir is one step to his opponent's side of the T.

Any angle shot by definition requires more careful placement and touch because it is a given fact that any shot that hits a sidewall will have a tendency to come back out into the center of the court. But squash is nothing if not a game of angles. Knowing how to make the sidewalls work for you from various positions on the court is imperative.

Let's look first at the corner shots.

Corner shots should strike the sidewall within two feet of the front wall and should be hit with a great deal of underspin and *slice* so that the ball is drawn sideways and down into the front wall, and bounces somewhat parallel to the front wall rather than out into the court.

Reverse corner shots are cross-court shots hit to the opposite sidewall within two feet of the front wall and that rebound in quick succession to the front wall and bounce parallel to the front wall. From behind you on the opposite side of the court, your opponent has a long

way to travel to get to the ball. With a rapierlike whip of the wrist to angle the ball, you can cover your shot until the last minute. Many players have a tendency to pull their leading leg away from the shot or pull their back leg around as they hit the ball, greatly reducing the power and direction of the shot. The feet should be set; use the wrist and upper body and the shoulders to swing around the outside of the ball to get the proper angle.

The power shots we've previously discussed are used to keep your opponent back and have the tendency to move him from side to side. Drops and corners are short shots—they move your opponent to the front of the court, the longest distance from the T. It's as important to think about moving your opponent up and back and along the diagonals of the court—the longest distance.

Any sidewall shot played from behind the floor service line can be termed a *slow angle*. Not too many players are using this shot—they're more likely to go for the three-wall nick. But it's a good shot when you're in the back and you've got time enough and room enough; you're basically trying to move your

SQUASH HOW TO PLAY, HOW TO WIN

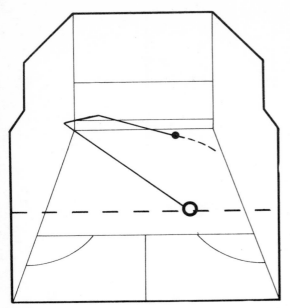

Reverse corner (reverse angle).

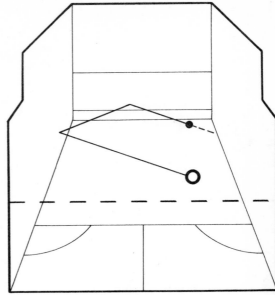

Reverse corner, closer to front wall.

opponent, but if you can get that second bounce in the crack, you may have a winner as well. What you have to think of on the slow angles is the distance to the front wall. You have to hit the ball up into the sidewall so it will go the distance, hoping it will be coming down when it gets to the front wall, dropping into the nick at the opposite sidewall on the second bounce. Merely by virtue of hitting a sidewall before the front wall, some of the "starch" is taken out of the shot, and it drops from loss of velocity. This is what you're capitalizing on in using the sidewall. The sometimes forgotten *roll corner*, a sort of enlarged corner shot, hitting the sidewall quite far back, angling to the front wall and dropping near the opposite sidewall, is a slow angle shot.

Once you're up in the forecourt, you have a good chance to hit what might be called a *masked angle*—that is, one that bamboozles your opponent; you can't fool him very much from backcourt, but from up front, you can fool him a lot. It's a completely different shot from the slow angle. When you're up front your opponent is expecting a drop or a reverse

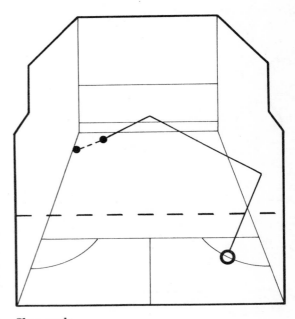

Slow angle.

corner, and he's probably moved a bit in front of the T. Then you take a big swing and it looks like you're putting the ball right down the line; as soon as he's leaning that way, you drop the racquet head and just graze the side

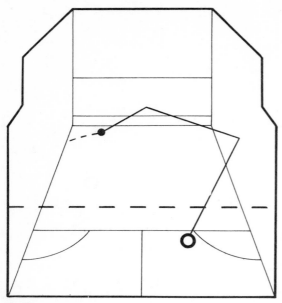

Roll corner.

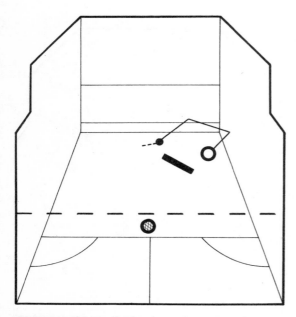

Masked angle.

Drop.

stance with your back to your opponent, the ball will for all intents and purposes be hidden until it strikes the sidewall, and then as you step back toward the center, it's covered even longer. The deception is very important here. If you give it away, your opponent has plenty of time to get to it, and you're caught in the forecourt. But well played, it can be a winner.

DROP SHOTS

The operative word in speaking of drop shots is finesse: The ball is hit with the right amount of firmness and underspin so that it drops and dies upon reaching the front wall.

A versatile, potential winning touch shot, it is the one the Khans made famous. The Khans rarely play fancy corners—just perfectly timed, deadly, straight drops.

Timing, ball contact, underspin, and a slow, firm stroke and follow-through are the hallmarks of the drop shot. The racquet strings must be drawn under the ball with the racquet face very open, as the ball is struck with a slow, lifting motion. There is very little back-

of the ball so that you can still hit quickly into the sidewall and follow through quite fast toward the front wall. It hits the front wall at a good pace and finishes pretty close to the center of the court near the front wall. In an open

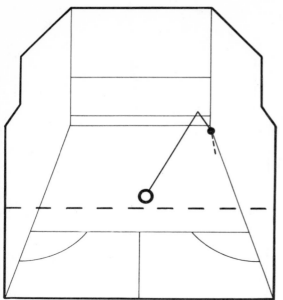

Drop (into the nick).

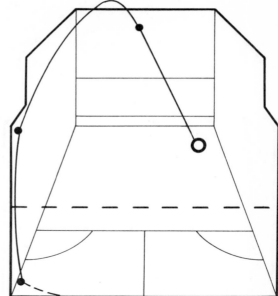

Lob. Covering the court.

swing. The actual functioning path of the swing starts at a point ahead of your leading knee, and the racquet is lifted on the follow-through to the point where you're aiming the shot. The grip should never be loosened for a touch shot.

This shot is sometimes confused with a type of drive that is hit down and under the ball so sharply that the ball is "stunned" on hitting the front wall with such a great deal of spin, and it drops quickly into the nick and dies. Although this shot is technically a drop shot—requiring careful timing combined with pace—it is the slow touch shot described above that is the "classic" drop.

A straight drop, from any position of the court, should be hit so that it is already dropping sharply when it hits the front wall, ideally ten to twelve inches from the sidewall you're facing. If it doesn't rebound directly into the nick, it will hug the sidewall after it makes its first bounce.

Once you've mastered the execution of the drop-shot motion, you can try any of the many variations: cross-court drops, for example, that hit the front wall near the opposite sidewall.

Start right away to practice drop shots. Developing the feel for the timing, spin, and lifting motion on the drop will take considerable practice, so don't wait. You don't have to use the shot in actual play until it feels right, but only time will give you confidence.

LOBS

The lob is a largely overlooked and underestimated shot. With the increase in heated courts and with the livelier balls creeping into the North American game, the lob should be played more than before.

A lob is hit as described in the section on the lob serve, from low and out in front of the body, with a lifting motion of the wrist, and should be angled to bounce near the sidewall behind the service line and make its second bounce before reaching the backwall. The ball must be lobbed *up* into the front wall so that it loops up and back too high for your opponent to volley.

While usually thought of as a defensive shot —one that requires little power and that gives

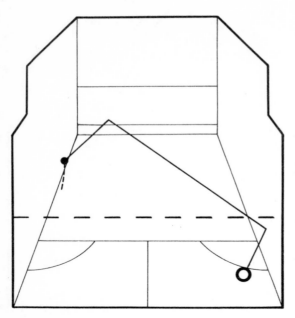

Three-wall nick.

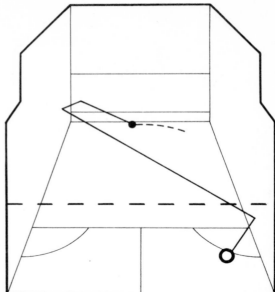

Double boast.

you some time to regain your balance, your breath, and your position on the T—it can be an offensive shot. Against an opponent who likes to play at a fast pace and who has powerful drive shots, the lob can be very frustrating and can effectively throw off his timing. On defense it should be a staple response. Offensively, it must be played with deception. When played from the front of the court it should be made to look like a drop shot, and you should lift the ball up into the wall at the last second. Hopefully you will have the pleasure of seeing your opponent watch the ball sail over his head as he runs forward for the drop.

BOASTS

Boasts are three-wall shots. The most common are the boast for nick (or three-wall nick), the double boast, and the Philadelphia (or Germantown) boast.

Boasts require power (except for the three-wall nick) and direction. Power because every time the ball hits a wall, it slows considerably; it's got to be able to go the distance. Direction

because you've got to understand the angles. If it ricochets all over and never makes it to the front wall, it's useless.

Boast for nick: This three-wall nick is used to pull your opponent out of position, a standard reply for the advanced player when faced with a shot into the sidewall. Given its element of surprise and its difficulty in retrieving, it's also increasingly viewed as a point-maker—a point that Niederhoffer has proved often enough. The shot is hit from the backcourt; your angle depends on your distance from the sidewall. The racquet face is open so that you hit fast and up into the wall with a full wrist snap so that the sidewall carries it higher on its flight to the front wall. The ball flies diagonally to hit the front wall near the opposite sidewall above the tin and quickly drops into the nick. Even with an early start, your opponent will have to cover a lot of ground to get there. Unless you're very deft, playing a three-wall nick in the mid-court or forecourt is more risky. Unless the pace and touch are just right, it's going to come back into the center of the court and right at *you.*

Double boast: When you've got a setup on

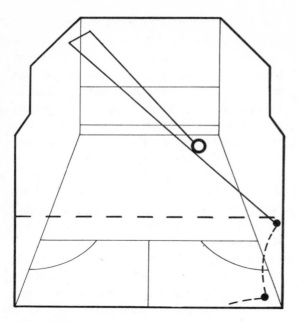

Philadelphia boast.

an easy ball coming off the sidewall, or your opponent is moving back a bit or on his heels, you can think about hitting the double boast. As with all boasts, the surprise element—the change of pace and direction—is all-important. The double boast is angled into the sidewall so it travels at a more acute angle diagonally to the opposite sidewall, and rebounds so obliquely toward the front wall that the subsequent bounce is almost parallel to it. Against someone who is very fast or who anticipates well, you've got to be careful on this shot, because if he gets a head start on it, he'll not only get there, but he'll also make a little short shot for a winner. You want to have the shot in readiness when the opportunity presents itself on a crucial point, but you don't give it away at the beginning of the match.

Philadelphia boast: Not by any means the shot of brotherly love, the Philadelphia is a boast made from the front of the court. The ball is hit hard and high to the front wall near the sidewall on the opposite side of the court from which you are standing, caroms quickly to the near sidewall near the front wall, sails diagonally to the back corner, hits the opposite

sidewall, and drops to the floor parallel to the backwall and into the nick. If your opponent is very quick, he may be able to volley the return as it cuts its diagonal path across the court, but it's a difficult volley. If he's moved up on you in the forecourt he's going to have to scramble to the backwall. As with all boasts, the element of surprise is as important as the shot itself.

Just a word about backwall boasts. In keeping with the philosophy that goes "The backwall is just like any other wall," remember that when you're not only up against the wall but also turned in the wrong direction, the backwall counts.

BACKWALL SHOTS

Players have a tendency to think of backwall shots as last resorts—something to play when the ball's gotten past, when the only way they can get the ball back is by slamming it into the backwall and praying it makes it to the front. In reality, the backwall is just another wall, and backwall shots are but another variation. Just knowing that there is such a shot, and knowing how to play it, take the mystery out of it. Most of the time it *is* a defensive shot. You've been passed on a high volley or maybe your backhand and it's into the backwall. You don't have time to get behind it again so you turn on it and hit it into the backwall. You can't afford to put it an inch above the tin because the chances are you'll miss it, but you can play it strategically. There are times when you want it just inches above the tin and other times when you want it high on the front wall. For instance, if you're involved in a long match at the end of a long rally and suddenly you're faced with the backwall shot, then you want to put the ball up high and give yourself a bit of a breather. So you hit, with an upward motion, up into the backwall; the wall will put backspin on it and take it up to the front wall, where it will quickly drop to the floor. If the situation is reversed and your opponent's had the worse of it, then you want to keep the pressure on and put it as low as you safely dare.

The shot can even be an offensive one. If you've learned in warm-up or in play that your opponent doesn't always look around, there's a great element of surprise in playing the back-wall shot. You just have to realize that it's a possibility and be ready to use it.

The point should be made, too, that shots made against a *glass* backwall must be hit harder than those made on hard cement or fiberglass court. Glass is a slower surface.

●

CHARLIE UFFORD: Mind you, at the top level of play the guts of the game is driving, and you've got to hit your rails along the wall, and your cross courts have to be wide so that they bounce right on the sidewall and die in a corner when the other guy wants to hit them, so that he's always of an uncertain mind as to whether he has to take them before they get to the backwall or whether he can allow them to get to the backwall and have enough time to retrieve them. When I was at the top of my game, winning some tournaments, I was able to delay the drive, and I hit it hard. Once you set up the drive, then the other shots count. Then you have those glorious days when you're getting the drives in length and every-thing is going and you just hit every shot under the sun; it's a joy. But if you don't have that ability to drive hard up and down the walls, you're just not going to be able to win on a long-court shot. I'm not an overpowering hitter. . . . You can hit a drive so hard that when the ball hits the backwall it comes down. There's no chance to get your racquet in there. That's power; I never had that. So my game really is more use of shots. Probably, the back-hand reverse corners I felt most confident about. If I don't know how to hit this shot, then it's time to quit. And so, I snuck out of a couple of matches with that in a tight spot when I should have had no business to hit it. It's not in the percentages.

I don't think it is necessary to have all the shots to be on top. You look at someone like Anil Nayar, who came in and won our cham-pionships for three years straight—he was just an extraordinary physical specimen. What he could do is, he could get to the ball so quickly, and do a very difficult shot to return, when you weren't quite sure that he was even going to get it. He would get there with such ex-traordinary quickness that he could turn it around and make the shot that you could not possibly expect him to make. You just didn't think that anybody could get there to retrieve it, let alone do what he did with it. So he didn't have all the shots by any means: He had a straight drop, and he learned a three-wall nick after a while, and the rest was done on quickness and changing the ball to a different direction and picking up the tempo. There aren't too many players who have played the full complement of shots.

ROLAND ODDY: First of all you have to iden-tify the shots; second, you have to teach a per-son how to hit them; and third, you have to teach a person when to hit them. Going back to the beginning, I believe that two shots at a time are more than any person can reasonably expect to learn. What I try to do in each case is to teach a short shot and a long shot, so that they add a way of driving their opponent back, and they add a way of taking their opponent forward—or, of course, making outright win-ners. Once the person has the basics in his sys-tem, the first two shots he should learn, or the first two shots I teach are the rail shots so he can get control of the center of the court and the roll corner. The roll corner is not used very much by Americans; it's more of an English shot. I like to teach it first because, although it takes touch, it's a fairly easy shot to hit. Also, Americans are not used to it; they're not look-ing for it, so it has the extra element of sur-prise. The second group that I like to teach are the cross courts and drop shots; the three-wall boast and the lob is the third combina-tion. The reverse corner is also a shot that was

SQUASH HOW TO PLAY, HOW TO WIN

largely used for a long time a great deal, but isn't used very much anymore because of the nature of the ball we're using; it's also, I think, a very low-percentage shot. It's very flashy, it looks fantastic when it goes in, but it's very easy to make errors. I think that people are basically afraid of leaving the ball in the middle, and roll corner, if you hit it too hard, will come out in the middle. Obviously, what you're trying to do is make it bounce twice before it gets to the sidewall. The reverse corner comes right out into the middle; the straight drop shot doesn't.

VICTOR NIEDERHOFFER: Conditioning is most important and then strokes and patience are very important next, and having a good killer instinct. Now, how important is a full repertoire of shots? Well, this brings a tremendous satisfaction: utilizing all your resources. The average player may not have a full repertoire of shots. What's more important is having several shots that can move your opponent to every area of the court. You should be able to hit him deep on both sides and short on both sides from any part of the court. Now, if you can do that with two or three shots from your repertoire, then that's great. For example, in my own case I have a pretty darn good repertoire of shots, and what's particularly important, from the same position I am able to hit the ball to opposite sides of the court. I think each player has his favorite shot, one that he developed pretty much, and it's nice to really concentrate on that. The most important shot in the game is the three-wall; you could make a point at any time that would very rarely lead to an error. So then the straight drops are next most important.

JOHN REESE: Very few of our champions have all the great shots. They understand all the shots, but very few will use them all in a given match. Normally they will utilize whatever shot they feel is the most effective for them against a given individual. Also, they will recognize that they perform certain shots not as well as others and as a result that knowl-

Jay Nelson.

edge will prevent them from using the full array of shots that exist in the game. I think there are very few players whom you can say have a total repertoire. I don't think that's a handicap. I think the biggest handicap is to think that you *do* have the repertoire. Utilize that in your playing strategies and you'll come a cropper pretty quickly on that basis.

SHARIF KHAN: I think you can get by with the minimum of shots just so long as the game . . . is basic and you keep a sound game. I don't think that I'm a fantastic stroke player as compared to, say, Niederhoffer. I do try to rely on a few winning shots. Otherwise, the pattern is very simple and the strategy is very plain.

MIKE PIERCE: I concentrate on what I do best. I can hit all the shots, though I can't hit one particular shot as well as another shot. I think most players work on the shots they feel most comfortable with. Now, I do not hit many boasts . . . you have to be a very hard hitter, a very strong player to hit good offensive boasts. No, that is not a big shot in my game. I hit a lot of reverse corners, and a lot of low, straight drop shots, and lobs. I lob probably more than anyone in the game of doubles.

I'm not a hard hitter, and I feel that a lob is a very offensive shot. It's a doubles shot, but I feel that most people who play doubles don't use the lob because they don't believe it's an offensive shot.

JUAN DE VILLAFRANCA: I think that each person has a favorite shot, and you have to work on your shots and try to develop or "combinate" your best shots and put them into work. I don't think any player has all the shots working very well. You have to build them. You need some shots to move the guy up front. Somebody uses the drop shot, other people like to use the two-wall shots, and some people like to hit the double boast to move the guy up front. The main thing is to move the opponent from one side of the court to the other, keep him off balance. And each person has his own shots. You have such a large variety of shots because of the wall—compared to tennis, where you have no walls . . . you have a lot of angles.

DIEHL MATEER: I think there has been too much emphasis recently put on having great shots. If you can't hit the ball up and down the wall, if you don't have the basics, the shots really mean very little. If the other guy can beat you up and down the wall consistently, he can go in and play zero shots, and he'll win nine times out of ten. I very recently, at Episcopal, tried to count the number of errors in an intravarsity university match because I felt I had to come up with some way of eliminating errors. Everyone was playing three-wall boasts and triple reverse-corners . . . and the errors averaged eight a game. That's a pretty big handicap to start with: down 8-love. So I spent the next day talking to the boys, told them I was going to play the No. 1 player, I was not going to make any errors, and I was not going to play any shots and that he was going to determine who won and lost the point. Just to try to prove to him . . . I wasn't even going to hit any cross courts, I was only going to hit it up and down the rails. I did win the first game. I didn't win the next two, but I was trying to demonstrate that if

you don't have the basics you don't need the tricks, that you've got to have the basics before you can start to add the icing on the cake.

BARBARA MALTBY: I think it's very important to have a variety of shots. I've seen a lot of players who have very good games, but they don't have any winners. You have to be able to put the ball away—that's part of the game. I mean, you can have all the power in the world and keep them digging in the back corner all day, but if you can't put the ball away, what good is it? You've got to be able to hit the winner when you have the opportunity. And of course the more different ways you can hit the winner, the harder it is for your opponent to retrieve it because he doesn't know what shot you're going to hit. So I think it's first of all very important to have a winner, even if it's only one or two shots, and then of course the more winning shots you have, the higher you can actually progress.

JOHN REESE: I think length is probably as important as anything when you talk about pace. I think there's no question that the people who hit the ball the hardest are not necessarily the best players, because by and large you want a ball to die toward the back of the court. The big power players who take enormous swings so that the ball comes shooting back to the middle court often find that they've gone from the offense to the defense. So, in many cases, a very strong individual will be hitting at three-quarter speed. I will not hit much faster than three-quarter speed. Occasionally I'll overhit the ball, with the net result being that I often lose the point.

DIEHL MATEER: Unless you're five, six, seven points ahead, when everything works, you're sailing along, you can't afford to take chances with a shot you're not absolutely sure of. When you're down and you're even, if you're going to play a shot, it better be one you're pretty confident in. I've never hit, or very seldom—because of experience—I've never hit a boast when I was down because I found that I made more errors.

Zachariah has a long way to chase Barbara Maltby's short reverse corner.

I had some good advice from one of the better players in the game, Neil Sullivan, who won the Nationals two or three times. I had played a match in Atlantic City, the first major tournament I ever competed in, and I played the National Intercollegiate champion in the first round. I felt, here I am playing the National Intercollegiate champion, I've got to go in there and play a lot of shots to win the match. Well, it turned out I won the match, I think, by one point in the fifth. And that night, at the cocktail party, Neil Sullivan came up to me and said, "That was the worst exhibition of squash I've ever seen in my life." He pulled me off into a side room, and I didn't know whether he was going to poke me in the nose or what. I said, "What do you mean?" And he said, "I never saw all those crazy shots. What are you trying, to be fancy or something?" I started explaining that I didn't know how I was going to beat this guy without playing a lot of fancy shots. And he said, "No. This game is the basics—up and down the walls." I've played Sullivan many times and he had all the shots in the world and he never beat me in an important match. And I think he was entirely right.

BARBARA MALTBY: I'm sort of working on my deep game, my power game, and I hope to make that a little better because I think I have a decent amount of finesse. It's just a matter of playing your shots the right time, which is not that easy—knowing when to play your various shots and what patterns to play, and when to break your patterns. For example, your opponent is off balance, you want to hit a shot to the opposite corner of the court, but then again if he's anticipating that, then sometimes it's better to wrong-foot him or something. It's very hard. I think one of the other important things is relaxing when you play. When you're at a certain level you can actually relax and still get a lot of shots.

Shots

With racquet fully prepared, Victor Niederhoffer heads to the forecourt for a short shot.

11

•

Tactics, Strategy, and Using Your Head

To play squash well you've got to use your head as well as your racquet. You must apply your wits, wiles, imagination, and judgment in order to put your physical abilities and racquet skills to best use.

Like a battle or a game of chess—to both of which squash is often compared—sound tactics and strategy maximize your physical capabilities. You need to have a clear picture of your own and your opponent's abilities, and take advantage of your strengths and his weaknesses. You must know what shots to hit and when. You must be able to cover your shots and anticipate his. You have to know when to be patient and when to go for the winner. Your game must be flexible enough to adjust to varied playing conditions and situations.

SHOT SELECTION

The teaching of shots and strokes presumes ideal conditions: the ideal position, the perfect swing, and no one else on the court to contend with. In actual play, you are hitting and thinking on the run, and you are battling your opponent for court position.

Your object is to hit a shot your opponent can't return. But first you have to soften him up and move him out of position so that he won't be able to return your winning shot. For this you need reliable rails and cross courts, and the patience to play them doggedly until you find an opening.

Hit the ball to where your opponent *isn't*. To do this, you must already know where he *is* (without looking directly as you make your shot). Hit the ball into the area of the corners of the court, and those corners that make him run the longest distance. Hit a shot that allows you to hold or retake the T.

Hit shots that you have confidence in. Your front-wall shots should be trouble-free. If you have confidence on your forehand drop, use it. Don't play shots that are as yet beyond your abilities. As you master additional shots, add them. Don't rush. There's something to be said for the steady player who plays only what he knows—no fancy stuff that still needs practice. It's tough playing against someone who just hits every shot six inches above the tin and who you know isn't going to miss, isn't going to fluff the shot. The percentages are on his side. You feel forced mentally and psychologically to keep trying to put the ball away, to cut it closer and closer, until you're the one making the errors.

Don't be impatient to end the point. In a game of percentages, the odds are with your rails and cross courts. Don't hit your winner until you are able to find a good placement and are able to get a good shot at it. A misjudged finesse shot can be a winner for your opponent.

●

PETER BOSTWICK: I would say basically I try to play percentage squash and sound squash. I used to have a tendency not to go for a shot quickly enough. But that was because my shots were not very good in the beginning, and whenever I did go for a shot I was apt to make an error. I was better off perhaps just trying to grind them out with rails and cross courts, which is good to a certain point. But basically I would say that I do try to play percentage squash and not try ridiculous shots at bad times.

JAY NELSON: Whereas when I was coming up, the idea in my head was, "Don't do any of that fancy stuff; just play your rails and cross

courts, because the only way you can win is if *he* makes the error," it was a real prohibition I had to set up for myself. Well, player percentage is good advice any time except if the percentages have changed as you get better. In fact, it starts to reverse with players that are good enough, and the defensive shot in certain circumstances is the nonpercentage shot. It gets to a certain point where you have to play shots if you want to beat certain guys because you want to show them the whole court. Sometimes you'll play very safe, and you have to forget it because the guy's too good. He'll be delighted to have you play defensively. You can't make every shot cling to the wall. This is another Barnaby thing: *Do it to him before he does it to you first.* When you play Sam Howe, for example, the guy's shots are just too good to play a defensive game.

GRETCHEN SPRUANCE: You find that the person who makes the mistakes is the one who is going to lose. But that's my problem. I have a tendency to go for the shots; I have to exercise a great deal of discipline. Actually, the courts are so cold now it's unbearable to play the game. It's not in my personality to go on forever and ever. I'm in fairly good shape but I'm not in really, really good shape. I don't know how long I can go.

●

Find your opponent's weakness and take advantage of it. If his backhand is weak, hit every shot to the backhand. If he is slow, make him run—and mostly to the front of the court.

Be unpredictable. Don't always hit the same shot in the same situation. Have an alternative. Don't go for the winner every time you have a chance. Keep 'em guessing.

Change the pace. Follow up a series of fast drives with a slow drop; try to break the rhythm.

●

CHARLES UFFORD: In an all-around sense squash takes basic hand/eye co-ordination, certainly very quick footwork. But at the same time, it makes greater demands on your mental abilities than tennis. I keep comparing it with tennis because it's a popular, well-known, recognized sport around the world. But in squash, there is a far greater variety of effective shots that can be played from any position on the court, and it comes down to the ability to select among this greater variety. You have maybe three or four different shots to be played at any given time, different shots at any given time on a position on the court, whereas in tennis, it is usually one or two. Tennis is a game where you hit it down one side and then the other, and if you're better than your opponent, you win. It's very simple. In squash, you can play the rails or cross courts—your basic shots in tennis. In addition, you can play the reverse corners, you can play the roll corners, you can play two types of drop shots, and you can play your three-wall nick. And occasionally, if you think you're really hot stuff, you can play a double boast. The fun is picking up the right one at the right time. In this position last time you played such and such, but this time it's going to be different. Each time you start in the same way, but you put more underspin into the stroke and leave it short. It's a feel for the combination of possibilities, selecting alternative shots from the same position, tailoring the selection to the weaknesses you think you discern in your opponent's game and certain natural combinations of one shot with another—your reverse corner combined with a cross-court drive (particularly, in my case, from the backhand side . . . as that's probably my stronger shot), but if you think about it, you can line up and you can hit it cross court and that takes him back to the far right-hand corner, or snap it around a little more into the reverse corner.

That's one of the things to teach in this game; people get the notion that there's the driving game, and then there are shots. . . .

O'Toole vs. Zachariah.

Everything is a shot. Every drive, every retrieve is designed to do a particular, precise thing. And you never hit the ball without an exact notion of what you're trying to accomplish with that particular shot. So if you have this approach, it helps to focus your concentration, and it also gets you over that terrible divided state of mind. A shot, particularly the reverse corners and roll corners, should be nothing more than redirected drives; just like the drive, they are conceptually no different except that you put more of the force of the stroke into imparting a spin on the ball than imparting forward speed on it.

PETER BOSTWICK: I would say that not all the champions have all the shots. But they have certain shots that they seem to hit better than others, and they still win the championships. I don't think that everybody who's been at the top in squash has every shot down pat. The Khans, for instance, play very few angles and reverse corners. They play an awful lot of drop shots, three-wall nicks, rails, cross courts—just bread-and-butter stuff—and they've been the best in the world. At the same time, I would think the more variation you have and the more shots you have, the better off you are. I started late in squash . . . I never practiced shots until the past couple of years. So I only had one or two shots, and perhaps that's why I didn't get to the top. . . .

GORDON ANDERSON: Knowing what shot to hit when becomes natural; because the game is so quick, you can't think of that. You can think of that when you practice it, because you don't really have to think of winning. When you have a good game with somebody and when you hit a particular shot up into the right-hand corner and the other fellow hits a winner, and if you're thinking all the time, you'll say, "Why did he hit a winner?" It's because of what *you* hit! As a junior player you say, "What a terrific shot! The guy hit a winner!" But you forgot that you hit the ball right to him. Now, why didn't you hit the ball down the wall, which can move him from the center of the court and let him do whatever he wants because you're in position? But so many guys run up and down the court and are just thinking about hitting the ball and they run up and whack it, and they've forgotten that there's a wall on that side. It's very hard to go up from that stage of playing. There are lots of guys in my club who can hit the ball really, really well, and you can tell in a warm-up. . . . I'm hitting the ball to you and you've got a good stroke and everything; O.K. The people up in the gallery are saying, "Those two look quite equal." And then the game starts and one creams the other person. Why? Because one fellow is not too sure what to do once the ball gets turning around the court a bit.

●

DECEPTION

Deception is the flip side of anticipation.

Most players, even good ones, don't consider deception enough. They telegraph their message, their intent, long before they hit the ball. Excellent shots are diminished if your op-

Anything that hits the front wall counts.

ponent can see exactly what you're doing. There is a definite way to make your shot in such a way that the ball is partially hidden by part of your body, whether it be your head, chest, or legs, *at the moment you contact the ball.* This way your opponent doesn't see the ball until it's halfway to the front wall. No matter where you are on the court you want your back to your opponent. This means that on the backcourt you assume a closed stance, and in the center-court area your feet will be more parallel. In the front court, you'll have a more open stance. It's worth it, for what you might lose in power you gain in deception value.

Too, every shot should be prepared in exactly the same way—with a full backswing with the feet the same distance apart (about the length of a racquet handle). You should hold your shot until the last possible second, keeping your opponent guessing. Your swing should be the same for every shot, but the particular shot you use will employ only the necessary piece of the full arc for its actual execution. The particulars that distinguish one shot from another are very subtle to all but the most accomplished and watchful player—the slowed swing, the turned wrist, the shoulders pivoted at the last minute.

The direction of your swing changes the path of the ball and is difficult to see. The swing is always in a straight line, but where the line begins and ends is changeable, like throwing a ball across the court, down the line, or into the sidewall. For a cross court your swing would begin away from your body, contact the ball slightly on the outside, and finish across the body. A down-the-line swing would start and end parallel to the sidewall. The swing for an angle shot would start close to the body and finish away from the body. (See illustration, page 72.)

●

BARBARA MALTBY: I mean you may cover the ball well, but if you can't hesitate you're much less effective. If you can get there in time and have enough presence of mind not just to hit it but also to hesitate for a moment, it makes your opponent commit too early, to be off balance because he can't figure out what you're doing. If you can just hold your shot till the last second it really makes a big difference. Very effective and also very deceptive.

ROLAND ODDY: The secret to deception basically is that you should try to hit all shots or most shots with the same motion or the same swing. I think that Sam Howe was the real expert at this: I could never tell what he was going to hit; he hit them all the same. There may have been a slight difference, but one you couldn't detect. I think you can do an awful lot of them with the same motion. I know that when I line up to hit a forehand, a rail shot, a straight drop, and a roll corner, I hit them with the same motion, but I hit the soft shots a little easier; I still have to follow through a little bit, because if you stop the head of your racquet on contact with the ball, the ball just bounces off it. So you have to go through. But I hit those three the same way. Sometimes it may be how your feet are lined up—that might be a clue.

JAY NELSON: Most people don't work enough on deception. I can't do it as well as the other guys; that's sort of a weak point, but I'm doing a little better now. It's devastating if you can do it. And very few guys can. Most people just go up there and telegraph the hell out of the shot and hope they execute it well enough or hit it hard enough. But ideally, at least for short-ball setups, you want to get some pairing, where your stroke looks reasonably the same for a long enough period. That's good enough. I know sometimes in practice I'll try consciously to hold the guy. God, you can fake the hell out of it. All you have to do is get that first starting step. And actually the better they are the more chance you have to fool them. Because of their anticipation, they're so sure of what you're going to do. I think Niederhoffer, once by mistake, I think I hit my leg and he just went shooting by me . . . it was just a joke, and neither one of us could believe it. Like that backhand I've got here— I'll either hit the roll corner or hit it down the line. And again, that's the good pairing; the ball's either gonna hit there or there. Often my opponent will just see the roll and he'll start charging and I'll kind of hit it down here, down the rail. It is an effective kind of thing to be able to do, but it's very hard. I mean, you can imagine it's only for the guy who's really good at strokes. Really got 'em down. Reese is good at it. Ufford has great deception. I think that's physiological, though. His long arm. I spoke to him about this seven or eight years ago. I said to him, and this was when I was sort of a rookie . . . I think it's because of the length of your arms. He said, "You know, you may be right!" Everybody else was implying that it was all technique. He waited. . . . I said, "Yeah, that's all fine if your arms are about four feet long." He accurately recognized it early on. Of course, he gets a huge charge out of it, as anybody does. He's so big and he's got that great arm length that he'd be a fool not to. He's really a thinking player.

CHARLES UFFORD: I've been blessed with a

good wrist, and my style of play as taught to me by Barnaby up at Harvard is that you prepare every shot from the same basic position, and then you wait a fraction of a second longer than your opponent anticipates, and then change the direction of the ball. What this does is, it permits a deceptive stroke production so that you get your opponent off balance, so that he never quite can hit that ball. That's the state of mind I hope to induce. If you're really fortunate, you can sit there and play your shot, and your opponent will not move; what it means is that you've made up your mind what you're going to play this particular time, whereas you may have played that or that last time—this time, you're going to play this. You're positioned in such a way that you can play any of three, so that when you finally play your shot, he is not able to react at all, and you can leave him standing. The other thing, of course, is that you can also hit the ball one way and have the joy of seeing him run in the opposite direction. That is really the sheer delight of this whole game. In tennis you really can't do that very much. The length of interval of stroke is longer so that the guy sees the shot. The capacity of being able to do this comes from this business of preparing every stroke in the same fashion and taking just one wrist stance so that there is no clue as to which it's going to be this time. That is the ideal solution. As you play a variety of shots from that one position, which I have hopefully been able to develop, then you have this capacity. It's a terrific confrontation of minds involved as well as all the physical activity that goes along with it. But it's the mind, getting the guy uncertain as to where it's going.

It's also difficult to see around me. There's that little intricacy in the rule that interference with an opponent's sight is not cause for a let. For that reason, I will allow a ball that's coming off the wall to come in very close toward me, so that when I snap my wrist, they're not seeing much of the racquet. Seeing how the racquet approaches the ball is the key to knowing where it's going. If you don't see your opponent's racquet actually coming into contact with the ball you have very little hope of knowing what's happening. That helps to make it difficult to play. I don't know whether it's an unfair advantage. I suppose it is an unfair advantage, but then, I can't make the feet move.

PETER BOSTWICK: I don't think I've ever played anybody who could hold the ball as long as Charlie Ufford could. And this is something that some people seem to have and others don't. It seems to be an innate gift . . . although I think that everybody can probably improve it a little bit by concentrating on it. I just don't think too many people think about it too much. But Charlie was one of these guys who always, when he went to hit a ball, seemed to have you on hold for about two minutes, and you didn't know which way to go, and you always seemed to be jerked around the court. So it is a very important thing to hold a guy with the racquet and then change the direction at the last minute, and Charlie was a master. I never look forward to playing him; it's a difficult assignment.

●

PLAYING CONDITIONS AND THE BALL

The ball being played and the temperature on the court have a great influence on what kind of squash will be played on a given day. For years squash was played with the hard Cragin ball, which even at its liveliest was a shotmaker's ball. The current favorite, the West 70+ ball, is much livelier.

Your game should be flexible enough to adapt to the ball you're playing and the temperature. Some players tend to play the same game whether the temperature is 45 degrees or 75 degrees.

With a lively ball or on a hot court, conditions favor the runner rather than the shotmaker. The ball is not going to stay down when it's played for the nick. Sidewall shots become more difficult. On a hot court, the game shifts to the front walls. Angles and drops are forgotten, because if you miss them, you're in trouble.

On a cold court, you need power to move that ball. You may have to raise your placements higher above the tin to get the ball into the back corner. This is the time to go for those nicks and slow angles.

It's also possible that you'll go into the court at 45 degrees, and fifteen minutes later, with the heat of playing and 150 people in the gallery, the temperature shoots up and the ball starts bounding around the court, in which case you've got to readjust.

●

ROLAND ODDY: Psychologically, if you're playing on a warm court, you have to be prepared to run more; your mind has to be made up to that before you get in there. I think that if you've got the sort of temperament to make these decisions and know what's going to happen when you go in there, it's a big advantage. It's a lot of people who don't particularly want to play that way and then they go in there, and they really haven't thought it out—they're going to play it their way. So they play their way and they get into a lot of trouble. When it's warmer I think you probably go for more nicks. When it's cold you can achieve more with drives and touch; but when it's warm, a good player is going to pick all those drives and touch shots up, so you have to go for the nicks.

JAY NELSON: Certainly I've lost matches because I haven't adjusted to the fact that cold-court squash is different from warm-court squash—which is not to say that up until two or three years ago I had much of a choice. I mean, my strokes just weren't good enough. But during the past two or three years they have been good enough that I could have adapted if I had had the damn presence of mind. In many cases, even this year, I played Roger Alcaly in a league match on a freezing court, and I played hot-court squash. I had a little bit of a cold and he beat me anyway, but it wasn't until after the match that I caught on. If it's a cold, cold court you should adapt with a lot of short balls; you can cover that stuff.

BARBARA MALTBY: Sometimes you feel very confident and you can hit your shots all over the place and they all go, and at other times you're not as sharp and you kind of have to wait for them. I think that on a hot court you have to be more patient, and this is a very hot court. It will be interesting to see if you can hit any shots at all cause it's so hot. Some of the players will be slowing the shots down and some will be speeding them up; it will be pretty interesting.

Usually I will play my opponent instead of just going in and playing the game. You want you opponent to either play your game or a game he doesn't want to play. If you don't

Lisa Griffith flicks a shot from deep in the corner.

know what his strengths are, it's pretty silly to throw away one or two games trying to figure them out. By watching the strengths you can get an idea of what your opponent likes to do in certain situations. I consider myself more of a shotmaker than a power player, and I can change my game fairly quickly. I really depend a lot on variety, and I play different people with different plays.

Of course, I have my game, and I would like to play that. Because first of all, you have your own sort of game, and that's what you're used to and that's what you're best at. But if I have an opponent who has certain weaknesses and certain strengths that don't exactly jive, then I will consciously play a different sort of game. That is the important thing when you're not able to win at your game: to be able to switch to your opponent's game. If your game is changeable enough to react to anyone else's game, that's when your game has reached a high point.

•

GAME VERSATILITY AND STRATEGY

In addition to adapting your game to the ball and court conditions, it's important to analyze your opponent's game and develop a plan for playing him. You must also be able to change your game a bit if you're not able to impose your game on your opponent, or in a situation where a different type of game is called for. One should always keep a winning game and change a losing game.

A tremendously powerful hitter with great speed is usually able to hold his game; flexibility isn't that essential. Against a very hard hitter, it's difficult to get set and make good shots. He's inclined to ruin a good player's attributes. The only defense is to lob a lot so he can't take the ball low for his drives or to rob him of preparation time by volleying as much as possible. You in turn must prepare your shots very quickly to be ready for this attack.

Against a retriever you'll need the touch shots that are nearly impossible to return and that send him repeatedly to the forecourt, or drives deep into the corners. Against a touch player, you must hit shots that pull him deep into the backcourt where he can't make his placements, or volleys that make him run and that cut down the time he needs to prepare them.

You cannot fight fire with fire—you must know your abilities *relative* to your opponent. Don't try to outrun a retriever or overpower a power hitter—unless you're sure you're faster or more powerful. Know what abilities you have that work to counter what he has.

Once you decipher your opponent's weakness, whatever it is, play to that weakness and never let up. If you're leading 11–7 by playing 90 per cent of the shots to the left wall, you have the winning combination—the so-called answer. Eventually, of course, you're giving your opponent practice on that weak side, and you have to be on guard for when his weakness may become his strength. Also, he will be trying to hit shots that prevent you from playing to his weakness. There is a time—and you see it in almost every match—when two players are slugging it out, trying to see who has the weaker backhand (or whatever). Even at love-all, this becomes psychologically a very important rally.

•

MIKE PIERCE: Because we are analytical about how we play and whom we play, in the past few years my partner and I have been very successful. I have felt that every time we've gone onto a court there's no reason why we should lose a match. I take the pros very seriously. When I play against the pros who are hard hitters, my approach—because I do not hit the ball very hard myself—is to try to slow the ball down as much as possible by lobbing and hitting just lazy rail shots because I know I don't have the power.

I'll try to slow the game down so that they can't play the hard shots, because if I get caught in a hitting match with those guys, I'm going to be outclassed. And this is where, again, the thinking aspect comes into play very greatly.

JOHN REESE: To learn the game effectively, obviously the first part has to be the development of the stroking capability, etc. Tactics are things that you develop yourself in relationship to your abilities vs. those who you play. It's hard from the teaching point of view to develop the breadth of tactical experience that is necessary to play different styles. But it can be taught . . . what are the most fundamental approaches to the game, and what will most usually be effective against other players.

JAY NELSON: I think there are good paces to employ against different people. Maybe some people get a little bit confused. There are people who do not want a lot of time between strokes. They sound counterintuitive, but there are certain people I have beaten by slowing the game down and not making it particularly hard; just slowing the whole thing down. In other words, they want to sprint. And there are other people who are just the reverse. But as far as changing it, I don't say, "Now I'll change the pace on so and so" consciously. I may change the pace, but randomly, if I feel like it. I might change the pace, because I can play all kinds of different ways.

I'll tell you a funny thing about analyzing your opponent. I played a guy named Rob Dinnerman. I played him in one tournament where he was hurting me a lot with a particular shot, side/front, forehand side/front, and I wasn't seeing it. The next time we played I had somehow catalogued his shot. So without conscious thought I was picking it up much quicker. It is interesting the way your brain works. I wasn't even conscious of saying to myself, "Watch out for that side/front," but somewhere I had stored it away. So what I'm saying is that through experience you can add

patterns to recognize. It's not as though you put one in, you take one out. I just hadn't caught it the first time; the second time I'd known I'd seen it before. I wasn't looking for it in particular, but I remembered it. I would pick it up at two thirds of a second execution time instead of picking it up at one second, and you know, that made the difference.

But most of the guys who are known as runners, which I have been, that's their greatest strength, their speed off the mark. Give the guy a short ball and the ability to pick it up, go get it quick, and guys like Adair, myself, I think Dave Linden in New York—against most players, you have to be able to do that. Some people can take that a long way. You find that sometimes your opponent starts to cut it finer and finer. He says, "Hey, what's going on with my strokes? This isn't working today," and he gets a little frustrated. Then he starts to press if his best stuff doesn't work. That makes him start thinking, "What am I doing? I have to get back to the other side." You like to try to break the guy, change his game.

PETER BRIGGS: I think you have to incorporate all elements of the game (power, speed, touch, etc.). And you have to be able to have two or three kinds of game. A guy like Reese is a great shotmaker. But what happens if he goes out and his shots aren't working? He gets beaten. That's not really the way it should be. If you have one game that's not going for you, you should be able to turn it into another game. A guy who used to play over here, Anil Nayar, was great because he had two kinds of games. He was a very good shotmaker, but if that wasn't going very well, he was probably the fastest guy I've ever seen. And he could say, "O.K., I'll just keep hitting the ball four feet above the red line and I'll keep you out there for three hours." So he had two ways of playing, and he won both ways—according to which worked in that situation. I see myself trying to get into good enough condition to be able to do both . . . and not have to worry if one game is not working. . . . That builds up your confidence.

●

All of these things are easy to say but harder to do. Think of yourself as building a game, starting with a foundation of good conditioning, good strokes. As you learn each new shot, as you learn something new about the game, think about what it means, and put it to use. Cement it into the foundation. Don't get ahead of yourself or the foundation will have cracks and weaknesses.

●

SHARIF KHAN: To be at the top requires physical dedication; you try to excel physically. You're sort of in a race, a track race—and you must have the desire for excellence. When I first got started, I was strong physically—I used no brains. If I beat someone, I beat him by just drilling him into the ground. I learned a lot from this man sitting here [Yusuf Khan], my cousin, because he used to beat me very, very badly. I used to be able to hit the ball as hard as he did, as fast as he did, but I could never beat him. And the main thing is, I used to waste energy for shots I would hit straight back to him instead of making him work, wasting the volleys to hit it back to him. And then gradually, through hard experience, I tried to change my game and tried to use some strategy. And now I'm a strong believer in good strategy, good temperament. . . . I used to get mad, but now it's very rare that I get upset.

PETER BOSTWICK: All the guys who have been champions probably combine very good execution and are also mentally very tough at crucial times. I think everybody tries to figure out all the tactics and what you should do in a situation. But really, when you get into a match, your instincts sort of take over. There are some mental gymnastics because when you become a sophisticated player, you know every-

one else's game, so there's obviously a certain amount of tactics involved when you know somebody has a bad backhand so you hit more balls to his backhand. Maybe somebody is a little slow getting up front, so you play more short shots, etc. But I still feel that an awful lot comes down to your being able to apply yourself and execute well at the crucial times, which only happen when you've played a great deal of squash and have improved your shots and have good ball control and good conditioning.

I have a feeling that the guys who get to the top have a little more imagination at certain times. Therefore, I think it's important to try not to always play the same shot at the same time. You have to try to mix your game up a bit. If you get a loose ball, don't always hit a reverse corner on it; one time, try a reverse corner; maybe the next time, give him a cross court or something to keep him off balance. I think it's helpful if you can use your imagination a little bit and try to keep them guessing. It's very easy to say, but some people just don't have as good imagination as others on the courts.

JAY NELSON: As Barnaby told me, you should be delighted that the guy gets the shot back, not a poor shot, but you should be thinking that it cost him so much to get that, that two or three in a row each time. Barnaby used to say, "Great, I'm glad you got that one back, now chase this one," just for the confidence that ultimately if you play the game this way the other guy is going to wilt, regardless of how fit he was. This doesn't hold for every player, but if players are pretty equal you can win by outpositioning, outthinking, outplaying, or just frustrating him or just fatiguing your opponent. Ultimately you'll break the guy. You go into the match, the best thing, when you're really playing well. It's just "reaction"; you're not thinking at all. When you finally get broken, you start thinking a lot. What can I do? What should I do? You become very self-conscious, very aware of the choices you're making, wondering if you should do this or that. You just get confused, your plan has been broken. Very seldom have I been broken and been able to regroup, play a different game, and come back. The amazing thing is, I've been down a game and a half or two, changed my game, accurately figured out what should be a better game, changed it, but not been able to execute it as well. I become very aware of my play then, even though I hit upon the proper game. I did that against Reese in the Gold Racquets. I didn't execute it . . . the times that I would do it properly. You make errors, you go into the self-conscious mode, and you're almost dead then, against an equal player. You can always have a game handed to you, but if you have a guy who's whaling away, as Briggs says, and not thinking, sort of unconscious, then you have troubles. But I can't imagine anyone who would play better when he's very, very self-conscious of every shot. Maybe that's an approach you could take from the outset, "I'm gonna think so fast I'm gonna be totally aware of what's going on all the time and the choices I'm making," and still it's going to work. But it doesn't work that way with me. When you're in a position when you have a choice between two shots, when you're playing well, you never articulate the thought. We're getting into a gray area: When does a thought occur in your brain? You never really articulate the thought, "I think I will do this." In the end, you just do it. Obviously some decision is made somewhere in your brain, but it's not at a conscious level. When you practice, that's when you do your thinking. By the time the game comes you should try to blank your mind. At least I know I play best when I blank my mind. There's a nice loose flow when you're playing a practice match, or for fun. You're much more apt to lose track of the score, and you play almost each stroke at a time; whereas in a match that counts, you very seldom lose track of the score, and I think it might inhibit your

play. The same thing that makes you think of the score can inhibit your play. It's just that I noticed that when I'm really having a lot of fun, which is defined as playing someone you're pretty sure you're gonna beat, you're more open, less pressured; you take chances.

PETER BRIGGS: You're going to make mincemeat out of my approach to the game, but I'm perfectly happy, I like the game, I'm competitive, I enjoy it. I go in there and play, I enjoy it, and I don't think about everything. That's an approach as valid as anything else. It's valid for as long as I can continue to keep winning that way. If I start getting beaten all the time, then maybe I'll start re-evaluating. But you use whatever works for you as long as it can work, as long as you win more times than you lose.

VICTOR NIEDERHOFFER: Once you have the strokes and stamina, then you can start thinking about tactics and attitudes. They tend to fall into place. It's rare that you find someone with good strokes and stamina who doesn't evolve his game and work out a combination that fits in with his aptitudes and that can be winning. Correct form is not as important as having sound strokes. A great mistake that players make is concentrating on how they look, when they should be concentrating on the opportunities for strong shots that will come as a natural outgrowth of the basic strokes. As far as patience and mental attitude go, these are the types of things that over a five-game match can mean two or three points, each one of them, but most matches are won in usually four games. And it's very rare that you see a five-game match in the finals in a major tournament. I don't think there's been one in the North American Pro championships in the past ten years, so you must realize that we're dealing with usually an average difference between the players, which is mainly stamina and strokes.

Is there life after squash?

12

•

The Psychology of Winning

Squash has a tendency to reveal and reflect a player's character and personality. If you know your inner self the way you know your shots and physical capabilities, you can use your strong traits to work for you. You are the master of yourself. Knowing your weaknesses is just as important. In itself, playing squash tends to reinforce strength of character and positive traits.

Some players are dogged and methodical; they win by perseverance and patience. Others are flamboyant and creative—they do things others would never think of; they may be erratic, but they are occasionally brilliant. Some breathe fire on the court. Others are placid as a pond on a windless day. You have to make your temperament work *for* you and play your own game.

Certain qualities are mandatory: discipline, concentration, self-control, confidence, com-

petitiveness. You can learn these things by playing the game, by practice, as you would learn anything else. Without them you won't get far.

Squash is a fast game and demands full attention. Even momentary lapses of concentration can result in the loss of a point. Watch a match and you'll see that especially in the early stages of the game, one player will win several points, then slack off; then the other player will run up his score. Suddenly, at 10-all, the caliber of the game takes a great leap. Brilliant, hard-fought rallies ensue. This is because suddenly every point brings the game closer to the end, to a win-or-lose situation. Suddenly they're concentrating: Everything is focused on that point, everything works, no expenditure is too dear.

A good player is in there plugging every second. He bears down on his opponent from the

Pick waits, a little off-center, for Khalid Mir's volley return.

start. He does not get distracted or discouraged when he's made an error. He knows that the first point is as valuable as the last. He's unflappable when his opponent is trying to intimidate him or when he's making a big fuss over something. He's not overawed by his opponent: His enemy is the *ball*. He puts his energy and skill into every shot on every point. He is patient; he knows that most shots are retrievable, and he waits for his opportunity. No shot is considered irretrievable. No matter how desperate the retrieve looks, he tries for it. When he smells victory, he goes for it.

●

SHARIF KHAN: When you ask about the killer instinct, you're into the unknown. As far as I'm concerned, you can produce the most incredible painting, or you can't; or at best, you're mediocre. However, I aim—every time I step out, I'm a perfectionist. I want to perfect the art of the shot that I got back, retrieved, or made the last time. I want to improve the angles that I hit, the incredible number of angles and finesse shots, touch. And what I want to do each time obviously is to one-up the last time I did it—to go a little faster. It's like the Olympics—every four years, more records are

broken than are not broken, and what I'm trying to do is to go one step higher, one step beyond. That's what I really mean when I say that I want to keep my killer instinct going: develop, develop, and develop. There's no stopping; in life you don't stop developing, and you never stop learning. It's cat and mouse in squash, and every day I'm learning something. It's not just all repetition. To a lot of people it is repetition, and that's where they get bogged down. To me, it's a learning experience every single time. Something new to aim for. As long as I have that curiosity and that drive to go one step beyond into the unknown, I'll do all right.

DIEHL MATEER: Competitive instinct? I think it's mandatory. I've known just hundreds of players who've thrived on competition. I imagine that everybody competing in national tournaments is competitive. If you want to use percentages, I think there's a difference between somebody who's 99 to 100 per cent competitive vs. 91 per cent. It's got to be worth at least a point a game, or something like that. You've got to be above a certain percentile or you're never going to fight enough to do something.

CHARLES UFFORD: The psychology of the game is very elusive. I don't think anyone won the Nationals the year they were expected to

Jay Nelson ambles to take Yusuf Khan's serve.

do it. For some reason, it's been two or three years along the line, and then they sort of haphazardly happen to win it that year, and they may hold it for a while. But there are any number of players who have all the shots, all the physical equipment, they can run forever . . . and yet it's a few years later before they actually do it, and win the Nationals. That shows that if you just have a certain peace of mind when you get down to those tough plays at the end of the long matches in the National championships, that and that only counts, I suppose. I have a certain fatalistic attitude about these things: Let what's going to happen, happen.

JOHN REESE: I think you have to obviously have a competitive instinct to be good in a game where you are in very close proximity to your opponent. If you are not willing to stick in there fairly close to your opponent and compete with that individual—and this is just like being in an arena with a lion or face-to-face or hit-to-hit with your opponent, and you're swinging from the heels—you've got to have a great deal of desire to compete. I think that's important. A killer instinct? Yes, but a killer instinct that's refined, not primitive. It has to be one that is tempered by intelligence, I think.

JAY NELSON: The killer instinct gets civilized out of you; basically, killer instinct isn't a nice quality for human beings working their lives with one another. But you're not supposed to like to see someone squirm, to use Jimmy Carter's phrase. That's not a very appealing characteristic.

It's not necessary in squash, but it can be a plus. It really can. And I think to a large degree it did sort of get civilized out of me. I told you about the Little League thing: I definitely had it through ages eleven and twelve, where it was at its height. I used to love to strike kids out; well, any kid really would, I suppose. But through the years, somehow I guess I learned to try to be nice and not hit people when they're down, but this is pre-

Gretchen Spruance gets one back the hard way against Heather McKay.

cisely what the killer instinct is—to win every point, even if you're winning 14-love. Victor Niederhoffer has it. I don't think Victor has it off the court. Maybe, more precisely what he has is the ability to turn it on . . . to sort of call it out of the closet on special occasions, mainly squash matches.

PETER BRIGGS: You can have all sorts of reasons why a guy can be competitive. He can be competitive because he doesn't like his mother; I don't know. He can be competitive against another guy because he doesn't like the guy; he can be competitive because he wants to prove something to his girlfriend sitting up in the third row. But having a competitive spirit is very important, because of the intensity of the game. And the more intense the sport is, the more competitive you have to be.

GEOFF HUNT: If you can't concentrate, really, you lose. Especially I found with this hard ball as well as with the point system—all of a sudden the points go bang, bang, bang, and they're gone. . . . You've just got to concentrate. This is where someone like Hiddy Jahan has lost matches in the past because he loses his concentration. He gets someone on the go, he says something, and he gets all upset; he's lost concentration, and bam! He loses a few rallies, and he's lost the match.

To Victor go the spoils. Satterthwaite congratulates Niederhoffer.

13

·

Match Play

The Test of Champions

Match play should elicit your best performance. This is where you pull out all the stops, where you utilize everything you've learned.

You should go into a match fully prepared —physically, mentally, and psychologically. However nervous you are before the match, you should be fully alert and relaxed as soon as the referee says, "Play." At this moment, mind and body should shift into a kind of overdrive, purring along like a finely tuned auto.

BEFORE THE MATCH

Analyze your opponent. If you have never played him before or watched him play, ask those who have about him. What kind of player is he? A retriever? A shotmaker? A power hitter? Does he hit better before or after the ball hits the backwall? Is he fast? Slow? In top shape? Is he hot-tempered? Calm? What are his weaknesses? Do your homework before the match.

Analyze the court conditions. Is the court fast? Slow? Will the temperature rise during play or with addition of spectators?

Armed with this information and with the knowledge of your own game, form a basic strategy—a plan—for the match.

Always warm up thoroughly before a match. Never go onto the court "cold." Do your warm-up exercises and hit the ball around so that you're completely loose and limber. Use the on-court rallying before the match to get a final fix on your opponent and the court conditions and to refine your strategy. Let him see how loose you are.

Try to relax, and put everything but the match out of your mind.

Linden serves to Page in the Bancroft Men's Open in 1977.

DURING THE MATCH

Put your game plan immediately into effect. Remember, you want to win 15-love.

Immediately attack your opponent's weaknesses, and keep it up.

Think of each point as though it were an entire game, carefully setting up your winning shots. Never rush.

Put pressure on immediately. The first point is as valuable as the last point. Try to beat your opponent 15–0 in 3 straight games. Every point he gets puts him closer to winning. Never let up.

If you lose a couple of points, take a moment to re-evaluate. Change a losing game. Keep a winner's game.

Don't get ruffled. Never let your mistakes or your opponent's attitude get to you. Calm in the face of adversity.

Control your emotions. Don't let your opponent see that you are upset or tired. Everything you show can be used against you.

Don't be timid about calling lets. Don't question your opponent's let unless you're very sure of yourself.

Never give up on a shot. You'll be surprised at the irretrievable shots you can get to. Ex-

haustion and pain are part of competition. The player who pushes himself makes more points.

NEAR THE END OR CLOSE OF A GAME OR MATCH

Every point is crucial. Play very carefully and don't force the winner until you're absolutely sure. Just the fact of winning the point is a tremendous psychological advantage. However, if the opportunity presents itself, now is the time to pull out your surprise shot—the double boast, the Philadelphia, or even just your hard serve.

If the score reaches 13-all and you're setting, take stock. If you're very tired, call "no set." If he's looking the worse for wear, set 5. If you can go the distance and he's won the past few points, set 5, you're due for a streak.

If your opponent is setting, be prepared for his verdict and adjust your game accordingly. Don't be thrown by his abbreviating or extending the game against your wishes.

Near the end of a match, you will both be somewhat tired. Compensate for your decreased efficiency by preparing your shots extra early: tenaciously return to the T and get into the ready position.

●

VICTOR NIEDERHOFFER: I train by doing wind sprints, try to play every day, or ten months a year. I work out on the court by running up and back twenty or thirty times, running as fast as I can. That's what I should do, but I don't do enough of all these. How do I plan for an entire match? I prepare by resting up, trying to totally concentrate on the match. I try to eat a few hours before I play. I eat a diet high in carbohydrates, try to take care of all my ailments, which are numerous. I develop a certain game plan of a very general nature . . . whether to hit to the backhand or the forehand or to try to hit a lot of shots or use the hard serve or not. With most players I'm sufficiently better than they are so I don't have to go into game plans, it's just a matter of trying to impose my game on theirs, which I'm usually able to do. Since I don't make errors, really the only way to beat me is tie me down or make a lot of winners. My basic strategy is to keep the ball in play hard until I get an opening for a shot and use the great drop.

PETER BOSTWICK: Before a big tournament I just try to play a lot more than I would normally. You're always thinking a little bit about who you might play and what you might have to do. I would say it's pretty hard for me to get out there and watch a good player and really pick his game apart. I think among all the guys, you have to go to one of your friends and say, "Give me a few good pointers: How do you think I should play him?" As I said before, you can overdo trying to play a guy's weakness; with practice it becomes his strength. But I'm thinking of what I should be doing against different players.

MIKE PIERCE: In preparation for a match, my partner and I normally practice maybe once or twice the week before the tournament and get in a little practice. I find that the key to winning any big match is concentration and just being mentally prepared and knowing

Low to the ground and a complete follow-through—Zachariah vs. Barbara Maltby in the Bancroft Women's Open in 1977.

what you want to do when you get out there. The training part you have to do anyway. It's something you have to prepare for and the practice you have to do also.

I definitely think we're much better when we're ahead. I feel that Maurice [Hecksher] and I are a much stronger team when we're winning. Actually, when we fall behind, we're not as good a team. We play too conservatively.

SHARIF KHAN: You can play in practice, but that's not the same kind of pressure; your adrenalin is not flowing, you're not nervous. I try to get psyched up for a match, I try to be motivated. No special tricks—just by being a little bit of a masochist, forcing myself to go after every shot, not giving up on anything, trying to discourage the other man by getting his best shots back. I try to play a little psychology into it because up to a certain point it's physical, but then it's psychological. It's hard always to be psychologically ready. It's like a cycle. There are so many tournaments on the circuit —this [the Open] is the big one; I'm defending it again. I've played in so many tournaments, defended so many times that it's extremely tough for me to get psyched up for every single tournament every single time. I

Frank Satterthwaite on his toes for Victor Niederhoffer's hard serve.

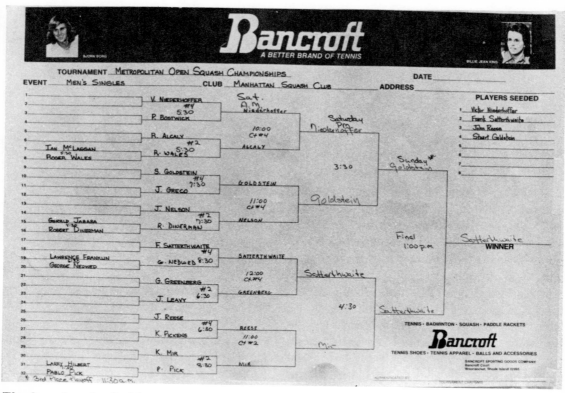

The draw sheet for the Metropolitan Open,
Manhattan Squash Club, 1977.

just try to be more consistent than the next guy, that's all. Golfers have a streak of three or four matches, and that's it, boom. Connors has a streak, and then boom. In squash, I know that I'm going to have a letdown. I know I'm capable of losing; what I want to do is be more consistent than the next guy. At a certain level a lot of players are about even: They're physically fit, psyched up. But up to a point. The thing is to be one degree higher than the other guy. You start playing with Mr. X and he's physically in good shape, he's got just as many good shots as I have. Then you try to watch out for every sign during the match—whether they're getting upset or frustrated, when he makes a few errors he shouldn't have, and you look for signals, a letdown. And once there's a letdown, you try to come in with the heavy artillery. It's the guy who mentally breaks down first. Then, if you're able to recognize the situ-

ation (that you've got him on the run, because sometimes a lot of guys have a mask on . . . but you've got to watch out for signs), then you come in and attack. Sometimes I may be feeling the pain just like he is, but I wouldn't let him know. I would cover it and mask it better. And then he would show it a little earlier than I would; then I'll know that I've got him. And then what I do is try to prolong it for an even stronger attack. Sometimes your opponent may not physically give up, but there are signs. Sometimes they are not very obvious, but you can tell. It's just like a boxer: You look in his eyes. You look for the drainage; there are signs. It's like a fight.

When I'm behind, I play tighter. Obviously when I'm ahead there's a chance I can get relaxed and sort of complacent. I try not to, but it's hard. When I'm behind, I obviously have my back to the wall, and I fight harder. I tighten up my game, cut out the risky shots as much as I can.

ROLAND ODDY: In my opinion, if you are fit, and if you can run, and if you have a reasonable skill with the racquet, squash is 80 per cent the will to win. I always felt that when I was in an official match, my name was up—my record was at stake. And that makes you play an awful lot harder. It goes back, I think, to playing for one's city or country: There's a very definite difference in that than in playing for yourself. You may be a very experienced player, but when you're playing for your country, you're inclined to be nervous. I'm very calm in a match. My concentration, I think, is very good. I don't worry if I fall behind, at least the first game, because I've lost the first game in so many matches that I've won. Of course, it's nice to win 3–0. Definitely, when I smell victory in a match I play harder to get it, and try to put it away, and not give the guy a second chance. A lot of good players in squash will mop a guy up for two games and think it's over and not much trouble; they'll let down and the other person comes on.

One of the big mistakes people make is when they get behind, they press and make errors. When people come to me and tell me they're losing, my advice to them is usually: "Just play one point at a time. Forget everything else; just think about that one point. If you win that point, you move on to the next," etc. Everybody I have played, I always think about their game, or try to find chinks they have in the game. For instance, Niederhoffer and John Reese, I've always felt it was smarter to serve to their forehand. They've denied it. But I think Vic tried to use a little reverse psychology on me because it really is a good move to serve to his forehand, but he didn't want anyone else to know that. It makes sense, because 99 per cent of the time people serve first to the backhand anyway, so they get all the practice on the backhand.

If someone is knocking the hell out of the ball, and killing me, I will try to change the pace and lob. The greatest exhibition of the lob I ever saw was at the Gold Racquets about three years ago, when Satterthwaite was being slaughtered by Briggs. Satterthwaite was down two games and about 7–2 in the third, and he looked like it was all over. He was exhausted—and all he did was change the pace: He lobbed. And Briggs made a stupid move—instead of getting on with his game, he changed, he lobbed too. And before he knew where he was, he was beaten 15–2 in the fifth game!

PETER BOSTWICK: I would say that I'm pretty calm in a match, and my concentration is usually good. Basically, I would say I have a good disposition for a game. I don't get particularly riled up; I don't get upset when I make a bad shot, and I seem to be able to hang in there when things aren't going well. I stay fairly calm. . . . I'm not saying that I don't get a little nervous at certain times, but that's good. I get less nervous than I used to, and I think it probably hurts my game a little bit because when you're keyed up, it means more to you, you want to do well, sometimes you react a little faster and you run a little harder . . . when your adrenalin is pumping. But normally I'd say I'm fairly calm and complacent and my concentration is good.

I think I play perfectly well when I'm behind. But I think I'm probably tougher when I'm ahead. . . . Usually when you're going

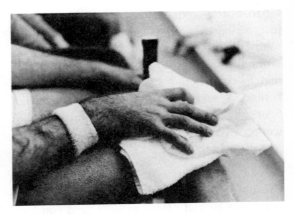

Niederhoffer's knee.

well, it's a little easier to play well. There are people who get ahead and they have a mental lapse. I would say that happens to me very seldom. . . . Very seldom do I have lapses when I'm ahead, where I let up and get careless.

PETER BRIGGS: Each match is like a specific learning experience where you learn one particular thing, cause when you look back on it you can re-create the situation and you learn either one particular thing about yourself or the other guy or how you react under pressure, or just about the game.

It's important, when you're young and trying to play competitively, to make the jump. All it really is, is playing tournaments when you play above your head and beat people you're not supposed to beat. And I can think of hundreds of guys who always have that potential to make it, but never got a big win at the right time. They blew it somehow. Or they just beat that guy they just didn't think they'd beat. Everything reaches certain plateaus. . . . Sometimes a big victory will go to your head for a while, and you'll start getting beaten by people who you shouldn't lose to. All you've really done is jumped up a notch, which is great.

You really have to keep playing matches. I hadn't played a tournament in two months before the Open. I didn't even play a match. That annoyed me. Physically, I was in good enough shape to win the tournament, because I played with Hunt up here; three days before, I had beaten him. I took about a month to just really train, but I hadn't played under tournament conditions. I'll learn next time. Normally, I always played ten times better in match conditions. I play better when I'm behind. I take more chances. I just sort of figure that I've been chicken up until then. It works. I have no concentration, I just play. I just really like to play.

JUAN DE VILLAFRANCA: Even when you're playing against a friend, when you get into the court you go and play very hard, and you kind of have to a little bit hate your opponent be-

Happy is the man who can beat Victor Niederhoffer (Stu Goldstein).

fore playing a match. I think you've got to get there thinking you're going to kill the other guy. Give no opportunities—believe that you can beat him 15-love every single game you play.

GORDON ANDERSON: I'm usually worst the first game, and I'm always best when I'm down, by about 7 or 8 points. I love it coming from behind. If I know I've only got 1 point before I lose a game, I'll get to the next 6. If it's even at 5-all or something, then I fall asleep. The mind wanders; my concentration wanders. As a result, when I'm down 14–9, in my mind, I probably won't lose that point, hopefully.

CHARLES UFFORD: After my initial years, after I had gotten to what we'll say is the top of my game, from there on during my thirties, before I hit the fence (and even thereafter), I've always been a player who's played in streaks. Very rarely do I ever beat anyone 3-love . . . it's always been in streaks. I would say that 80 per cent of the time if I will run a streak of points and get to 14, I will lose the next point. Very bad on the finishing, the finishing instinct. I don't know why. You know perfectly well what you should do. It should be just like any other point, and there should be not one iota of lapse in concentration. Yet for some reason, more often than not, I'll lose that silly point. And there have been some remarkable episodes. . . .

How do I prepare for a match? In college, the problem was sleeping. That was just a disaster area. The night before a match—I got to the finals of the National Intercollegiate in my sophomore year—I didn't sleep a wink. What used to happen was this ball would circle around you; and you would play one interminable point. Just get to the shot and retrieve it, get to the next. . . . That's the reverse side of the coin: psyching yourself down. I was never at ease in my life, generally, at the big tournaments. I think if I had gone out and had a couple of stiff belts of scotch, maybe, but I never actually tried that out.

You see, the whole notion was that if I could play my game the way that I wanted to, the rest of it would take care of itself. My problem has always been largely incidental. I would be aware of the style of my opponent's game, but as far as how to get mentally prepared, it's a matter of being able to relax. Certainly the adrenalin, get that going. You sort of have to have an equilibrium so that you're able to concentrate on looking at the ball, thinking about your variety of strokes,

where the shot should go this time as opposed to where it went last time. And when my game was going, why, it was fine . . . the feet do most of the running. I play better when I'm down. Basically defensive. When my conditioning was there you would wait until the opportunity presented itself. . . .

GRETCHEN SPRUANCE: I try very hard to get to the point where I'm thinking about where my opponent is and getting it where he's not, just trying to think on that level. I've been practicing very hard, but either you feel it or you don't feel it; it's something that's so fast and furious that you don't know. Normally I think what I want to do and work very hard. I'm very determined, and I talk to myself occasionally—that sort of gets me going. I cope fairly well under match conditions, but I haven't played in very many tournaments, and that makes a big difference. Playing men isn't the same thing as playing women; with men, there's no pressure on me whatsoever. When I get behind I tend to force things, and really that's bad. It's hard for me to think cause I haven't really played that many matches this year, but the fact is I would get behind in a game and there would be no coming back, and that was it. In practice you can't really tell. I've realized that no matter who I play, I just have to play *my* game; I've realized that over the years. You've got to stop going for shots if you have a warmer court. You have to change your game. I love to roll shots into the wall, but they're not very effective unless you have the person guessing at the wrong thing. It's really a matter of guessing. It seems that every shot can be gotten into the middle on a warm court.

GEOFF HUNT: After all the years that I've been playing . . . since 1965, the time I represented Australia—I get keyed up anyway. Last year in the championships I had never been so nervous playing a tournament because it meant so much to me to win it. It was the first world-wide open championship we had, and I still played well, once I got into the match.

Weymuller and Michel joust for position.

Niederhoffer waits to see what Alcaly, well positioned on the T, will do. PHOTO: RAIMONDO BOREA.

What I do now is get on the court five minutes beforehand and just get myself warmed up a bit hitting the ball, and that helps me a good deal. Too many times I come to the court and if I don't do that, I'm more nervous.

I think everybody gets upset, but sometimes you can't help it. I try not to let it worry me. As to whether I do better when I'm ahead or behind, well, I think you fight better, obviously, when you're behind. Usually when you are behind that's the time you usually concentrate the hardest. It's not necessarily the right thing to do. If you're ahead, you really are not quite sure you're going to win it. Once you're ahead, you should just keep it. But you do lose concentration, and when you are behind you've got to pull out all the stops to win it. You see, I'm a bit of a gambler. If I'm down whatever, I'll try for everything unless, of course, I'm very, very tired and there's one more game to go, and I know it . . . then I'll kill myself.

JAY NELSON: I've got lists you wouldn't believe. That's what I get a kick out of . . . most of my lists start with "Don't." Things like, "Don't think it's going to be easy." I'll fall into that and I'll have to re-educate myself to the fact that this is the kind of game where you re-

ally have to almost expect that the guy's gonna get it. And if he gets it pretty well, it'll help if you can not be real down, that you say to yourself, "Hey, that's pretty good. You really beat me in that one." If you can have a sort of joy in playing, it'll help. As I've said before, that's fine in practice, it's almost impossible in a game, but at least neutrality in a game, rather than "Oh God, he got that." . . . when you really have to say, "I'm better than he is."

I've had a lot of matches where I've played lousy and won. I felt lousy, I just brutalized it out, I just hung in there, wasn't running well, had stiff legs, nothing was working particularly well, and I expected to lose—but I just hung in there and somehow pulled it out. Hanging in there seems to be a key to the game.

I think you just sprint at the end of a match, when it's close. You're not consciously saving the energy for that sprint, theoretically, but I think you are somehow saving something. I think you're not going 100 per cent flat out. I think it's maybe it's like the sprint at the end of an 880. I mean, an 880, people say it's nearly a sprint the whole way, but not quite. But I know that you can muster up energy at the end, particularly if you decide to go on a run-and-grind approach: Forget the subtleties. I sometimes will do that at the end of a match: I'm just gonna run and hit hard, and if something pops into my mind, fine. But I've got my mind thinking defense. Getting it when he hits and then hitting hard . . . and yeah, you can pull it up.

BARBARA MALTBY: I consider myself very competitive. On the court I try to see everything very objectively; I try to be very cool. If you get too much into the competitiveness you can't see what the other person is trying to do and what you're doing wrong. You have to be able to look at yourself and see what you're doing wrong. You have to get an overall viewpoint.

It's very hard to concentrate completely for the whole match. Some tournaments you find it easy to concentrate, and others, no. Some tournaments you hope your opponent hits every ball back because you're ready and you want to hit again, and some tournaments you hope your opponent misses because you just don't want to hit it again. It's all how mentally up you are. I found that by playing too many tournaments in a row you just get mentally tired, you sort of get into routines, you react the same way to every shot. You get in patterns, and it's much easier for your opponent to play you when you get into patterns than when you're changing. It's really important to be mentally sharp as well as physically sharp. Another thing I wanted to say about the physical part is that in the first couple of years I played I didn't train that hard, and I found that sometimes I would be so tired that I would be unable to take advantage of the short shots. In essence you are so tired you're unable to hit the winner; you can only return the ball. If you have to play a person just on stamina alone, you should be able to do it. Another thing: It really helps you for not getting injuries to be in good condition. A lot of minor pulled muscles and sprained ankles and just getting hit occur because you're so tired, and can be eliminated through good condition. . . .

Doubles. PHOTOS: RAIMONDO BOREA.

14

•

Doubles

As in tennis, the game of squash doubles differs markedly from singles, and, despite the limited number of doubles courts, has a great number of partisans, fans, distinguished champions, and a full tournament schedule.

Played on a larger court (45 feet by 25 feet) with a livelier ball and a heavier racquet, the game demands a quite different complement of skills and strategies from singles. Many squash singles champions have found that they do not excel in doubles, and many of the very best all-time doubles players have never been seeded singles players. Victor Niederhoffer and Peter Briggs have been successful at both games, as has Diehl Mateer. Mike Pierce and Roland Oddy are doubles "specialists."

Patience, teamwork, and stamina are hallmarks of winning doubles.

A good doubles team is formed by a good balance of capabilities and understanding. Po-sitioning in doubles involves the sides of the court (rather than the center, as in singles); there is a left-wall player and a right-wall player. The team may involve a strong backhand on the left, a forehand on the right, with the center covered by the forehand of the left-court player. A left-handed player (Briggs) and a right-handed player (Howe) often make a powerful doubles team and make it hard for their opponents to watch the ball. In many cases, one is a power hitter who sets up the play; the other is a touch player who makes the winning shots. One member usually acts as the captain, doing a lot of calling, saying, "I've got it," "It's yours," "Let it go," "Coming around," and that sort of thing. So each member of the team must know the other's capabilities in a given situation, as well as know the opponents' predictable response.

A doubles team is only as strong as its

weaker link. Early in a warm-up or a match, or in discussion of the opponents, you decide who the weaker player is and send 80 per cent of the balls his way, because hopefully he's not only going to miss some of the shots, he's also going to tire. Sometimes this backfires in that as you give him more practice, he rises to the occasion and turns out to be the better player. So you have to discern when you reach this point, and forget him for a while. The technique, generally, is to assault the weaker player so that his partner gets the feeling, "They're ignoring me, I can't get a chance to make a point." Then you put the winner away on *him* because he's moving around covering his partner.

If, for instance, the right-wall player is weak, the left-wall man will be hanging around behind trying to get anything the other fellow misses, so he's always a little out of position. Once you've got him compensating for the right-wall player and he's just diddling shots back, you then make the drop shot on him— the left-wall man—and he looks bad. He got one chance at the ball and couldn't make it.

Technique and strategy are quite different. In doubles, you're never really on the T. The two left-court opponents are rotating, changing places, to the left of the T; the right-court players are doing the same on the right. It's very difficult to pass your opponents in doubles: It's a long court, and there are two retrievers. Sometimes, particularly if the ball comes off the wall and the first guy misses it, his partner can come around and pick it up. So the technique is often to put the ball right at your opponent, so he's defending himself from being hit by the ball.

You've got to be psychologically prepared in doubles to be very patient and to play for a long time. The length of each rally is generally longer because two retrievers can get just about any ball back; and because the ball is livelier, it is a game of doggedly hitting those cross courts, rails, and lobs, and waiting for the opening for the winner. It is definitely a percentage game.

The nature of doubles exaggerates the importance of both power and touch. The size of the court requires much stronger hitting (and higher placement) of the cross courts and rails, and the putaway itself requires expert timing and placement.

To step up the pace, you have to volley a lot more and give your opponents less time to prepare. A lot of balls are hit high in doubles: On the doubles court, it is nearly impossible to hit the ball six inches above the tin and have it go to the backwall. To get that length you really are hitting about a foot under the service line. If somebody puts a drive inches above the tin in doubles, it's like a drop shot—it's finished ten feet from the front wall, a long run from the backcourt. And the lob, provided the court has high ceilings, is used a lot, because you stall a lot in doubles, and you also want to move your opponents to the far reaches of the court.

The putaway shots in doubles can be the drop, the Philadelphia, or sometimes a rail shot. But it is what you do to get to the point where you're ready to go for the shot that counts, patiently setting up with a series of shots that finally move both opponents so far out of position that the winner is a sure thing, for a misjudgment of your opponents' ability to retrieve it can easily result in a winner for *them*.

●

DIEHL MATEER

Q.: What makes a good doubles team?

A.: It's two people who know the game. Doubles is a game of being able to have good pace on the ball, being able to volley it, and adding the shots to it. If you can't volley in doubles, then you can't win—the court's too big; if you're going to let every ball go to the backwall, you're going to be out in left field. You've got to be able to hit the ball on the volley, with good pace, particularly cross court —doubles is a cross-court game in comparison to singles, which is up and down the walls. I think one of the reasons Peter Briggs is tougher in doubles this year than he was last year or the year before is that he's volleying more and more. I saw him play Niederhoffer in exhibition at the National Juniors; Briggs played the best squash I thought than anybody for two games. I was a judge, and I felt: "How can anybody play the game better?" It was just awesome, fantastic; and Niederhoffer just kept plugging away, making bread-and-butter shots, and Peter would make an error here and there. Niederhoffer won it in five games; it was a great exhibition. But for the first two games, Briggs was unbelievable.

Q.: How analytical are you about the people you are going to play; about your opponent in a match that's coming up?

A.: I've always tried to sit down with my partner, before a match, and analyze what the opponents do well and what we should do to negate that and what we should do to win the match. In singles, you can really in five or ten minutes decide what the job at hand is. I always found it very difficult to judge two players as a team. I find that I didn't do nearly as well the first time I played someone; my confidence level after playing someone once went way up, because I knew really what the job was I had to do.

As a team, you have to decide what each person's responsibility is—based on the opponent. You're usually playing opponents you know—that have a good straight drop . . . or a good reverse corner, hit a hard cross court well, so each person has his responsibility not to feed them balls that give them the opportunity to play their favorite shot, and the other person has the job to defend against that shot when it comes. Mike Pierce has as good shot-making ability as anybody in the game, in the doubles court, whereas Maurice Heckscher doesn't have the shots, but he has the big, fast cross court. In 1975, the year that we lost to them in the Nationals (Gilbert and I), it was the second match of the day, and I was maybe half a step slow in defending against the cross court, and if I had defended the cross court a

little better, we would have had a better shot at it than we did.

Q.: Why do you like doubles so well?

A.: It's got to be, outside of tennis doubles, the greatest fun game that was ever devised, and I can't tell you which one is more fun. . . .

Q.: What is your mental attitude in a match?

A.: I never had any problems concentrating; that comes fairly easily. I think the reason I've done well in doubles is that having a team effort, working with a partner—I've enjoyed that . . . I've seen teams lose doubles matches because they're at odds with each other. Even more, you can sort of see a player's game go downhill because he's lost confidence in his partner. Whereas, in fact, in doubles (I remember Hunter [Lott] saying this), when one guy's having problems, that's when the other guy has got to be up there, or then you really are in difficulty.

I remember many matches where a partner was having problems. John Ince had a bad back one year and he couldn't really bend over to get a ball that was six inches off the floor, but he was in there trying. Of course he couldn't run, and it was something that I can't say I enjoyed the fact that he had a bad back, but I did enjoy competing with that problem to see if we could overcome it.

Q.: Do you think there's any advantage of a left-handed/right-handed combination in doubles?

A.: There's no advantage other than the fact that if you have a left-handed player on the back left wall he should be able to cut off balls, have a little better reach, etc. It's not a big advantage. It's still dependent on the player's ability on that left wall. That's the whole thing. It can be a disadvantage . . . this might be one of the reasons why I've had as much success as I've had in doubles, in the fact that I had the forehand in the middle, the strong stroke in the middle. And I've played a lot of balls from that forehand and been able to convert a potential losing point into a winning point with the strong forehand. It's important to have the center of the court well protected. Mike Pierce may have told you he relies a lot on hitting the ball down the middle. When you have a ball set up and everybody is anticipating something on the walls, a lot of points can be won down the middle of the court.

Q.: Is there any basic strategy about position on the court in doubles?

A.: The biggest mistake that many players make in the doubles court is that they play too close to the walls. With the game being a cross-court game, you've got to play well off the wall to give yourself the ability to adjust to where the ball is going to end up when it comes off that wall.

Q.: Is there anything comparable to one-on-one playing in doubles?

A.: Oh yes. Now, I like to stand in front of my opponent, unless he's standing on the front wall; so I would say that 85 to 90 per cent of the time, I'm standing in front of my opponent on the left side. There have been a few opponents who, I think, have been a little upset. Of course, they have the option if they want to, to stand in front of me. I have my spot; if they want to stand in front of me, they're welcome. They may be a little too far forward, but I like to stand dead center in the court with respect to the sidewalls, because I feel that way, there's no way someone can break the ball off the wall and jam me to the point where I'm going to make an error; this way I know I'm always stepping into the ball and not backing away from it. And if you're out front in the center of the court, you have full view of everything that's going on. If your partner happens to get caught short and he can't cover a shot from the forehand front corner, you're not too far away from it. I covered quite a few balls out there.

ROLAND ODDY

Q.: What is doubles about?

A.: Doubles is basically two things: patience and teamwork; teamwork in the fact that two people work together trying to achieve a winning result. They do this greatly through patience—they don't hit shots unless they have the openings, and they don't always hit shots when they *do* have the openings. They may play more defensively than that. What can happen in doubles is that people lose a little bit of track if the match is going badly and they press and they hit far too many shots. And the ball has to travel a long way on the doubles court, so you should be in a pretty good position on the court, and it should feel good to you; your body position should feel good, so that when you do try for a shot you have every chance of making it if you're well balanced. If you're not balanced, you make errors.

Q.: What is the strategy of positioning of team partners on the court?

A.: Basically, people play side by side; but certain hard-hit cross-court balls are much better left to the opposite-court player, which is part of teamwork. You get to know whose ball this is. And a very big weapon is for the left-court player to hit forehands down the middle.

Q.: What makes a great squash team? Why do two particular people make a good team?

A.: Well, I think to play well together you must have a basic respect for one another. Very unusual players sometimes make good doubles teams because they know they're good individual players and they feel that if they really make an effort to combine and team and work with someone else, the end result will be good. All of it comes down to the "will complex." You get two guys who have a lot of pride who have worked at the game and are fierce competitors.

On almost every good doubles team I know, one is always hard-hitting, and the other is a smart player who can make all the points if he gets the openings. Or he sets up the hard hitter—it depends. If you take the top teams now (Pierce and Heckscher, for example), Michael Pierce is not that hard a hitter; Maurice Heckscher is a very hard hitter. Briggs and

Howe won the Nationals last year, and Briggs is a hard hitter. Also, you get a lot of people who are good at one game and not the other. I think as far as doubles is concerned, it makes a lot of sense, particularly in today's squash world and with the growth of the game, to be a doubles specialist and not play competitive singles. You have to play a certain amount of singles for conditioning. Basically, neither Pierce nor Heckscher are serious singles players; they're both good doubles players.

MIKE PIERCE

Q.: What's squash doubles about?

A.: I think doubles is a greater spectator game than squash singles. Squash singles comes down to endurance, who's in better shape, who's better prepared for a match. You get four good doubles players, I think it is possible for so many variables . . . so many different situations because there are two extra players. And there's just so much more that can be done out there.

Q.: What makes a good team out of you and Maurice [Heckscher]?

A.: I would say primarily he can hit as hard as anyone in the doubles game. I do not hit very hard, but I have very good touch; I play all the shots, so I think that's where the blend works out very well. My partner has many shots, don't let me mislead you, but he's the strength. With his hard hitting he's able to open up the court, and if he creates an opening it's up to me to make the shot or put the ball away. And if I'm doing that, we should win most of the time.

The most important strategy in doubles is, in starting off the point, getting the ball past the red line. The way Maurice [Heckscher] and I do it is through cross courts. . . . I lob . . . the cross-court lob primarily over my

The Rowes celebrate their win against Clement and Baccalao. PHOTO: RAIMONDO BOREA.

right-hand-court opponent's shoulder, to get him back, and Maurice hits a hard cross court, breaking it off around the red line, and making sure he backs the left player to the backwall. If we're doing that well, it's hard to open the court, and our opponents hit loose shots up front, and that's when we move in for the kill. It's basically pretty simple. We also play a lot of balls down the middle of the court.

Q.: Do you think that doubles will catch on? Do you think that they'll be building enough doubles courts to make it grow at all?

A.: No way. No, I don't think that they'll build enough doubles courts. I wish they would . . . but it's impractical at this point. I would like to see some of these new clubs put up doubles courts, because I think from the spectator point it's very exciting. . . . I'm kind of unique in a way—I've devoted all my time to being good at doubles. The past six or seven years everybody else has worked very hard on singles. I play a lot of singles to stay in shape and I compete, but not on the same level as the top singles players.

Sue Newman and Heather McKay . . . and their trophies.

15

·

The English Game

On the surface, the differences between the North American hard-ball game and the English soft-ball game—which is played everywhere outside North America and increasingly in Canada—don't seem very radical.

In the English game, the court is 2½ feet wider. The sidewall slopes, rather than steps, down to the backwall, and the service box is a square rather than a quarter circle.

The ball is smaller and softer; it bounces higher and comes farther out off the walls. The racquet is usually a bit lighter.

A game is scored only to 9 points, but a player can only win a point on his own serve. At 8-all the loser of the tying point can declare "no set" or "set 2." On the serve the receiver may elect to return a serve that would have been a fault (would not have landed in the service area); in so doing, the serve becomes valid. A first serve that hits the ceiling, lights, or that hits above the backwall line is considered a double fault.

The cumulative effect of these seemingly small differences is quite substantial, however, and the game in fact differs markedly in its requirements of skills and tactics.

What the English game demands most of all is an incredible level of physical fitness and stamina. The ball is slower, but the play is faster. Because the ball is so much more bouncy, it is easier to retrieve but more difficult to put away. Once you've passed your opponent with the hard ball, you're much closer to having scored the point than with the English ball. Rallies tend to last a long time and require patient setting up of the putaway —moving your opponent over the larger court, making him run, wearing him down. Endurance is essential. Since points can only be won by the server, the games are longer as strings of long rallies go by without a point being scored. A much bigger, harder swing is required to power the slow ball at the pace necessary to set up the winner. Quick reflexes and mobility are essential, but the accent is on reaching rather than running, to conserve precious energy. The English game is played with arm's-length strokes and the elbow out from the body.

Most hard-ball players are caught flat-footed, and exhausted, by the demands of the soft-ball game. We keep fit at the level required by our game; for many players, playing the game is enough to keep fit. Champions of the soft-ball game must maintain much more rigorous programs of conditioning and training.

Partisans on both sides argue the superiority of their brand of squash, but it's a moot question: They're two different animals. In the soft-ball game, it often boils down to pure will, endurance, and conditioning. For this reason, it's usually easier for a soft-ball player to adapt to the hard-ball game. To make the transition the other way, a player has to train to a much higher level of fitness—no matter how smart or adept a player he may be in the hard-ball game.

●

SHARIF KHAN: I think it's easier to switch from the International game to the American game. If you've been playing the International game, you're more fit, and you've had a good grounding in basic shots, whereas in the American game you lack that kind of conditioning, and your strokes are very different and very abrupt. So there's much more of an advantage for somebody from the International game. But there's no such thing as *the* best game. It's a question of what you're looking for in the game; it's like saying what's the best, NFL football or soccer? How can you compare two games so diverse? Sure, both use a leather ball, but they're different games.

CHARLES UFFORD: The English game and the American game are so different. I've been fortunate enough to play both and over a period of time. And they are just so different. I mean the lob . . . it's a thing of beauty—it's a joy; it's an attacking shot—you can tear your opponent's tummy out: All of a sudden, there it is. In our game, the lob—well, if you're in trouble, all you're trying to do is hit it along the wall so that it doesn't do too much harm. Properly speaking, the stroke production is different—I think it's very difficult for a player, any player, to develop the different type of stroke production that is ultimately required for each game. The English game employs terrific length of arc between your starting the stroke and the impact on the ball, whereas in the American game, you generate more speed with a wrist snap. If you're going to hit the ball hard in the English game, you really have to take a full-blooded swat at the ball; it's hard to learn how to do it. Some of our players, if they learn the American game very easily, then try to go over and learn the English game. But they're going to have a very hard time ever catching up to the top players of the English game.

The English players have a better chance of making a better showing in our game; not that they play our game, but the basic equipment of the English game will go farther than the basic equipment of the American game takes you in the English game. That turns largely on the degree of fitness. There is nothing in the American game that will tire the English squash player. The most telling example of that is when Len Carran and the Australian team came over here in '72 or '73, and he and John Jacobson played—Carran won that. That was against good, top, solid, elite players; not the top twenty in the country, just good. The next weekend he played in the National championships; he went to the semifinals, and lost a long tough one; the third weekend, he won the Canadian Nationals. He sort of covered the court like a crab . . . he was all over the place. He hit the ball with such speed that they couldn't quite return the shots. . . .

PETER BRIGGS: I went over and played the International game for two months last spring, and I like it. But it would take about two years for a good American player to get into good enough condition to compete on the same level as he was playing here. It's all conditioning. The American game is a lot more racquet-work because the ball is faster.

GORDON ANDERSON

Q.: Do you think in Canada they're going to swing toward the International game?

A.: They are already. Any new clubs that are being built in Toronto and the area are at least 50 per cent English courts; at one new club, now there are eight courts, four English courts, one with a gallery, and then one American court with a gallery. And now, in the next installation, they're probably going to build all English courts because commercial squash is big in Canada, and especially in Toronto. And I work in a club that is commercial and I teach completely soft ball, and none of the new players want to play hard ball even though they're playing on an American-size court, which makes it a sort of bastard type of game. It seems they would definitely rather play English squash; girls would rather play it. There are a lot of reasons. It's easier to learn, and just more exciting from their point of view, because they can hit the ball right away.

Q.: What are the real differences in the game?

A.: The main difference is that in our caliber of squash, if I want to be No. 1 in England, I have to concentrate far harder on fitness in the English game, far harder. When we were in Pakistan watching the world's singles, after about half an hour, when the top two in the world were playing, guys like Hunt and Alaudin, it came down to the fitness, and to the fellow who's worked the hardest, whereas our game doesn't show that. A guy like Niederhoffer, who is really clumsy on the court, and moves the ball around, and is very smart, can beat a guy like Caldwell or somebody who is very fit and has been working out and run-

ning miles every day. He's more fit, but he can't beat Niederhoffer, because he doesn't have the shots yet.

And I like the American game for that reason. It's more exciting, more shots, and if there's an opening in the court and he's beside me, bang! I can hit it down the wall. Whereas in English squash, even if he's there, if he can just step behind me and run, he'll get to the ball. I'm sure in the years to come that they also will try to work on getting more shots into the International game. They've got a great game right now because the size of the court is super; that's my argument. Their court, with the extra 2½ feet, is much safer with all these new guys playing. There aren't enough coaches and teachers to supply all the new people playing. We've had cuts on our club, lacerations above the eye—and that destroys the game, makes it dangerous.

GEOFF HUNT: The hard-ball game is very different. The degrees of strength and fitness required are not nearly as high. And the ball does go faster. I think our game has a lot to offer, but they're two different styles of game altogether.

The first big difference is the ball. Now, the hard ball . . . you can't compress it very much; it goes through very fast. It hits the wall and still keeps coming off, whereas, the soft ball doesn't go through nearly as fast, hits a sidewall, and slows down; and it comes off at a different angle, so it means that to convert

Heather McKay, No. 1 in the soft-ball game for more than fifteen years, and Sue Newman, Australia's No. 1-ranked amateur.

from one game to the other, you've got to get used to where the ball is going. I think that aspect of the hard ball is more difficult because the ball is flying around more instead of pulling up. In our game, we've got to generate racquet headspin to get the ball to go hard, whereas in the hard ball, there's not so much of that. For that reason, we swing a lot bigger, and sometimes that gets us into a little bit of trouble with the hard ball. I could change; it would take me a while. I've been playing seven or eight years with the soft ball. Nearly all the top players on the hard ball originally came up on the soft-ball game. Sharif, for instance, was No. 1 as an amateur in England before he came over to play the hard ball. Look at the players—even in this tournament, many of them have been good soft-ball players before they picked up this game.

Q.: In the game last night, you didn't even seem to be breathing hard by the end of the match.

A.: I always breathe hard anyway; but I don't let my opponent see that I'm breathing hard. You get more breaks and opportunities to recover in this game, and I'm conditioned to play a lot harder squash. Momentarily you get out of breath; it doesn't last as long when you're playing our game.

Q.: In the International game, what do you think are the ingredients that make a top player?

A.: I think you've got to have reasonably good ball sense. Some people can't hit a ball, no matter what they do. You also need, I think, speed and quickness, which means quick reflexes generally. This doesn't always occur; some of the good players haven't got quick reflexes, but they still get up to a certain level. The really top players are all very quick and fast around the court and can move very adroitly, change direction. Our game particularly requires fitness, which we have to attain by extensive training. Because of this, even if you're not that gifted at stroking the ball, you can always learn by practicing and applying yourself. And I think dedication to the game is a lot, whether or not you've got the speed and everything else. Sometimes if you dedicate yourself and practice and train hard, you can still get there. This has been proven in a number of instances.

Stroke execution is very important. Our game is a combination of stroking (learning to hit the ball) and fitness. Now, you can be the fittest guy in the world but you can never win a squash match. It depends on how you hit the ball. Stroking is quite complex and takes quite a lot to learn, and it's a constant battle to keep your stroking up. There is quite a large variety of strokes in our game. One of our best shots is the one that goes into the nick. We play for that all the time; that's how we're going to win it. When someone is fast and you get him out of position, that's a great shot. You must develop the ability to hit the ball to the area of the court the opponent isn't. To be able to hit the ball softly or hard takes a lot of strategy. You also have to wait a longer time for a winning shot because of the ball. You've got to work your opponent out of position. One thing I've found with the hard ball: It's easier to go for a winner. Also, the lesser player can often hit winners, whereas in our game, unless you hit the ball really well, it's difficult

SQUASH HOW TO PLAY, HOW TO WIN

to hit a winner against someone who is good.

Q.: How mental and analytical is the game, given good conditioning and good strokes?

A.: That has a lot to do with it. Some matches will last up to two hours. It's a constant battle. Top players in our game are masters of confidence and positioning and concentration. I believe it's like a game of chess; you're maneuvering your opponent out of position off the wall, whereas in the hard ball you can have the fellow out of position and yet he can still produce the winner. Now, this doesn't happen in our game at all. You've got to maneuver him out of position before you're really able to put the ball away. Because of the speed of the game, you've got to think ahead. You've got to make sure you make your opponent run; you've got to soften him up a bit by moving him; part of the game is really working him around the court. I think it's the same in this game as well, but not to the same degree. Everybody who plays the English game at a top level can go the distance very easily in the American game, because the game isn't wear your opponent out. But your standard of fitness is only the standard required for this game, so you really only train yourself for that. That's why someone like Sharif would work his opponent's guts out: Obviously his tactics on the court are maneuvering the opponent around, slamming the ball, and hammering him into the ground.

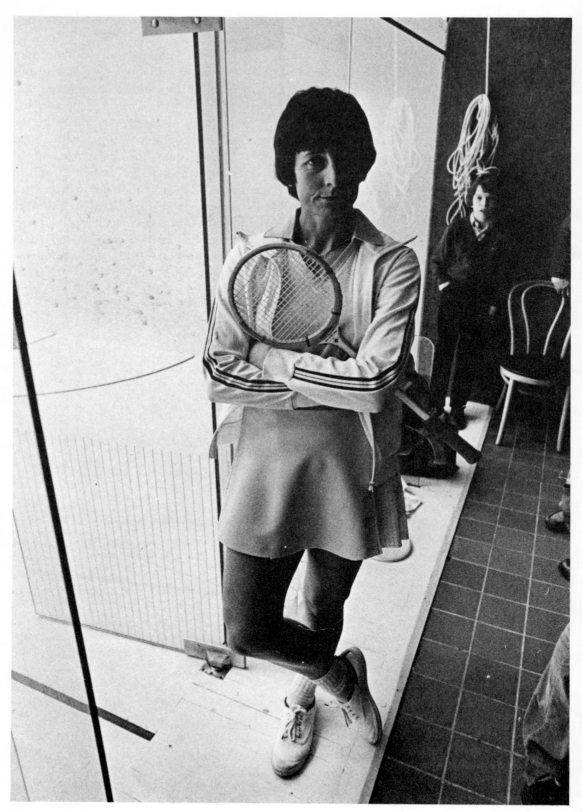

Heather McKay.

16

•

The Experts
Player Biographies and Commentary

In this section are pictures and brief profiles of the players whose commentaries are found throughout the book, followed by some additional remarks about their own game.

For reference, all interviews in this book took place during the two weeks surrounding the 1977 North American Open Singles Championship in Philadelphia and the Bancroft Women's Open Singles Championship in New York.

GORDON ANDERSON
Born: 1949

Twenty-eight-year-old Gordon Anderson is a teaching professional at the Bay Street Racquet Club in Toronto, where both the hard- and soft-ball games are played. In 1971, his first year out of college, he won the Canadian Amateur championship. In 1972 he repeated the feat, and he was a finalist in the U. S. Amateur championships. He is known for his size (tall), his power (formidable), his stamina (endless), and a playing style both exciting and erratic.

Q.: What do you think is the strength of your game?

A.: Probably the strength of my game is relaxation on the court. Like I'll go for a shot whenever I can, and I'm probably more exciting to watch than somebody who's deadly—up and down the wall type of game. . . .

Q.: So, you're not a percentage player, then?

A.: No. I've won some big matches, and I've lost some bad matches; like, I've beaten Sharif twice on a particular day. When I get excited enough (and I like crowds), I'm just calm and

Gordon Anderson. PHOTO: BANCROFT SPORTING GOODS CO.

easy. If I try to get uptight, that's when I choke.

Q.: So you think that, in the end, by taking risks you sometimes win matches that you wouldn't otherwise win, and probably blow matches that you would have won?

A.: That's right. I'm up and down. If you saw a record, I'm sort of a bad person to bet against. But my other strength is being able to hit the ball hard—good timing to hit the ball so that the majority of players in this tournament couldn't hit a forehand as hard if they were given the opportunity, and sometimes when I lay into it, it's gone—you know, the hard ball.

PETER BOSTWICK
Born: 1934

Pete Bostwick's sports accomplishments, especially in racquet sports, are awesome.

In court tennis, he has won six National Amateur championships, three U. S. Opens, two U. S. Amateur doubles, three U. S. Open doubles, and three Tuxedo Gold Racquets (all doubles with his brother Jimmy).

In racquets Pete has won two U. S. Opens and three Tuxedo Gold Racquets, two in the same meet in which he won the court tennis championships), four Gold Racquets, and was World Champion, 1969–72.

In tennis he was a ranked junior, and in 1972–74 he played in the Junior Veteran Division of the U. S. Open at Forest Hills.

He is also a golfer and has played in five National Amateurs, the British Amateur, and the U. S. Open, and he is a hockey player—captain, coach, and currently leading scorer of the St. Nicholas Hockey Club, the oldest amateur hockey club in the United States.

He started playing squash seriously, and has been a ranked player since 1971, was the No. 1 Veteran player in 1975, and was No. 2 in 1976.

Q.: How would you describe your game?

A.: I've never really seen myself play. You do a lot of things you probably don't realize you're doing; your strokes look a lot different than you mentally fix them. I don't really know what kind of game I have. I'm sort of a scrambler. I have a sort of bastard game because I play so many different sports that I occasionally revert to a racquet shot—a hard racquet shot—instead of a squash shot; at the same time, having played a lot of different games, it can be helpful because it does something a bit orthodox that people aren't used to, and it bothers them from time to time. Basically, I would say that I'm a pretty good scrambler in there, and I have a pretty quick racquet; I'm not a particularly hard hitter . . . not a power hitter, although I hit the ball fairly crisply when I'm playing well. I now can play almost all of the classic shots in squash racquets.

Q.: Would you say that you're a touch player?

A: Yes. I am a touch player, and my touch has probably gotten better as I've played more. . . . I have a little better feel for the shots now. Basically, when I won my first big tournament and was ranked in the first ten in the United States, I was pretty much just a hitter and a scrambler, with just one or two shots. Obviously you have to be in pretty good shape.

Q.: You don't think you play a particularly mental or analytical game?

A.: No. I'm not experienced enough. . . . I'm not saying that my instincts aren't pretty good out there. I've never really studied the game very closely or given it much thought that way. That's not to say that I'm not thinking in there of what I'm trying to do. This is probably a weakness in my game. I probably should spend more time on figuring where the other guy is weak, get at his weaknesses, analyze shots and patterns. . . . I find I seem to play my best when I go in there and play the best from my ability and the shots that I have and let my instincts take care of the rest of it. If I execute well that particular day, I seem to be pretty competitive.

Q.: What do you consider the strength of your game?

A.: That's a tough one. I guess I have a pretty quick racquet. I volley quite a bit; I cut off a lot of balls, so I put quite a bit of pressure on a player. I cut off as many balls as I can, and—just by doing that—you kind of rush the other guy a bit. But I would say that's probably the thing I do the best. When I go up front, when I'm moving well—and that isn't always—I seem to have a pretty good racquet up front; I can change the direction of the ball, or my selection of shot is pretty good up there. I'm more of a shotmaker now than I was a few years ago. Probably because as I've gotten older, I've gotten more experience. . . . I never used to practice; I just used to play before a tournament and now, occasionally, I do go on the court by myself and hit some practice shots. I'm a little more of a shotmaker than I was, and I have a little better touch. You kind of hope that as you get older and slow up that maybe you'll get smarter and your shots get better; you can make more winners, and you don't have to run quite as

much. . . . Basically, that's what I'd like to have happen. I don't know whether it will, because the legs are very important.

Q.: Do you think that there's a weakness in your game?

A.: Yes, I'm sure that I have a lot of weaknesses or I would be a better player than I am. I would say I lack a little power on the backhand . . . although it is more consistent than my forehand, although I can't hit it quite as hard. I would say that my serve is pretty good, but my underhand serve could be a little better if I practiced it a bit, which I hardly ever do. I have trouble covering a lot of the court when I've been playing hockey, because my legs are tired and I don't move very well, but most of the time I seem to be pretty agile around the court; but everybody can also probably improve their agility a bit by working at it. I would say a lack of power is a weakness if you were to ask advanced players who have played against me.

Q.: What's your best shot?

A.: Before they changed the ball . . . the one shot that I could really count on was a fast corner shot, I think because it's sort of a semiracquet shot and I think I have a very good wrist and I could put a lot of spin on it and I could hit it very quickly in the corner and it would squirt out and stay very low. It was, I think, the one shot that bothered all the

Peter Bostwick.

guys I ever played. And with this ball, which is an excellent ball, it's a little harder to put it away. It's a fast angle shot, I guess. It doesn't take quite as well; it doesn't squirt quite as quickly; it doesn't stay quite as low. Although it still is one of my better shots, it's not quite as damaging as it was.

PETER BRIGGS
Born: 1951

Peter Briggs had made his mark on the national squash scene before he graduated from Harvard in 1973, where he served as team captain during his senior year. He won the Intercollegiate championships in both 1972 and 1973 and played in enough national competitions to be ranked No. 5. He was a finalist to Niederhoffer in both the U. S. and Canadian Nationals in 1974. In 1976, he won both the National singles and (with partner Ralph Howe) doubles championships. One of the most dynamic players in the game today, Peter Briggs is considered a "natural" and a great racquet handler. He joined the pro ranks in 1976.

Q.: What kind of player are you?
A.: I just play. This is sort of different.

Peter Briggs. PHOTO: ROBERT LEHMAN.

Niederhoffer has his whole thing on how he thinks and plays—he just puts three or four times more into it than anybody else. I'd probably do better if I had a regimen. But the way I play is fine for me. I'm perfectly happy with it. I don't really think you start playing your best squash until you're twenty-nine, thirty, or thirty-one, but I think my game would tend to go downhill as I get older. . . .

Q.: You're saying that if you're able to go on the court and be able to continue to do what you do, then you'll stay in the game?

A.: No, I'll have to do more than all right. I want to be one of the five or six best in North America. It's going to mean putting a lot more physical conditioning into the game. But there are two ways of doing things; Niederhoffer has his way, which has obviously proven to be very effective; but I can't change the way I am. I sort of go out and just play—I can't explain it. You have to just keep working at it. That's why I'm saying my concentration is so bad. Niederhoffer plays a consistent kind of game. He doesn't change. He is incapable of being quicker than a lot of the guys. I can be quicker than a lot of guys and just outlast them. But then I can't say I'm just going to concentrate a lot harder. That's what I can't do, but he can't do something that I can. The problem is I have to get it together to figure out *my game:* What is Peter Briggs' game? Right now, it's a myriad of things. And I've just sort of realized that recently, actually. For while I can play about four or five different games, the problem is that you become a jack of all trades and a master of none. But then I go through another idea, that in a way it's almost more fun to do it different ways, if you can. It makes it more interesting. Sometimes I look at a lot of guys playing and it looks like a substitute for going to a convention; I just don't think they're really having fun. A guy like Peter Bostwick has got a perfect attitude. An older guy, a very good athlete, he's continually curious, he knows there's a whole lot of people who know a lot more than he does about it, but he keeps learning. His outlook on athletics is very good.

SQUASH HOW TO PLAY, HOW TO WIN

And Gordy Anderson is another type. He has almost as bad a concentration span as I do. He'll play really well for three or four points where nobody in the world could ever touch him. Then he'll look at somebody or think about something else and his whole game goes out the window.

Q.: How would you present material in a squash book?

A.: I would write a squash book not from a theoretical standpoint or from a strategy standpoint. I would write it in a more novelistic approach, knowing the players as I do, cause I've been playing about eight years now in tournaments. Even when I was at Harvard I got let off a lot to play. I've traveled a lot playing the game and seeing different countries—how they approach the game, how they relate, what physical competition is to somebody, whether it's a sex outlet to someone else, whether it's this or that. I would write it from a novelistic standpoint, using the characters I know, but using different names. A good example is when we were in Mexico two years ago for the North American Open. You basically had sixteen guys from totally divergent backgrounds. All met together in Mexico City, which was a foreign place to everybody, where the papers got into it, the fans got into it. It's a hot-blooded country, it was hot outside. It was a very interesting tournament.

JUAN DE VILLAFRANCA
Born: 1954

Law student Juan de Villafranca comes from a squash-playing family and lives in Mexico City, where the air is thin and where squash therefore demands tremendous stamina. In 1974 he won the U. S. Intercollegiate championship and finished high in several other tournaments, which included the U. S. Amateur championship. In 1975 he was semifinalist in both the U. S. and Canadian singles championship. The No. 1-ranked player in Mexico for the past four years, he has won the Mex-

Juan de Villafranca. PHOTO: BANCROFT SPORTING GOODS CO.

ican Nationals Open and the Mexican Nationals. Juan is a very fit power hitter who likes to mix his strokes.

Q.: What do you think is the strength of your game?

A.: Well, I like to hit the harder ball. Basically, I'm in pretty good shape. I'm working and improving my strokes, my shots. But basically, I hit the ball hard, and I'm in good condition.

Q.: Do you play any touch shots?

A.: I'm developing that. I play some drop shots, straight drop shots. I hardly play any reverse corners. I play many drop shots, and two-walls and three-walls, and mix up and down the walls, and cross courts.

GEOFF HUNT
Born: 1947

To see No. 1 International player Geoff Hunt play our hard-ball game is to immediately see the difference in the two games. A truly profes-

Geoff Hunt.

sional athlete, in top condition, he learned the game in his native Australia, and is now a full-time playing and touring pro. Geoff has won every title available in the soft-ball game, and, on his first try here in the 1977 Nationals, he made it to the finals, where he was finally defeated by Sharif Khan.

Q.: What is the strength of your game?

A.: My strongest shot is intercepting the ball, volleying, in particular the forehand volley . . . and also my backhand drives, and backhand boasting is one of my best assets. The backhand side becomes easier; I don't know about the hard ball, but definitely in our game. The backhand is an easy shot, and I'll put a lot of work into the forehand to get it as good as the backhand. There are things, especially in the past twelve months, that I've really tried to bring into my game—a lot of undercutting the ball, which I didn't do much of before. It's a whole new side of my game that I'm developing.

Q.: You haven't played the North American game very long. How much have you played the game?

A.: That's right. It was 1964, I played a couple of weeks . . . and I've had a few odd games over the past few years. A couple of

weeks ago I came out here, and now, eight or nine days. I played a tournament at the Merion Club here in Philadelphia, and then I went back to New York for a couple of days to get some practice against some of the best players, because it's a different game for us. I decided to come in and give it a go at the hard ball.

Q.: What do you think your future in the game is?

A.: Look, my income is generated by the English game, so I'll probably stick to the International game. It's been good for me to come here and have a try and have a go at the tournament and see how I do. However, I am not that keen on making the hard ball my game. I like the other game better. I was brought up on it, and I'd like to see our game go ahead—the International game. And the money got bigger and bigger in the United States, with the hard ball, and you have to consider that, obviously. I'm planning to go on with our game a little bit longer, and I doubt that at that stage I would change over to the hard ball; I think I would have had enough of touring around like that and settle down. I'm not really keen to play forever as a professional sportsman, although I love it now. It's just too much living out of your suitcase. I enjoy squash as much as when I first took it up; while I'm keen to train hard and the dedication is there, I'll do all right. But once that goes, I think that's the end of me, or any player.

SHARIF KHAN
Born: 1945

A champion in both the hard- and soft-ball games, Hashim's oldest son has won the North American Open eight times and the North American Professional championship eight times. In short, he has dominated the game as no one has since his father's reign. The word for Sharif's game is incredible—incredible power, stamina, speed, and gamesmanship.

Q.: Are you competitive within your family?

A.: Probably much more competitive than outside it—much more so, much more intense. I look up to my father . . . in fact, we all got going because of my father. He kind of put Pakistan on the map. And as a result, the dedication is there, the tradition is there—it's an awesome task. There's a sort of fantastic tradition of the whole family; it's unique in sports.

Q.: Do you feel that you're maintaining a family name or national tradition?

A.: Oh, very much so. We're very much aware, every time we step onto a court—and that sort of drives us harder than, say, someone else. Also, where we come from, the physical conditions are quite harsh; the climate is quite hot and very humid . . . so when you compete against someone in North America or England, it's like Christmas—competitively speaking. Also, a lot of it is within ourselves, the motivation . . . just the desire to be better.

Q.: Did you actually learn the game from your father?

A.: In one way or another. He didn't actually teach us how to formally hold the racquet and show how to step up. We used to watch him a lot and by example . . .

Q.: Did he strongly urge you to play the game and be good at it?

A.: No . . . after he trained his brothers, cousins, and nephews, he said, "Look, guys, we've got enough Khans; you guys should go do something else—be doctors and engineers. . . ." But squash is in our blood. We can't just suddenly divorce ourselves from squash. All of us are quite into squash.

Q.: But there must be something absolutely exotic about your country and your family, not only to play squash, but also to excel at it?

A.: I can't explain it; it's just one of those things that you can't explain that one family can dominate for so long that it's such a tradition. Like in hockey, or football, you may get two or three from a family; in tennis . . . that's about all. We go back twenty years, in large numbers. Every tournament we get four or five representatives. We have about six here.

Sharif Khan. PHOTO: BANCROFT SPORTING GOODS CO.

BARBARA MALTBY
Born: 1949

Barbara is the classic example of the new breed of American woman squash player—disciplined, determined, and devoted to the game and to excelling at it. She was a finalist in the U. S. National singles in 1975 and 1976, and was the No. 1-ranked U.S. player in 1976.

Q.: What's your game?

A.: Well, you probably have to ask someone else that.

Q.: Do you consider yourself a power hitter, a shotmaker, a retriever, a defensive player?

A.: I'm a combination of a shotmaker, sort of, and a fairly quick player; I wouldn't exactly call myself a retriever. I get a lot of balls; I'm more of a finesse player than a power hitter, I'd say. I just don't have the overwhelming power that a lot of players do. I'm sort of working on my deep game, my power game, and I hope to make that a little better cause I think I have a decent amount of finesse; it's just a matter of playing your shots the right time, which is not that easy. Knowing when to play your various shots and what patterns to play, and when to break your patterns—that is, your opponent is off balance, you want to hit a shot to the opposite corner of the court, but then again if he's anticipating that sometimes it's better to wrong-foot him or something like that. It's very hard. I think one of the other things is relaxing when you play. If you . . . when you're at a certain level you can actually relax and still get a lot of shots.

Q.: What's happening with the women's game? Are we going to develop a high level of women's squash with a great number of women playing?

A.: What I think is going to happen is that it's going to change over the next few years quite a bit cause what you're going to have is more of the professional squash player who plays squash primarily, instead of secondarily to something else: playing after work, weekends, stuff like that. Just the fact that you're spending more time at it and training for it makes a big difference. When they get into

Barbara Maltby.

the training and practicing a lot more, the depth is really going to improve.

Q.: Is there a difference between the women's game and the men's game?

A.: Yeah. I would say the men's game is more power; they try to overpower each other a little bit more, but I think the women's game is a little bit more finesse. In the next five years there's just going to be more larger numbers. Can you see us in our forties and fifties? . . . Also, people are going to be training a little bit more in the off-season, work with weights, sort of building up in the off-season. Heather [McKay], I think, probably does; she hits the ball very hard. I think that's where it's going.

DIEHL MATEER
Born: 1928

Diehl Mateer is often called "the greatest doubles player in the history of squash racquets." He won the U. S. doubles championship eleven times, with five different partners. Winner of the U. S. Amateur championships in 1954, 1956, and 1960, and the U. S. Open in 1955 and 1959, Diehl was ranked No. 1 from 1953 to 1956. He's also won the Gold Racquets six times and the Harry Cowles five times. He's shown here with son Gil, one of a long line of Mateers still to come—and runner-up in the National doubles in 1977.

Q.: How would you describe yourself as a player?

A.: Well, I was not a shotmaker; I really never was, although I had enough shots to back up the pace I kept on the ball. But I really felt that getting out front and volleying, volleying was No. 1, and keeping the balls on the walls was the basic part of the game that was going to win for you. I didn't depend on shots . . . I happen to have had a combination of power and touch—whether it was 90–10 or 80–20, I really can't tell.

Diehl Mateer with son Gilbert. PHOTO: JOHN
PRIETO.

Q.: People have always described your game
as "classic," which is a very nice compliment.

A.: Well, that's strictly, I think, from the
fact that I was fortunate enough—thanks to
George Cummings—to have the feet in position and never taking that wild swing; trying
not to take that wild swing at the ball that you
see so many players doing.

Q.: How analytical are you about your
game? Do you think about where you're going
to play the next shot, the next string of shots?

A.: I would say that my singles game is not
analytical; in other words, I'm in there to put
the other player in the back of the court and
get out in front and then win the point up
front. Now, especially, when you're playing
better in squash, you can win the point up
front a little more easily than you use to; but I
think doubles has to be far more analytical
than singles because it's a team effort and
requires continuity between the two partners.

Q.: Why do they call you the greatest doubles player in the history of the game?

A.: I really can't tell you. . . . I've won the
Nationals more than anyone else. . . . I think
that I've related well with the people I've gone
into the court with; I've enjoyed the team
effort, and I've played well with my partners. I
never got upset with them; that, and the fact
that I'm tall enough and had the ability to hit
a moving object. I believe I probably volleyed
better from the aspect of doubles than most
people. From the standpoint of my playing the
game better than anybody else, I don't think
there's any way they can say I played the game
better than Hunter [Lott] did. I played the
backhand side, and he played the forehand
side; the two are as different as black and white.
If I go over on the forehand side, I'm in the
"D" League. You get used to a ball on the
left side, the ball is traveling counterclockwise
looking down, and the forehand in the singles
court, my forehand, is probably 25 per cent
stronger than my backhand. But put it on that
right wall, I refuse to go there anymore; I don't
like people sitting in the gallery laughing at me.
I played one tournament on the forehand side
in doubles with German Glidden, I had to
play there because he was left-handed, and we
won the tournament; but it must have been a
weak tournament.

JAY NELSON
Born: 1941

Jay ranked No. 7 at Harvard when he graduated in 1962, but he did not really hit his
stride in the game until the seventies. In 1973,
he was captain of the U.S. team in the World
Amateur and Team championships and
ranked No. 2 nationally in 1974. Recent articles in *Racquet* magazine testify to his knowledge and articulation of the game.

Q.: How would you describe your game?

A.: My basic game is defensive, and so I always have a little bit of reluctance to rely on
the short balls even though now my game has
become better, and I get a lot of good short
shots. But I still would prefer to go the other
way.

Q.: Do you have a favorite shot?

A.: I used to favor a three-wall shot, but with the West ball I don't hit it as well. I guess the roll corners, actually both sides, are my favorites. See, I'm one of these guys who didn't play a lot of tennis as a kid, and for most people who didn't play, regardless of what the book says, the backhand is harder to learn. Everyone always says, "Well, the backhand is easier because you just rotate." Well, that's baloney. For most people, the backhand is harder, and I didn't have a backhand, so I really had to build a backhand. I was watching a lot of good players and really tried to analyze piece by piece, to break the whole stroke down, and see who did what. So now I get a kick out of hitting backhand roll corners for a winner because I didn't used to have any kind of backhand. I don't lob much. I think it's unfortunate that you can't lob in our game very well. I've tried it, and either the ball gets too hard or the court does something. But whatever it is, most of the time it comes off the backwall so it sets up for the other guy. It's too bad, really. I mean, once in a while you can luck out, but it's a nonpercentage shot.

VICTOR NIEDERHOFFER
Born: 1943

Victor Niederhoffer is the legendary boy from Brooklyn who learned the game under Harvard's Jack Barnaby and brought a whole new style and method of play to the game while winning just about every title and honor the game has to offer. He has won the U. S. Amateur championship five times, the Open once, and the doubles championship, and hopes to win the Professional title away from Sharif just one year. Niederhoffer and Sharif Khan have fought over the top squash ranking for many years now, each with his distinctive weapons. Victor's game is uniquely his own—a methodical, mental, strategic, cerebral one— one that has won great respect, admiration, and imitation in the squash world.

Jay Nelson

Q.: What kind of player do you consider yourself to be?

A.: As far as what kind of player I am, I'm a conservative player, a player of good character; of extraordinary integrity and one who doesn't make many errors; I probably have the highest ratio of winners to errors in the history of the game. My major strengths are that I basically hit pretty hard and I've developed some new concepts to the game with the hard serve and the nick. My forehand has been pretty good for a long time. My major weakness is my backhand. I don't have enough power; also, I tend to get stiff frequently. My game is not set, it's constantly evolving. I'm always changing. I recently learned to volley. I've developed a new underhanded serve, which I have a "patent" on. My future in squash is that I'm over the hill. Right now as I'm talking, I'm hanging by my toes trying to see the skin on my feet, trying to stay with it one or two more years. There's an opportunity probably if I work as hard as I might to stay at the top a little more time, but I'm rapidly declining, and I'm just an old dog right now. Before they put the nails

Victor Niederhoffer. PHOTO: RAIMONDO BOREA.

Roland Oddy.

on my coffin, I think I can get Sharif Khan once or twice more, but it's going to have to be soon.

Q.: At what age do you reach your peak in this game?

A.: The best players seem to be around twenty-six or twenty-seven. Of course, when you're young you don't have to worry about your condition, and if you have had experience by that age it would be great. Then you start losing your condition as you get into your twenties and you have to work out if you want to stay in condition, whereas before, you didn't. I think that a good player should be able to stay at his maximum from, let's say, twenty-five to thirty-one. The best way to answer would be to look at the average age of the champions. I've managed to stay in the picture for a long time, so I think there's a strong possibility that because of the mental aspects of squash, it is possible to stay with it much longer than most other sports. By the time you get to thirty-two or thirty-three, you've slowed down enough to lose about four points per game.

ROLAND ODDY
Born: 1934

Doubles is Roland Oddy's game. A seeded singles player from 1966 to 1972, he has been a ranked doubles player since 1965, was twice the National Team Champion and Metropolitan Doubles Champion, and is now a high-ranking veteran doubles player. A great spokesman for and informal historian of the contemporary game, he has taught the game extensively and served as president of the Metropolitan Squash Racquets Association from 1973 to 1975. Stamina and determination are the hallmarks of his game.

I've had a great number of memorable matches. I would say that one of my most pleasurable matches was in the quarter finals against my so-called nemesis, Charles Ufford. I'd only beaten Charlie once out of sixteen times at that point. We got to 9-all in the fifth game, and he ran four straight points, and I said, "My God, I've been here before." And I don't know what happened. . . . I felt I was probably beaten. But I didn't give up; I got in the next two points. They were excruciating rallies for the both of us—they were so long, and it was hot. I got to 11–13 and I thought, "My God, you can beat him." So I dug, I went in. It got to 13-all and I knew he was going to set 5; I didn't want him to—I wanted set 2. During our many matches we had been to 13-all in the fifth game twice before; and both times he had set 5, and both times he had won. My computer said to me, "I know what his computer's thinking, so that when he says 'set 5,' I'm not going to be surprised." And sure enough, he said "set 5," and I had him 3–2, set 5, and I had a ball very deep, probably classified as the greatest shot I ever hit. It was on the left side, a little back of the red line. And it shaped up for a three-wall boast. But Charlie was on the red line on the right side, and it missed the nick—it was 3-all, because he put the ball away . . . and we had a couple of lets, and then I won, 18–15. As a follow-up, when we got into the locker room, Charlie said he was glad that I won because I played well. But there was only one problem: Charlie said, "I'm going to have to hear about it for the rest of my life!"

MIKE PIERCE

Mike Pierce, active in the squash world, was chairman of the 1977 National Open singles tournament in Philadelphia. Long a ranked doubles player (with partner Maurice Heckscher), he was ranked No. 1 in 1975 and No. 2 in 1976. He has the touch to back up Heckscher's power.

Q.: What do you think is the strength of your game?

A.: I would probably say my consistency in doubles; I make very few errors . . . consistent and patient. Doubles is a game of patience. I find that if I rush myself into a shot, that's when we play very bad squash. If you play pa-

Mike Pierce. PHOTO: ROBERT LEHMAN.

tiently, and wait for the proper opening, that's when we play our best game.

Q.: Who hits the winners—whoever's there?

A.: In most doubles teams, it's up to the left-court player to really make the majority of the winners. And, I would say, of Maurice and I, I probably make the majority of winners. But he makes his fair share. His winning production on the right-hand side is far greater than the average right-court player. So he's very capable of making shots as well.

Q.: You say you're not a power hitter. Do you think that hampers you in many instances?

A.: I think, probably, if I could hit the ball a little harder, it would probably improve my game a lot. But I've never really been able to get more power into my game. I haven't really tried too hard. . . . I think my forehand is definitely weak. . . . If I had to improve, I think I would work on the forehand.

Q.: What's your best shot?

A.: I think it's my reverse backhand, especially off a return of serve. I hit a shot with a lot of players, a Germantown or a Philadelphia. Maurice and I probably hit that more than any other doubles team that plays.

Q.: At what age do you hit the top of your game?

A.: I think everything comes together probably anywhere between twenty-eight and thirty-two; at least that was true of the old game. But as the game becomes more international in nature, as the ball changes, I think you're going to find younger and younger champions. I think that you have a number of very good older players—and when I say older, between thirty and thirty-five—Vic Niederhoffer is that age, Sharif Khan is that age, primarily because the game has never taken off. As a result, your best players have stayed around for many, many years, and they're still around. I think that they're going to have to give way very shortly.

JOHN REESE
Born: 1944

John was captain of the University of Pennsylvania squash team when he graduated in 1966, and has been ranked nationally since 1970. A hip injury took him out of the game for a while in 1972 (after being ranked No. 1 in 1971) at the top of his game, but he has managed to remain a top contender, with his classic form and racquet handling: He was the No. 1 ranked amateur in 1976. A past president of the Metropolitan Squash Racquets Association, he is very interested in the game's growth and future.

Q.: What kind of squash player do you think you are? How would you describe your game?

A.: I would think that I would be thought of as a power player. But I am what I would call "of the old school" of power player. I rely heavily on angle shots and power drop shots. I have not a great deal of finesse, in the sense of touch, and yet I am thought of by my opponents as a shotmaker—and a power shotmaker. In my prime I was known as a very good retriever. I'm quite a bit different because of my height being six-three to six-four. There have never been more than two or three great players of squash of my height. One reason is that the game calls for so much twisting that a person with long arms and legs takes a fraction longer, no matter how quick he is, to change directions. Another reason is that taller, skinnier people have a tendency not to have quite the stamina of stockier, shorter individuals. But, being tall, I have certain advantages. One is that I can take one stretch and touch almost any part of the court. Retrieving, or let's put it in a different sense, playing defensively, only on a very rare occasion do you completely dominate a match . . . you're always going to have to do some defensive work, and I don't think there's ever been a great champion of the sport who did not know how to run, who did not know how to retrieve a shot. I am more of a stretcher than a runner. And I would say that when I play my best, I am playing my defensive squash at my best. If I defend well, I'm going to win most matches.

Q.: How mental is your game? How analytical are you about the game as you play, before you play?

A.: Particularly since I'm a veteran player in the game, I think that a lot of it is subconscious as to my analysis of players; I know the styles of play I'll be facing. I appreciate what works well against certain styles of play. I do not sit down and meditate before a match. I think I recognize that for me to win, I probably have to execute and do what I do well, and if I do that, I feel that I can beat 99 per cent of the players I play. But I do try to be moderately cerebral when I go out on the court.

Q.: What do you consider your strengths? The strongest part of your game?

A.: My consistency; my level-headed attitude toward the game. I try not to get too excited about what's happening at a given point. I am capable of fairly high-level squash, even verging on brilliant squash for a period of time,

John Reese. PHOTO: ROBERT LEHMAN.

which is enough sometimes to break a match open and give me the advantage. My concentration, which weakens with age, at one time was very, very good, along with my running ability.

Q.: What do you consider the weakness in your game, if there is any?

A.: Right now, no question: my mobility around the court. I have a deteriorating hip joint, which forced me to stop playing the game after I had enjoyed my best year, back in 1971 and 1972. What's happened that has allowed me to return to the game is that the ball has changed. It has gone to a livelier ball that stays up longer, not as dead a ball, which means that I don't have to turn quite as fast, and I don't have to run quite as quickly to the ball. But there's no question that over time or over the length of the match, my mobility is what I am most concerned with.

Q.: What's your best shot? What's the shot you like to play?

A.: I think I have two shots that my peers would think excellent. One is the backhand

reverse corner shot, which is rarely seen today with the livelier ball, and that is why I sometimes consider myself an old-time, classical kind of player. It used to be used a great deal on colder, country-club courts. When the court is hot, you can't do it. The second shot I use effectively is a straight drop, which is not hit like a piece of cotton to the front wall; it is hit as if I were hitting a normal ground stroke, but I have so much draw on the ball that it hits the front wall and dies as it comes off, so that a player who is looking for a power drive ends up finding the ball not coming back to him. And I will use that a great deal in a match.

Q.: Do you prepare for a match in any particular way? Do you train in any particular way? Do you train by exercise?

A.: After I got out of college, I allowed my youthful vitality to carry me through. Since I laid off two years, my prime years, around when I was twenty-nine or thirty (I'm thirty-one), I find now that I must do certain exercises to improve my overall efficiency on a court, and also because the game demands more stamina. Playing is not always enough. I will run painfully when I don't play. I will do sitting-up exercises and stretching exercises, but I am not a glutton for punishment.

Q.: Do you feel that your game is set, that there is anywhere to go with your game? Do you think that your game will change?

A.: I think there's no question that if I had the time or the underlying desire, I could improve my game. The biggest problem that people who are amateur or part-time players have is that they cannot put in the time necessary to improve or hone their abilities. In my case, I suspect that I am in more of a holding pattern. My understanding of my weaknesses is probably at its height, and therefore a lot of people might say that I'm doing better, that I'm playing better than in the past, but I know for a fact that I've leveled off and that I'm not apt to be going up by any stretch.

Q.: Do you have any particular memorable moment—one match in a game?

A.: My most memorable events surround tragedies. I twice lost in the finals of the Nationals; those were very bitter pills to swallow. I think winning my first tournament at a time when I never expected to be a great squash player was very exciting. In fact, the first tournament I ever won was the Metropolitan Open Tournament, and I beat Roland Oddy. Winning my final match against Harvard when I was at the University of Pennsylvania —being showered with scarves and mittens and caps from the crowd at the end of that was very exhilarating. I think perhaps from the point of view of just sheer excitement, my wins in 1971 when I was ranked No. 1, over Anil Nyar, who was undefeated at that point; no American had beaten him in three years. I beat him twice—once in the Nationals; and winning over Sam Howe, who was twice the National champion. Each time, I beat them when my vision of myself as a player was such that I didn't think it was possible. The more egotistical or more content one becomes with one's own ability, the fewer memorable moments one has. I think that I'm at the point now where many of my most memorable moments will be bitter ones, because now I am vulnerable to the upset, and people are shooting at me rather than myself shooting at them.

Q.: But you plan to continue to play?

A.: I will certainly play this year, and I would like nothing more than winning the National championship. I would suspect that this may well be my last year, but I have a very competitive nature, and I think that in the future I will be more of a local player than a national or international player. I'll always continue to participate, but I don't think that I'll travel as much or put in quite as much time as I have in the past. It is sort of a lonely task to get yourself in shape, and the rewards are few, albeit they're psychic in the sense that it sure is nice to be feeling healthy. But at some point you move on to try something else.

Q.: What do you think it takes to be a top squash player?

A.: I think that you've got to feel that you're better than your opponents. I particularly am always afraid of everyone I play, but that sometimes, perhaps, helps me as well as hurts me. I go on feeling at times that I may suffer a loss rather than just looking at it the opposite way: that I'm going to win. What it does mean is that I'm usually ready to play when I play, but I may not quite reach the heights that I should. I think that's also a function of being on top of the ladder; on top of the heap rather than at the bottom of the heap. There's no place to go but down—and it's an empty elevator shaft, too. I think that when the fall comes, it will be very, very fast. But maybe my grandchildren or children will be pleased to know the fact that I was No. 1 in 1971 and won't ask what the competition was.

GRETCHEN SPRUANCE
Born: 1946

Tremendous athletic ability, exuberance, and a keen competitive spirit mark Gretchen's game. She has won the National singles title four times, the National doubles (with her mother, Bunny Vosters) four times, and the National mixed doubles twice (with Kit Spahr of Philadelphia).

Q.: How would you describe your game? Do you consider yourself a power hitter, a shot player?

A.: Shots. And I do have strength, but I don't think I overpower anybody. But I do like to make shots. And I like to volley.

Q.: Is there a weakness in your game? I mean, is there anything that you would work on?

A.: Well, I played a tournament earlier this year in which I played Barbara Maltby and lost to her very badly and she was doing hard serves, slice serves, and I worked on that quite a bit. Hardly anybody at home would do that. I'm going to continue to play. It's a grueling

Gretchen Spruance.

game. I mean, here I am over thirty, and I'm continuing to play. What am I doing? Killing myself. But you feel in much better shape, in much better condition; I just love that feeling.

CHARLES UFFORD
Born: 1931

Charles Ufford started his squash career by winning the Intercollegiate title twice, and in recent years he has won the Veterans title twice. In between, he won just about everything but the U. S. Nationals—he was New York State champion six times, has won the Gold Racquets Invitational, Appawamis, Harry Cowles, and the Metropolitan "A" League championships, and has ranked No. 1 in North America (1963). When squash players talk about Charlie Ufford's game, they always mention deception—he could fool most of the people some of the time.

Q.: What kind of player are you? Are you a power player? A retriever? How would you describe your game?

A.: . . . I might give away a few secrets. . . . I would like to say that I once played a game roughly similar to Niederhoffer's in concept. But that's a disparaging comparison as far as Victor's games go. He's developed what I've sort of tried to work at to a much higher degree in terms of anticipation—of knowing where the other guy is going to hit the ball. That's defensively. He had the greatest anticipation . . . the times I played him, even before he had achieved his stature and he had won the Intercollegiates and his first few years in the Nationals—and I beat him in a couple of matches, and then he beat me in the Nationals up in Hartford in that quarter-final match in five games, and I never caught him thereafter. It's as if he had finally figured out what to do, and once he had solved that problem, then I could be dismissed. . . . It's his anticipation . . . his feeling and sensing the way you were going to hit the ball before you

Charles Ufford. PHOTO: ROBERT LEHMAN.

SQUASH HOW TO PLAY, HOW TO WIN

even knew it yourself . . . there's a distinctly different feeling being on the court with him. But that's one thing—learning to anticipate—analyze your opponent's stroke production so that you sense where he is going to play his shots. As far as my own strokes go, the greatest advantage I have—to my knowledge—is that because of my height and reach, I can make a long stretch, and get around and hit the ball in a different direction from what would normally be expected.

Q.: Whom do you admire in the game?

A.: Henri Salaun. The great thing about Salaun is you're on with him, and you don't even know he's on the court with you. And you're in torment, just torment; you are invariably going the extra half foot to get to the next shot. Somehow, you're always going a little bit farther than you care to go. And there's no one in your way, and you have no sense of him being anywhere on the court with you. He's just wonderful. And my admiration for his game and abilities, and his knowledge of playing this particular shot as opposed to that one. I've played him innumerable times over the years, and I've had one or two fortunate wins, which I attribute somehow to sort of a lapse in the eternal order of things . . . I never had any feeling that I should ever beat him. I've always enjoyed trying except when I'm actually in there trying because beating the man and trying . . . is fantastic; it doesn't do much for your ego. I've had less of that kind of a feeling about Mateer's game because I've always thought, Diehl's being stronger and being able to dominate the play, it seems sort of logical that he should dominate you and make you do most of the running and retrieving. But you're very much aware that you're in the court with Mateer, because there he is, he's a large presence in the court. There's no denying that he is largely responsible for the difficulties that you encounter; with Salaun, it's magic. . . .

Appendixes

Doubles. PHOTO: RAIMONDO BOREA.

Rules of Eligibility

1. *General Rule:* An amateur squash racquets player is a person who plays or teaches the game solely for pleasure, recreation, or honor, without seeking or obtaining from it financial or material gain, directly or indirectly, either for himself or another.

2. *Specific Rules:* A. A person shall be eligible as an amateur squash racquets player if he is a citizen, subject, or national of a foreign country, unless he has been determined to be ineligible as an amateur squash racquets player by the national amateur squash racquets association of such foreign country or by the Executive Committee.

B. Subject to the provisions of subdivision C., a person shall be eligible as an amateur squash racquets player although he is declared ineligible as an amateur player by the governing body of any other racquet sport or game.

C. A person shall be ineligible as an amateur squash racquets player if:

1. he accepts, directly or indirectly, money or other valuable consideration for playing or teaching the game of squash racquets, except that a person shall not be ineligible by reason of

(a) the acceptance of a trophy or prize consisting of merchandise having a value not in excess of $300, except as the temporary holder of a permanent trophy or prize; or

(b) the acceptance from a Tournament Committee of reasonable travel expenses; or

(c) employment as a member of the faculty of any high school, secondary or preparatory school, the duties of which include, among others, the coaching of the game of squash racquets; or

(d) employment as a member of the faculty or staff of any college, university or institution of higher learning, the duties of which are primarily other than coaching the game of (i) squash racquets, or (ii) the game of squash racquets and tennis; or

(e) employment during the summer vacation period as a member of the staff of any courts, club, athletic association or other similar organization while enrolled as a full-time student at any school, college or university, provided the compensation therefore is on a fixed periodic basis; or

(f) employment by or management of

(i) a manufacturer or merchant primarily of equipment or clothing for squash racquets or for squash racquets and tennis, or

(ii) a store or shop which sells primarily equipment or clothing for squash racquets or for squash racquets and tennis, or

(iii) a public squash racquets court, or any club or center which includes one or more squash racquets courts;
provided, however, that for the duration of such employment or management he shall not
teach squash racquets, or
play squash racquets (A) during the normal working hours of such employment or management, or (B) in clinics or exhibitions of the game; or

(g) ownership of a financial interest directly or indirectly in

(i) a manufacturer or merchant primarily of equipment or clothing for squash racquets or for squash racquets and tennis, or

(ii) a store or shop which sells primarily equipment or clothing for squash racquets or for squash racquets and tennis, or

(iii) a public squash racquets court, or any club or center which includes one or more squash racquets courts;
provided, however, that for the duration of such ownership he shall not
teach squash racquets or
play squash racquets in clinics or exhibitions of the game.

2. he accepts, directly or indirectly, money or other valuable consideration for acting as the subject of any article, column, book or television, movie or slide film presentation of or on the game of squash racquets.

3. he accepts, directly or indirectly, money or other valuable consideration for writing any article, column, book or radio or television presentation of or on the game of squash racquets primarily for instructional rather than descriptive or historical purposes.

4. he permits his name, likeness or initials:

(a) as a squash racquets participant to be used in advertising which promotes the use of the merchandise of a manufacturer or merchant other than as a participant in a tournament under commercial sponsorship approved by the Executive Committee.

(b) to be placed on any squash racquets equipment or clothing.

5. he becomes an active playing or teaching member of any professional squash racquets association or organization.

Playing Rules

Official Playing Rules of the United States Squash Racquets Association.
Revised October 1974.

SINGLES RULES

1. SERVER
At the start of a match the choice to serve or receive shall be decided by the spin of a racquet. The server retains the serve until he loses a point, in which event he loses the serve.

2. SERVICE
(a) The server, until the ball has left the racquet from the service, must stand with at least one foot on the floor within and not touching the line surrounding the service box and serve the ball onto the front wall above the service line and below the 16′ line before it touches any other part of the court, so that on its rebound (return) it first strikes the floor within, but not touching, the lines of the opposite service court, either before or after touching any other wall or walls within the court. A ball so served is a good service, otherwise it is a Fault.

(b) If the first service is a Fault, the server shall serve again from the same side. If the server makes two consecutive Faults, he loses the point. A service called a Fault may not be played, but the receiver may volley any service which has struck the front wall in accordance with this rule.

(c) At the beginning of each game, and each time there is a new server, the ball shall be served by the winner of the previous point from whichever service box the server elects and thereafter alternately until the service is lost or until the end of the game. If the server serves from the wrong box there shall be no penalty and the service shall count as if served from the correct box, provided, however, that if the receiver does not attempt to return the service, he may demand that it be served from the other box, or if, before the receiver attempts to return the service, the Referee calls a Let (See Rule 9), the service shall be made from the other box.

(d) A ball is in play from the moment at which it is delivered in service until (1) the point is decided; (2) a Fault, as defined in 2(a) is made; or (3) a Let or Let Point occurs (See Rules 9 and 10).

3. RETURN OF SERVICE AND SUBSEQUENT PLAY

(a) A return is deemed to be made at the instant the ball touches the racquet of the player making the return. To make a good return of a service or of a subsequent return the ball must be struck on the volley or before it has touched the floor twice, and reach the front wall on the fly above the tell-tale and below the 16′ line, and it may touch any wall or walls within the court before or after reaching the front wall. On any return the ball may be struck only once. It may not be "carried" or "double-hit."

(b) If the receiver fails to make a good return of a good service, the server wins the point. If the receiver makes a good return of service, the players shall alternate making returns until one player fails to make a good return. The player failing to make a good return loses the point.

(c) Until the ball has been touched or has hit the floor twice, it may be struck at any number of times.

(d) If at any time after a service the ball hits outside the playing surfaces of the court (the ceiling and/or lights, or on or above a line marking the perimeters of the playing surfaces of the court), the player so hitting the ball loses the point, unless a Let or a Let Point occurs. (See Rules 9 and 10.)

4. SCORE

Each point won by a player shall add one to his score.

5. GAME

The player who first scores fifteen points wins the game excepting that:

(a) At "thirteen all" the player who has first reached the score of thirteen must elect one of the following before the next serve:

(1) Set to five points—making the game eighteen points.

(2) Set to three points—making the game sixteen points.

(3) No set, in which event the game remains fifteen points.

(b) At "fourteen all" provided the score has not been "thirteen all" the player who has first reached the score of fourteen must elect one of the following before the next serve:

(1) Set to three points—making the game seventeen points.

(2) No set, in which event the game remains fifteen points.

6. MATCH

The player who first wins three games wins the match, except that a player may be awarded the match at any time upon the retirement, default or disqualification of an opponent.

7. RIGHT TO PLAY BALL

Immediately after striking the ball a player must get out of an opponent's way and must:

(a) Give an opponent a fair view of the ball, provided, however, interference purely with an opponent's vision in following the flight of the ball is not a Let (See Rule 9).

(b) Give an opponent a fair opportunity to get to and/or strike at the ball in and from any position on the court elected by the opponent; and

(c) Allow an opponent to play the ball to any part of the front wall or to either side wall near the front wall.

8. BALL IN PLAY TOUCHING PLAYER

(a) If a ball in play, after hitting the front wall, but before being returned again, shall touch either player, or anything he wears or carries (other than the racquet of the player who makes the return) the player so touched loses the point except as provided in Rule 9(a) or 9(b).

(b) If a ball in play touches the player who last returned it or anything he wears or carries before it hits the front wall, the player so touched loses the point.

(c) If a ball in play, after being struck by a player on a return, hits the player's opponent or anything the opponent wears or carries before reaching the front wall:

(1) The player who made the return shall lose the point if the return would not have been good.

(2) The player who made the return shall win the point if the ball would have gone directly from the racquet of the player making the return to the front wall without first touching any other wall.

Appendixes

(3) The point shall be a Let (see Rule 9) if the return except for such interference would have hit the front wall fairly and (1) would have touched some other wall before so hitting the front wall, or (2) has hit some other wall before hitting the player's opponent or anything he wears or carries.

When there is no referee, if the player who made the return does not concede that the return would not have been good, or, alternatively, the player's opponent does not concede that the ball has hit him (or anything he wears or carries) and would have gone directly to the front wall without first touching any other wall, the point shall be a Let.

9. LET

A Let is the playing over of a point.

On the replay of the point the server (1) is entitled to two serves even if a Fault was called on the original point, (2) must serve from the correct box even if he served from the wrong box on the original point, and (3) provided he is a new server, may serve from a service box other than the one selected on the original point.

In addition to the Lets described in Rules 2(c) and 8(c) (3), the following are Lets if the player whose turn it is to strike the ball could otherwise have made a good return:

(a) When such player's opponent violates Rule 7.

(b) When owing to the position of such player, his opponent is unable to avoid being touched by the ball.

(c) When such player refrains from striking at the ball because of a reasonable fear of injuring his opponent.

(d) When such player before or during the act of striking or striking at the ball is touched by his opponent, his racquet or anything he wears or carries.

(e) When on the first bounce from the floor the ball hits on or above the six and one half foot line on the back wall; and

(f) When a ball in play breaks. If a player thinks the ball has broken while play is in progress he must nevertheless complete the point and then immediately request a Let, giving the ball to the Referee for inspection. The Referee shall allow a Let only upon such immediate request if the ball in fact proves to be broken (See Rule 13(c).)

A player may request a Let or a Let Point (See Rule 10). A request by a player for a Let shall automatically include a request for a Let Point. Upon such request, the Referee shall allow a Let, Let Point or no Let.

No Let shall be allowed on any stroke a player makes unless he requests such before or during the act of striking or striking at the Ball.

The Referee may not call or allow a Let as defined in this Rule 9 unless such Let is requested by a player; provided, however, the Referee may call a Let at any time (1) when there is interference with play caused by any factor beyond the control of the players, or (2) when he fears that a player is about to suffer severe physical injury.

10. LET POINT

A Let Point is the awarding of a point to a player when an opponent unnecessarily violates Rule 7(b) or 7(c).

An unnecessary violation occurs (1) when the player fails to make the necessary effort within the scope of his normal ability to avoid the violation, thereby depriving his opponent of a clear opportunity to attempt a winning shot, or (2) when the player has repeatedly failed to make the necessary effort within the scope of his normal ability to avoid such violations.

The Referee may not award a Let Point as defined in this Rule 10 unless such Let Point or a Let (see Rule 9) is requested by a player.

When there is no referee, if a player does not concede that he has unnecessarily violated Rule 7(b) or 7(c), the point shall be a Let.

11. CONTINUITY OF PLAY

Play shall be continuous from the first service of each game until the game is concluded. Play shall never be suspended solely to allow a player to recover his strength or wind. The provisions of this Rule 11 shall be strictly construed. The referee shall be the sole judge of intentional delay, and, after giving due warning, he must default the offender.

Between each game play may be suspended by either player for a period not to exceed two minutes. Between the third and fourth games play may be suspended by either player for a period not to exceed five minutes. Except during the five minute period at the end of the third game, no player may leave the court without permission of the referee.

Except as otherwise specified in this Rule 11, the Referee may suspend play for such reason and for such period of time as he may consider necessary.

If play is suspended by the Referee because of an injury to one of the players, such player must resume play within one hour from the point and game score existing at the time play was suspended or default the match, provided, however, if a player suffers cramps or pulled muscles, play may be suspended by the Referee once during a match for such player for a period not to exceed five minutes after which time such player must resume play or default the match.

In the event the Referee suspends play other than for injury to a player, play shall be resumed when the Referee determines the cause of such suspension of play has been eliminated, provided, however, if such cause of delay cannot be rectified within one hour, the match shall be postponed to such time as the Tournament Committee determines. Any such suspended match shall be resumed from the point and game score existing at the time the match was stopped unless the Referee and both players unanimously agree to play the entire match or any part of it over.

12. ATTIRE AND EQUIPMENT

(a) A player's attire must be white except that a solid, pastel color shirt may be worn. The Referee's decision as to a player's attire shall be final.

In the absence of a Referee, if a player's opponent objects to a colored shirt, white shall be worn.

(b) The standard singles ball as specified in the Court, Racquet and Ball Specifications of this Association shall be used.

(c) A racquet as specified in the Court, Racquet and Ball Specifications of this Association shall be used.

13. CONDITION OF BALL

(a) No ball, before or during a match, may be artificially treated, that is, heated or chilled.

(b) At any time, when not in the actual play of a point, another ball may be substituted by the mutual consent of the players or by decision of the Referee.

(c) A ball shall be determined broken when it has a crack which extends through both its inner and outer surfaces. The ball may be squeezed only enough to determine the extent of the crack. A broken ball shall be replaced and the preceding point shall be a Let (See Rule 9(f)).

(d) A cracked (but not broken) ball may be replaced by the mutual consent of the players or by decision of the Referee, and the preceding point shall stand.

14. COURT

(a) The singles court shall be as specified in the Court, Racquet, and Ball Specifications of this Association.

(b) No equipment of any sort shall be permitted to remain in the court during a match other than the ball used in play, the racquets being used by the players, and the clothes worn by them. All other equipment, such as extra balls, extra racquets, sweaters when not being worn, towels, bathrobes, etc., must be left outside the court. A player who requires a towel or cloth to wipe himself or anything he wears or carries should keep same in his pocket or securely fastened to his belt or waist.

15. REFEREE

(a) A Referee shall control the game. This control shall be exercised from time the players enter the court. The Referee may limit the time of the warm-up period to five minutes, or shall terminate a longer warm-up period so that the match commences at the scheduled time.

(b) The Referee's decision on all questions of play shall be final except as provided in Rule 15(c).

(c) Two judges may be appointed to act on any appeal by a player to a decision of the Referee. When such judges are acting in a match, a player may appeal any decision of the Referee to the judges, except a decision under Rule 11, 12(a), 13, 15(a) and 15(f). If one judge agrees with the Referee, the Referee's decision stands; if both judges disagree with the Referee, the judges' decision is final. The judges shall make no ruling unless an appeal has been made. The decision of the judges shall be announced promptly by the Referee.

(d) A player may not request the removal or replacement of the Referee or a judge during a match.

(e) A player shall not state his reason for his

request under Rule 9 for a Let or Let Point or for his appeal from any decision of the Referee provided, however, that the Referee may request the player to state his reasons.

(f) A Referee serving without judges, after giving due warning of the penalty of this Rule 15 (f), in his discretion may disqualify a player for speech or conduct unbecoming to the game of squash racquets, provided that a player may be disqualified without warning if, in the opinion of such referee, he has deliberately caused physical injury to his opponent.

When two judges are acting in a match, the Referee in his discretion, upon the agreement of both judges, may disqualify a player with or without prior warning for speech or conduct unbecoming to the game of squash racquets.

DOUBLES RULES

1. SERVER
At the start of a match the choice to serve or receive shall be decided by the spin of a racquet.

Each side or team shall consist of two players. The two partners of a side shall serve in succession, the first retaining his serve until his side has lost a point. On the loss of the next point the side shall be declared "out" and the serve revert to the opponents. On the first serve of every game, however, the "in" side shall be declared "out" after it has lost one point only.

The order of serving within a side shall not be changed during the progress of a game.

At the end of a game the side which has won the game shall have the choice of serving or receiving to commence the next game.

2. SERVICE
(a) The server, until the ball has left the racquet from the service, must stand with at least one foot on the floor within and not touching the line surrounding the service box and serve the ball onto the front wall above the service line and below the 20′ line before it touches any other part of the court, so that on its rebound (return) it first strikes the floor within, but not touching, the lines of the opposite service court, either before or after touching any other wall or walls within the court. A ball so served is a good service, otherwise it is a Fault.

(b) If the first service is a Fault, the server shall serve again from the same side. If the server makes two consecutive Faults, he loses the point. A service called a Fault may not be played, but the receiver may volley any service which has struck the front wall in accordance with this rule.

(c) At the beginning of each game and each time a side becomes "in" the ball shall be served from whichever service box the first server for the side elects, and thereafter alternately until the side is "out" or until the end of the game. If the server serves from the wrong box there shall be no penalty and the service shall count and the play shall proceed as if the box served from was the correct box, provided, however, that if the receiver does not attempt to return the service, he may demand that it be served from the other box, or if, before the receiver attempts to return the service, the Referee calls a Let (See Rule 9), the service shall be made from the other box.

(d) A ball is in play from the moment at which it is delivered in service until (1) the point is decided; (2) a Fault as defined in 2(a) is made; or (3) a Let or Let Point occurs (See Rules 9 and 10).

3. RETURN OF SERVICE AND SUBSEQUENT PLAY
(a) A return is deemed to be made the instant the ball touches the racquet of the player making the return. To make a good return of a service or of a subsequent return the ball must be struck on the volley or before it has touched the floor twice and reach the front wall on the fly above the telltale and below the 20′ line, and it may touch any wall or walls within the court before or after reaching the front wall. On any return the ball may be struck only once. It may not be "carried" or "double-hit."

(b) At the beginning of each game each side shall designate one of its players to receive service in the right hand service court and the other to receive service in the left hand service court and throughout the course of such game the service must be received by the players so designated.

(c) If the designated receiver fails to make a good return of a good service, the serving side wins the point. If the designated receiver makes a good return of service the sides shall alternate making returns until one side fails to make a good return. The side failing to make a good return loses the point.

(d) Until the ball has been touched or has hit the floor twice, it may be struck at any number of times by either player on a side.

(e) If at any time after a service the ball hits outside the playing surfaces of the court (the ceiling and/or lights, or on or above a line marking the perimeters of the playing surfaces of the court) the side so hitting the ball loses the point, unless a Let or a Let Point occurs. (See Rules 9 and 10.)

4. SCORE

Each point won by either side shall add one to its score.

5. GAME

The side which first scores fifteen points wins the game excepting that;

(a) At "thirteen all" the side which has first reached the score of thirteen must elect one of the following before the next serve:

(1) Set to five points—making the game eighteen points.

(2) Set to three points—making the game sixteen points.

(3) No set, in which event the game remains fifteen points.

(b) At "fourteen all," provided the score has not been "thirteen all," the side which has first reached the score of fourteen must elect one of the following before the next serve;

(1) Set to three points—making the game seventeen points.

(2) No set, in which event the game remains fifteen points.

6. MATCH

The side which first wins three games wins the match, except that a side may be awarded the match at any time upon the retirement, default or disqualification of the opposing side.

7. RIGHT TO PLAY THE BALL

Immediately after he or his partner has struck the ball, each player must get out of his opponents' way and must:

(a) Give his opponents a fair view of the ball, provided, however, interference purely with an opponent's vision in following the flight of the ball is not a Let (See Rule 9).

(b) Give his opponents a fair opportunity to get to and/or strike at the ball in and from any position on the court elected by an opponent; and;

(c) Allow either opponent to play the ball to any part of the front wall or to either side wall near the front wall.

8. BALL IN PLAY TOUCHING PLAYER

(a) If a ball in play, after hitting the front wall, but before being returned again, shall touch any player, or anything he wears or carries (other than the racquet of the player who makes the return) the side of the player so touched loses the point, except as provided in Rule 9(a) or 9(b).

(b) If a ball in play touches the player who last returned it or his partner or anything either of them wears or carries before it hits the front wall, the side of the player so touched loses the point.

(c) If a ball in play, after being struck by a player on a return, hits either of the player's opponents or anything either of them wears or carries before reaching the front wall;

(1) The side of the player who made the return shall lose the point if the return would not have been good.

(2) The point shall be a Let (See Rule 9) if the return would have hit the front wall fairly except for such interference.

9. LET

A Let is the playing over a point.

On the replay of the point the server (1) is entitled to two serves even if a Fault was called on the original point, (2) must serve from the correct box even if he served from the wrong box on the original point, and (3) provided he is a new server, may serve from a service box other than the one selected on the original point.

In addition to the Lets described in Rules 2 (2) and 8(c) (2), the following are Lets if the player on the side whose turn it is to strike the ball could otherwise have made a good return:

(a) When an opponent of such player violates Rule 7.

(b) When owing to the position of such player, either of his opponents is unable to avoid being touched by the ball.

(c) When such player refrains from striking at the ball because of a reasonable fear of injuring his opponent.

(d) When such player before or during the act

of striking or striking at the ball is touched by either of his opponents, their racquets or anything either of them wear or carry.

(e) When on the first bounce from the floor the ball hits on or above the seven foot line on the back wall; and,

(f) When a ball in play breaks. If a player thinks the ball has broken while play is in progress he must nevertheless complete the point and then immediately request a Let, giving the ball to the Referee for inspection. The Referee shall allow a Let only upon such immediate request if the ball in fact proves to be broken. (See Rule 13(c)).

A player may request a Let or a Let Point (See Rule 10). A request by a player for a Let shall automatically include a request for a Let Point. Upon such request, the Referee shall allow a Let, Let Point or not Let.

No Let shall be allowed on any stroke a player makes unless he requests such before or during the act of striking or striking at the ball.

The Referee may not call or allow a Let as defined in this Rule 9 unless such Let is requested by a player; provided, however, the Referee may call a Let at any time (1) when there is interference with play caused by any factor beyond the control of the players, or (2) when he fears that a player is about to suffer severe physical injury.

10. LET POINT

A Let Point is the awarding of a point to a side when an opponent unnecessarily violates Rule 7(b) or 7(c).

An unnecessary violation occurs (1) when the player fails to make the necessary effort within the scope of his normal ability to avoid the violation, thereby depriving an opponent of a clear opportunity to attempt a winning shot, or (2) when the player has repeatedly failed to make the necessary effort within the scope of his normal ability to avoid such violations.

The Referee may not award a Let Point as defined in this Rule 10 unless such Let Point or a Let (See Rule 9) is requested by a player.

When there is no Referee, if a player does not concede that he has unnecessarily violated Rule 7(b) or 7(c), the point shall be a Let.

11. CONTINUITY OF PLAY

Play shall be continuous from the first service of each game until the game is concluded. Play shall never be suspended solely to allow a player to recover his strength or wind. The provisions of this Rule 11 shall be strictly construed. The Referee shall be the sole judge of intentional delay, and, after giving due warning, he must default the offender.

Between each game play may be suspended by any player for a period not to exceed two minutes. Between the third and fourth games play may be suspended by any player for a period not to exceed five minutes. Except during the five minute period at the end of the third game, no player may leave the court without permission of the Referee.

Except as otherwise specified in this Rule 11, the Referee may suspend play for such reason and for such period of time as he may consider necessary.

If play is suspended by the Referee because of an injury to one of the players, such player must resume play within one hour from the point and game score existing at the time play was suspended or his side shall default the match, provided, however, if a player suffers cramps or pulled muscles, play may be suspended by the Referee once during a match for each such player for a period not to exceed five minutes after which time such player must resume play or his side shall default the match.

In the event the Referee suspends play other than for injury to a player, play shall be resumed when the Referee determines the cause of such suspension of play has been eliminated, provided, however, if such cause of delay cannot be rectified within one hour, the match shall be postponed to such time as the Tournament Committee determines. Any such suspended match shall be resumed from the point and game score existing at the time the match was stopped unless the Referee and both sides unanimously agree to play the entire match or any part of it over.

12. ATTIRE AND EQUIPMENT

(a) A side's attire must be white except that matching solid, pastel color shirts may be worn. The Referee's decision as to a side's attire shall be final.

In the absence of a Referee, if a side objects to its opponents' colored shirts, white shall be worn.

(b) The standard doubles ball as specified in

the Court, Racquet and Ball Specifications of this Association shall be used.

(c) A racquet as specified in the Court, Racquet and Ball Specifications of this Association shall be used.

13. CONDITION OF BALL

(a) No ball, before or during a match, may be artificially treated, that is, heated or chilled.

(b) At any time, when not in the actual play of a point, another ball may be substituted by the mutual consent of the sides or by decision of the Referee.

(c) A ball shall be determined broken when it has a crack which extends through both its inner and outer surfaces. The ball may be squeezed only enough to determine the extent of the crack. A broken ball shall be replaced and the preceding point shall be a Let (See Rule 9 (f)).

(d) A cracked (but not broken) ball may be replaced by the mutual consent of the sides or by decision of the Referee, and the preceding point shall stand.

14. COURT

(a) The doubles court shall be as specified in the Court, Racquet, and Ball Specifications of this Association.

(b) No equipment of any sort shall be permitted to remain in the court during a match other than the ball used in play, the racquets being used by the players, and the clothes worn by them. All other equipment, such as extra balls, extra racquets, sweaters when not being worn, towels, bathrobes, etc., must be left outside the court. A player who requires a towel or cloth to wipe himself or anything he wears or carries should keep same in his pocket or securely fastened to his belt or waist.

15. REFEREE

(a) A Referee shall control the game. This control shall be exercised from the time the players enter the court. The Referee may limit the time of the warm up period to five minutes, or shall terminate a longer warm up period so that the match commences at the scheduled time.

(b) The Referee's decision on all questions of play shall be final except as provided in Rule 15(c).

(c) Two judges may be appointed to act on any appeal by a player to a decision of the Referee. When such judges are acting in a match, a player may appeal any decision of the Referee to the judges, except a decision under Rules 11, 12(a), 14, 15(a) and 15(f). If one judge agrees with the Referee, the Referee's decision stands; if both judges disagree with the Referee, the judges' decision is final. The judges shall make no ruling unless an appeal has been made. The decision of the judges shall be announced promptly by the Referee.

(d) A player may not request the removal or replacement of the Referee or a judge during a match.

(e) A player shall not state his reason for his request under Rule 9 for a Let or Let Point or for his appeal from any decision of the Referee provided, however, that the Referee may request the player to state his reasons.

(f) A Referee serving without judges, after giving due warning of the penalty of this Rule 15 (f), in his discretion may disqualify a side for speech or conduct by a player unbecoming to the game of squash racquets, provided that a side may be disqualified without warning if, in the opinion of such referee, a player has deliberately caused physical injury to his opponent.

Where two judges are acting in a match, the Referee in his discretion, upon the agreement of both judges, may disqualify a side with or without prior warning for speech or conduct unbecoming to the game of squash racquets.

Preparing a Draw

The U. S. S. R. A. Board of Directors officially approved the following method of preparing a tournament draw on October 12, 1959, revised October, 1974.

SEEDING

There shall be no more than one seeded player for every four players in the draw. Therefore, a draw of sixteen may have no more than four seeded players, a draw of thirty-two may have no more than eight seeded players, etc. All domestic seeded players in the upper half of the draw are placed at the top of their respective halves, quarters, or eighths. All domestic seeded players in the bottom half of the draw are placed at the bottom of their respective halves, quarters, or eighths. Number 1 domestic seed shall be in the top half and number 2 domestic seed in the lower half. Numbers 3 and 4 domestic seeds shall be drawn by lot to determine which is placed in the upper and lower halfs. Likewise, numbers 5, 6, 7, and 8 domestic seeds shall be drawn by lot to determine their respective locations by quarters. If there is a foreign seed, the foreign seeded players are arranged in reverse order on the above system, i.e. the number 1 foreign seed is placed at the top of the bottom half of the draw, etc.

BYES

If the number of entries is a power of 2 (4, 8, 16, 32, etc.) no byes are necessary. If the number of entries is not a power of two, the number of byes required is obtained by subtracting the number of entries from the next higher power of two. In the example draw there are twenty-three entries. The next higher power of two is thirty-two, thereby giving nine byes. If the number of byes is even, half are placed at the top of the draw and half at the bottom. If the number of byes is odd, one more bye is placed at the top of the draw than at the bottom. Byes are concentrated at the top and bottom of the draw and not distributed throughout.

Scoring Technique

A refined method of scoring developed by Edwin H. Bigelow adds interest to a difficult job.

There are in current use throughout the United States many different methods of marking (scoring) a squash racquets match which vary according to the tastes and training of the individual marker (scorer). The technique set forth below should not be considered as the Association's official method nor should its use be believed mandatory. It is, however, considered by some of the country's most experienced officials as the best system. To those accustomed to using the simpler "X" or "L" and "R" system, it may appear, at first to be slightly complex. It is believed, nevertheless, that practice and experience will show the user its many advantages.

	1	2	3	4
JONES	L	R	R	L
SMITH	R	L	R	R

√ (above col 2)   √ (above col 4)

JONES	1	2			3	4	
SMITH	0		1	2	3		4

√ (below)

Shown above are the first eight points of a theoretical match between Jones and Smith as scored using the common "L" and "R" method and the suggested technique. In this example, Jones wins the first two points, Smith the next three, Jones the next two, and then Smith ties the score at 4-all.

Using the suggested technique, Jones having won the first point, the digit "1" is entered in the first box opposite "Jones" and the digit "0" in the first box opposite "Smith." When Jones wins the second point, the digit "2" is entered in the second box after his name. When Smith wins the next point and the score is then 1-2, the digit "1" is entered in the third box after Smith's name. Subsequent points are entered in a like manner, thereby having no two points entered in the same set of vertical boxes. To indicate from which side the following service is to be made, a check mark is put above or below the box containing the score of the previous point, if the new service is from the left. If the next serve is to be from the right, no check mark is made. In the example, Jones served from the left after winning the first point.

The technique for doubles is the same with the exception that the marker writes on his sheet the order of service for each team. Only one line is used for the score of each team and not a line for each of the four players since points can not always be assigned to a particular player on a team.

With the suggested technique, the marker can more easily determine the score during a match in that it is written in digits and does not require reference to numbers over the boxes. Likewise, if a let occurs when the score is tied, the marker is aware of which player served last. In the example, the score was tied at 2-all, 3-all, and 4-all. The marker knows from the suggested technique that Jones is serving at 3-all and Smith is serving at 2-all and 4-all. As an added advantage, this technique indicates the margin by which one player or team has led the other player or team in points at any stage of the play. The completed score sheet is helpful in studying the trend in play after the match and should prove of value to the press in describing the match.

It is, of course, a cardinal principle that the marker and his score sheet must be accurate. It is suggested, therefore, that after each point the marker record the new score before announcing it. Also, it is of importance that the marker, in announcing the score, should do so in a loud voice, clearly audible to the players and the gallery.

National Champions

(Cities in parentheses indicated location of tournament)

SINGLES

1907—John A. Miskey   Philadelphia
1908—John A. Miskey   Philadelphia
1909—William L. Freeland   Philadelphia
1910—John A. Miskey   Philadelphia
1911—Francis S. White   Philadelphia
1912—Constantine Hutchins   Boston
1913—Morton L. Newhall   Philadelphia
1914—Constantine Hutchins   Boston
1915—Stanley W. Pearson   Philadelphia
1916—Stanley W. Pearson   Philadelphia
1917—Stanley W. Pearson   Philadelphia
1920—Charles C. Peabody   Boston
1921—Stanley W. Pearson   Philadelphia
1922—Stanley W. Pearson   Philadelphia
1923—Stanley W. Pearson   Philadelphia
1924—Gerald Robarts   London, England
1925—W. Palmer Dixon   Harvard University
1926—W. Palmer Dixon   New York
1927—Myles Baker   Boston

1928—Herbert N. Rawlins, Jr.   New York
1929—J. Lawrence Pool   New York
1930—Herbert N. Rawlins, Jr.   New York
1931—J. Lawrence Pool   New York
1932—Beekman H. Pool   Harvard University
1933—Beekman H. Pool   New York (Detroit)
1934—Neil J. Sullivan, II
                   Philadelphia (Boston)
1935—Donald Strachan
                Philadelphia (Pittsburgh)
1936—Germain G. Glidden
           Harvard University (Hartford)
1937—Germain G. Glidden
                 New York (Cleveland)
1938—Germain G. Glidden
                 New York (Baltimore)
1939—Donald Strachan
                 Philadelphia (Chicago)
1940—A. Willing Patterson
                Philadelphia (New York)

1941—CHARLES M. P. BRINTON
      Princeton University (Philadelphia)
1942—CHARLES M. P. BRINTON
      Princeton University (Buffalo)
1946—CHARLES M. P. BRINTON
      Philadelphia (Hartford)
1947—CHARLES M. P. BRINTON
      Philadelphia (Detroit)
1948—STANLEY W. PEARSON, JR.
      Philadelphia (Boston)
1949—H. HUNTER LOTT, JR.
      Philadelphia (Philadelphia)
1950—EDWARD J. HAHN   Detroit (New York)
1951—EDWARD J. HAHN   Detroit (Chicago)
1952—Pfc. HARRY B. CONLON
      USAF, Buffalo (New Haven)
1953—ERNEST HOWARD
      Toronto, Canada (Buffalo)
1954—G. DIEHL MATEER, JR.
      Philadelphia (Pittsburgh)
1955—HENRI R. SALAUN   Hartford (Detroit)
1956—G. DIEHL MATEER, JR.
      Philadelphia (Hartford)
1957—HENRI R. SALAUN   Boston (New York)
1958—HENRI R. SALAUN   Boston (Annapolis)
1959—BENJAMIN H. HECKSCHER
      Philadelphia (Boston)
1960—G. DIEHL MATEER, JR.
      Philadelphia (Rochester)
1961—HENRI R. SALAUN   Boston (Philadelphia)
1962—SAMUEL P. HOWE, III
      Philadelphia (Buffalo)
1963—BENJAMIN H. HECKSCHER
      Boston (Detroit)
1964—RALPH E. HOWE   New York (Annapolis)
1965—STEPHEN T. VEHSLAGE
      New York (Hartford)
1966—VICTOR NIEDERHOFFER
      Chicago (New York)
1967—SAMUEL P. HOWE, III
      Philadelphia (Chicago)
1968—COLIN ADAIR   Montreal (Boston)
1969—ANIL NAYAR
      Harvard University (Rochester)
1970—ANIL NAYAR   Boston (Philadelphia)
1971—COLIN ADAIR   Montreal (Buffalo)
1972—VICTOR NIEDERHOFFER
      New York (Detroit)
1973—VICTOR NIEDERHOFFER
      New York (Princeton)

1974—VICTOR NIEDERHOFFER
      New York (Annapolis)
1975—VICTOR NIEDERHOFFER
      New York (New York)
1976—PETER BRIGGS   New York (Philadelphia)
1977—VICTOR HARDING   Toronto (Chicago)

VETERANS SINGLES
(40 years of age and over)

1935—STANLEY W. PEARSON	Philadelphia
1936—RALPH T. POWERS	Monteville
1937—J. A. ROBINSON	Chicago
1938—A. M. SONNABEND	Boston
1939—J. M. WALSH	Philadelphia
1940—ROY R. COFFIN	Philadelphia
1941—JOSEPH JANOTTA	Chicago
1942—J. FREDERICK ROGERS	Buffalo
1946—RICHARD V. WAKEMAN	Boston
1947—CYRUS H. POLLEY	Philadelphia
1948—GEORGE WARING	Boston
1949—GEORGE WARING	Boston
1950—GEORGE WARING	Boston
1951—GEORGE WARING	Boston
1952—HAROLD W. KAESE	Boston
1953—HAROLD W. KAESE	Boston
1954—GERMAIN G. GLIDDEN	N.Y.
1955—GERMAIN G. GLIDDEN	N.Y.
1956—GERMAIN G. GLIDDEN	N.Y.
1957—ROGER M. BAKEY	Boston
1958—EDWARD J. HAHN	Detroit
1959—EDWARD J. HAHN	Detroit
1960—CALVIN MacCRACKEN	Englewood
1961—CALVIN MacCRACKEN	Englewood
1962—CALVIN MacCRACKEN	Englewood
1963—CALVIN MacCRACKEN	Englewood
1964—E. VICTOR SEIXAS, JR.	Philadelphia
1965—E. VICTOR SEIXAS, JR.	Philadelphia
1966—E. VICTOR SEIXAS, JR.	Philadelphia
1967—HENRI R. SALAUN	Boston
1968—HENRI R. SALAUN	Boston
1969—HENRI R. SALAUN	Boston
1970—HENRI R. SALAUN	Boston
1971—HENRI R. SALAUN	Boston
1972—CHARLES W. UFFORD, JR.	New York
1973—HENRI R. SALAUN	Boston

1974—CHARLES W. UFFORD, JR.
      New York (Annapolis)
1975—GEORGE H. BOSTWICK, JR.
      Locust Valley (New York)

1976—Richard Radloff
Seattle (Philadelphia)
1977—Les Harding
Seattle (Chicago)

SENIOR SINGLES
(50 years of age and over)

1968—Robert Wade   Vancouver
1969—Edward J. Hahn   New York
1970—Calvin MacCracken   Englewood
1971—Calvin MacCracken   Englewood
1972—Calvin MacCracken   Englewood
1973—Floyd Svensson   San Francisco
1974—Floyd Svensson   San Francisco
1975—Robert H. Stuckert
Milwaukee (New York)
1976—Robert H. Stuckert
Milwaukee (Philadelphia)
1977—Henri R. Salaun   Boston (Chicago)

INTERCOLLEGIATE

1932—Beekman H. Pool   Harvard (Trinity)
1933—William G. Foulke   Princeton (Yale)
1934—E. Rotan Sargent   Harvard (Trinity)
1935—Germain G. Glidden   Harvard (Yale)
1936—Germain G. Glidden
Harvard (Trinity)
1937—Richard M. Dorson
Harvard (Merion C. C.)
1938—Leroy M. Lewis   Pennsylvania (Yale)
1939—Stanley W. Pearson, Jr.
Princeton (Harvard)
1940—Kim deS. Canavarro
Harvard (Amherst)
1941—Charles M. P. Brinton
Princeton (Williams)
1942—Charles M. P. Brinton
Princeton (Yale)
1943—John C. Holt, II   Yale (Yale)
1946—Glenn Shively   Yale (M.I.T.)
1947—Peter Landry   McGill (Dartmouth)
1948—G. Diehl Mateer, Jr.
Haverford (Yale)
1949—G. Diehl Mateer, Jr.
Haverford (Princeton)
1950—Harold E. Hands   Yale (Amherst)
1951—Charles H. W. Foster, Jr.
Harvard (Williams)

1952—Charles W. Ufford, Jr.
Harvard (Harvard)
1953—Charles W. Ufford, Jr.
Harvard (U.S.M.A.)
1954—Roger L. Campbell
Princeton (Dartmouth)
1955—Roger L. Campbell
Princeton (U.S.N.A.)
1956—Benjamin H. Heckscher
Harvard (Wesleyan)
1957—Benjamin H. Heckscher
Harvard (M.I.T.)
1958—J. Smith Chapman
Sir George Williams (Yale)
1959—Stephen T. Vehslage
Princeton (Princeton)
1960—Stephen T. Vehslage
Princeton (Amherst)
1961—Stephen T. Vehslage
Princeton (Williams)
1962—Ralph Howe   Yale (Harvard)
1963—Ralph Howe   Yale (U.S.M.A.)
1964—Victor Niederhoffer
Harvard (Dartmouth)
1965—Walter Oehrlein
Army (Pennsylvania)
1966—Howard Coonley
Pennsylvania (U.S.N.A.)
1967—Anil Nayar   Harvard (Wesleyan)
1968—Anil Nayar   Harvard (M.I.T.)
1969—Anil Nayar   Harvard (Yale)
1970—Lawrence Terrell
Harvard (Princeton)
1971—Palmer Page   Pennsylvania (Williams)
1972—Peter Briggs   Harvard (U.S.M.C.)
1973—Peter Briggs   Harvard (U.S.N.A.)
1974—Juan de Villafranca
Mexico City (Pennsylvania)
1975—Juan de Villafranca
Mexico City (Princeton)
1976—Philip Mohtadi   Calgary (Philadelphia)
1977—Michael Desaulniers
Montreal (U.S.N.A.)

JUNIOR

1956—Stephen T. Vehslage
Philadelphia (New York)
1957—Stephen T. Vehslage
Philadelphia (Pittsburgh)

1958—STEPHEN T. VEHSLAGE
                  Philadelphia (New York)
1959—JAMES ZUG   Philadelphia (Philadelphia)
1960—RALPH HOWE   Philadelphia (Pittsburgh)
1961—WILLIAM B. MORRIS
                  Philadelphia (Hill School)
1962—VICTOR B. NIEDERHOFFER
                  Harvard (Middlesex School)
1963—JOHN C. WEST   Yale (U.S.M.A.)
1964—LAWRENCE S. HEATH, III
             Deerfield Academy (St. Paul School)
1965—JOSE GONZALES   Harvard (Amherst)
1966—JOSE GONZALES Harvard (Phillips Acad.)
1967—LAWRENCE TERRELL
                  Harvard (Philadelphia)
1968—FAROOQ MIR
             Greenville, S.C. (Kent School)
1969—FAROOQ MIR
             Greenville, S.C. (St. Paul's)
1970—CRAIG BENSON   Toronto (Hill School)
1971—IAN SHAW   Toronto (Middlesex School)
1972—IAN SHAW   Toronto (Buffalo)
1973—IAN SHAW   Toronto (Exeter)
1974—GILBERT MATEER
            Philadelphia (Shady Side Acad.)
1975—MICHAEL DESAULNIERS
              Montreal (Univ. of Penn.)
1976—MICHAEL DESAULNIERS
              Montreal (Rochester)
1977—MARIO SANCHEZ
              Mexico City (U.S.N.A.)

BOYS SINGLES

1973—THOMAS PAGE   Philadelphia (Exeter)
1974—MARIO SANCHEZ
            Mexico City (Shady Side Acad.)
1975—MARK TALBOTT
             Baltimore (Univ. of Penn.)
1976—MARK TALBOTT   Atlanta (Rochester)
1977—ALAN GRANT   Toronto (Detroit)

OPEN

1954—HENRI R. SALAUN   Boston (New York)
1955—G. DIEHL MATEER, JR.
                  Philadelphia (New York)
1956—HASHIM KHAN
            Peshawar, Pakistan (New York)
1957—HASHIM KHAN
            Peshawar, Pakistan (Cedarhurst)

1958—ROSHAN KHAN
            Karachi, Pakistan (Detroit)
1959—G. DIEHL MATEER, JR.
                  Philadelphia (Pittsburgh)
1960—ROSHAN KHAN
            Karachi, Pakistan (Hartford)
1961—ROSHAN KHAN
            Karachi, Pakistan (Indianapolis)
1962—AZAM KHAN
            London, England (Atlantic City)
1963—HASHIM KHAN   Detroit (New York)
1964—MOHIBULLAH KHAN   Boston (Buffalo)
1965—MOHIBULLAH KHAN
              Boston (Wilmington)
1966—MOHIBULLAH KHAN   Boston (Detroit)
1967—RALPH E. HOWE New York (Montreal)
1968—MOHIBULLAH KHAN
              Boston (Indianapolis)
1969—SHARIF KHAN   Toronto (Cincinnati)
1970—SHARIF KHAN   Toronto (Chicago)
1971—SHARIF KHAN   Toronto (Toronto)
1972—SHARIF KHAN   Toronto (Louisville)
1973—SHARIF KHAN   Toronto (Pittsburgh)
1974—SHARIF KHAN   Ontario (Toronto)
1975—VICTOR NIEDERHOFFER
              New York (Mexico City)
1976—SHARIF KHAN   Toronto (New York)
1977—SHARIF KHAN   Toronto (Philadelphia)

PROFESSIONAL

1930—JACK SUMMERS   Boston (Boston)
1931—JACK SUMMERS   Boston (Boston)
1932—JACK SUMMERS   Boston (New York)
1933—JOHN SKILLMAN Princeton (Philadelphia)
1934—JACK SUMMERS   Boston (Philadelphia)
1935—JOHN SKILLMAN   Rye (Pittsburgh)
1936—JAMES J. TULLY
              Pittsburgh (Philadelphia)
1937—JOHN SKILLMAN
             New Haven (Pittsburgh)
1938—AL RAMSAY   Cleveland (Philadelphia)
1939—LESTER CUMMINGS
             New York (Cleveland)
1940—AL RAMSAY   Cleveland (Detroit)
1941—LESTER CUMMINGS
             New York (Pittsburgh)
1942—LESTER CUMMINGS
             New York (Cleveland)
1946—LESTER CUMMINGS
             Greenwich (New York)

1947—EDWARD T. REID   Hartford (Cleveland)
1948—AL RAMSAY   Cleveland (Buffalo)
1949—EDWARD T. REID   Hartford (Detroit)
1950—EDWARD T. REID   Hartford (Hartford)
1951—JAMES J. TULLY
    Pittsburgh (Philadelphia)
1952—EDWARD T. REID   Hartford (Cleveland)
1953—JOHN WARZYCKI Philadelphia (Chicago)
1954—JOHN WARZYCKI   Chicago (New York)
1955—HASHIM KHAN
    Peshawar, Pakistan (New York)
1956—ALBERT E. CHASSARD
    Bethlehem (New York)
1957—MAHMOUD KERIM
    Montreal (Bethlehem)
1958—MAHMOUD KERIM   Montreal (Buffalo)
1959—ALBERT E. CHASSARD
    Bethlehem (New York)
1960—RAYMOND WIDELSKI
    Hamilton, Ont. (Detroit)
1961—ALBERT E. CHASSARD
    Bethlehem (Louisville)
1962—ALBERT E. CHASSARD
    Bethlehem (Cleveland)
1963—HASHIM KHAN   Detroit (Boston)
1964—HASHIM KHAN   Detroit (Indianapolis)

1965—MOHIBULLAH KHAN
    Boston (Pittsburgh)
1966—MOHIBULLAH KHAN   Boston (Toronto)
1967—MOHIBULLAH KHAN
    Boston (Milwaukee)
1968—MOHIBULLAH KHAN
    Boston (Washington, D.C.)
1969—MOHIBULLAH KHAN   Boston (Hartford)
1970—SHARIF KHAN   Toronto (Canada)
1971—SHARIF KHAN Toronto (Atlantic City)
1972—SHARIF KHAN   Toronto (Toronto)
1973—SHARIF KHAN   Toronto (Boston)
1974—SHARIF KHAN   Toronto (Toronto)
1975—SHARIF KHAN Toronto (Wilmington)
1976—SHARIF KHAN   Toronto (New York)
1977—SHARIF KHAN   Toronto (Detroit)

PROFESSIONAL VETERANS

1960–62	LESTER CUMMINGS
1963	LOU BALLATO
1964–65	FRANK IANNICELLI
1966–73	HASHIM KHAN
1974	KEVIN PARKER
1975	HASHIM KHAN
1976	HASHIM KHAN
1977	KENNETH BINNS

TEAM

1908—Philadelphia
1909—Philadelphia
1910—Philadelphia
1911—Philadelphia
1912—Boston
1913—Philadelphia
1914—Philadelphia
1915—Philadelphia
1916—Philadelphia
1917—Philadelphia
1920—Boston
1921—Philadelphia
1922—Philadelphia
1923—Boston
1924—Boston
1925—Harvard University
1926—Harvard University
1927—Harvard University
1928—New York
1929—New York
1930—Boston
1931—Harvard University

1932—Harvard University
1933—Philadelphia
1934—Cambridge
1935—Philadelphia
1936—Philadelphia
1937—Boston
1938—Boston
1939—Boston
1940—Boston
1941—Boston
1942—Detroit
1947—Detroit
1948—Philadelphia
1949—Boston
1950—Boston
1951—Harvard Univ.
1952—Philadelphia
1953—Philadelphia
1954—Pacific Coast
1955—New York
1956—New York
1957—Pacific Coast

1958—Philadelphia
1959—Yale University
1960—Canada
1961—Pacific Coast
1962—Philadelphia
1963—Harvard Univ.
1964—Washington, D.C.
1965—New York
1966—New York
1967—Quebec
1968—New York
1969—Ontario
1970—Ontario
1971—Toronto
1972—New York
1973—New York
1974—Pacific Coast
1975—New York
1976—Mexico
1977—Mexico

DOUBLES

1933—Roy R. Coffin and Neil J. Sullivan, II
Philadelphia (Greenwich)

1934—Roy R. Coffin and Neil J. Sullivan, II
Philadelphia (Philadelphia)

1935—Roy R. Coffin and Neil J. Sullivan, II
Philadelphia (Greenwich)

1936—Roy R. Coffin and Neil J. Sullivan, II
Philadelphia (Philadelphia)

1937—Roy R. Coffin and Neil J. Sullivan, II
Philadelphia (Buffalo)

1938—H. Hunter Lott, Jr. and William E.
Slack   Philadelphia (Phila.)

1939—H. Hunter Lott, Jr. and William E.
Slack   Philadelphia (Buffalo)

1940—H. Hunter Lott, Jr. and William E.
Slack   Philadelphia (Balt.)

1941—H. Hunter Lott, Jr. and William E.
Slack   Phila. (Cedarhurst)

1942—H. Hunter Lott, Jr. and William E.
Slack   Philadelphia (Balt.)

1946—Charles M. P. Brinton and Donald
Strachan   Phila., N.Y. (Balt.)

1947—Stanley W. Pearson, Jr. and David
McMullin   Phila. (Cedarhurst)

1948—Charles M. P. Brinton and Stanley W.
Pearson, Jr.   Phila. (Balt.)

1949—H. Hunter Lott, Jr. and G. Diehl
Mateer, Jr.   Philadelphia (Buffalo)

1950—H. Hunter Lott, Jr. and G. Diehl
Mateer, Jr.   Phila. (St. Louis)

1951—G. Diehl Mateer, Jr. and Calvin
MacCracken
Philadelphia, New York (Pittsburgh)

1952—Germain G. Glidden and Richard
Remsen   New York (Greenwich)

1953—H. Hunter Lott, Jr. and G. Diehl
Mateer, Jr.   Phila. (Baltimore)

1954—G. Diehl Mateer, Jr. and Richard C.
Souires   Phila., N.Y. (Boston)

1955—Joseph T. Hahn and Edward J. Hahn
Detroit (Philadelphia)

1956—Carlton M. Badger and James M.
Ethridge, III   Greenwich, (N.Y.)

1957—Carlton M. Badger and James M.
Ethridge, III   Greenwich (Minn.)

1958—G. Diehl Mateer, Jr. and John F.
Hentz   Philadelphia (Balt.)

1959—G. Diehl Mateer, Jr. and John F.
Hentz   Philadelphia (Buffalo)

1960—Howard A. Davis and James H.
Whitmoyer   Philadelphia (St. Louis)

1961—G. Diehl Mateer, Jr. and John F.
Hentz.   Phila. (Cedarhurst)

1962—G. Diehl Mateer, Jr. and John F.
Hentz   Philadelphia (Chicago)

1963—S. P. Howe, III and Wm. Danforth
Phila., Pittsburgh (Wilmington)

1964—S. P. Howe, III and Wm. Danforth
Phila., Pittsburgh (Minneapolis)

1965—G. Diehl Mateer, Jr. and Ralph E.
Howe   Phila., N.Y. (Balt.)

1966—G. Diehl Mateer, Jr. and Ralph E.
Howe   Phila., N.Y. (Phila.)

1967—S. P. Howe, III and Wm. Danforth
Phila., Pittsburgh (Buffalo)

1968—Victor Niederhoffer and Victor
Elmaleh   New York (St. Louis)

1969—S. P. Howe, III and Ralph E. Howe
Phila., N.Y. (Pittsburgh)

1970—S. P. Howe, III and Ralph E. Howe
Phila., N.Y. (New York)

1971—S. P. Howe, III and Ralph E. Howe
Phila., N.Y. (Wilmington)

1972—Larry Terrell and James Zug
Phila. (Minneapolis)

1973—James Zug and Victor Niederhoffer
Phila., N.Y. (Baltimore)

1974—Victor Niederhoffer and Colin Adair
N.Y., Montreal (Phila.)

1975—Michael J. Pierce and Maurice
Heckscher   Philadelphia (Buffalo)

1976—Peter Briggs and Ralph E. Howe
New York (Denver)

1977—Victor Harding and Peter Hall
Toronto; Hamilton, Ont. (St. Louis)

VETERANS DOUBLES
(40 years of age and over)

1971—Donald Leggat and Charles Wright
Toronto (Wilmington)

1972—G. Diehl Mateer, Jr. and William
Tully   Phila., New York (New York)

1973—James Bentley and William Bewley
Toronto (Rochester)

1974—Donald Leggat and Charles Wright
Toronto (Phila.)

1975—Donald Leggat and Charles Wright
Toronto (Buffalo)

1976—Donald Leggat and Charles Wright
Toronto (Denver)
1977—Thomas B. Jones and John Swann
New York, Toronto (St. Louis)

SENIOR DOUBLES
(50 years of age and over)

1962—Roger M. Bakey and Harold W. Kaese
Boston (Boston)
1963—William E. Lamble and George L.
Doetsch   Baltimore (Wilmington)
1964—Paul Ouimet and J. Milton Street
Quebec, Peterborough (N.Y.)
1965—William T. Ketcham, Jr. and James M.
Ethridge, III
New York, Greenwich (Baltimore)
1966—William T. Ketcham, Jr. and James M.
Ethridge, III
New York, Greenwich (Philadelphia)

1967—Howard A. Davis and Edward J. Hahn
Phila., Detroit (Buffalo)
1968—William T. Ketcham, Jr. and James M.
Ethridge, III   New York (St. Louis)
1969—William T. Ketcham, Jr. and James M.
Ethridge, III   New York (Pittsburgh)
1970—Newton Meade and Hastings Griffin
Philadelphia (N.Y.)
1971—William T. Ketcham, Jr. and Howard
A. Davis   New York (Wilmington)
1972—Jack Bowling and Jinx Johnson
Buffalo (Minneapolis)
1973—William Ketcham and Victor
Elmaleh   New York (Balitmore)
1974—William T. Ketcham and Newton
Meade   New York, Phila. (Phila.)
1975—Eugene O'Conor and Thomas
Schweizer   Baltimore (Buffalo)
1976—Gordon Guyatt and Eric Wiffen
Toronto (Denver)
1977—Gordon Guyatt and Eric Wiffen
Toronto (St. Louis)

Sharif Khan

Glossary

ACE A shot with which the receiver cannot even make contact with his racquet; used especially with reference to service.

ALLEY The area along the sidewalls. *See* RAIL.

AMATEUR A person who receives no money for playing, teaching, tournaments, endorsements, etc., as opposed to a PRO (*q.v.*).

ANGLE Any shot which hits a sidewall before hitting the front wall.

APPEAL A request by a player for the referee during match play to have the judges change his call (of "let," "let point," "not up," or a request for a time-out, etc.). If both judges concur with the player, the call is changed. If either judge sides with the referee, the original call is sustained.

AROUND *See* COMING AROUND.

BACKING ON THE BALL Backing up from the sidewall, especially on service, to take a ball that is coming out far from the side and/or back-wall.

BACKSPIN *See* SPIN.

BACKWALL SHOT Any shot that hits the backwall first.

BACKWALL BOAST A shot that hits the backwall and a sidewall (in either order) before reaching the front wall.

BOAST Any shot that hits three walls before bouncing.

BOAST FOR NICK A boast that lands in the NICK and DIES (*q.v.*).

COME OUT Used in reference to a ball that is mishit and instead of dying, dropping, or rolling from the nick, comes out again toward the center court for an easy retrieve.

COMING AROUND (also called TURNING ON THE BALL, *q.v.*) Making a 180-degree turn from one's forehand to backhand (or vice versa) to take a ball that is rebounding out from a sidewall or a backwall. The player alerts his opponent of his intent by saying, "around" or "coming around."

CORNER Any shot that hits a sidewall close to the front wall and then hits the front wall. *See* REVERSE CORNER.

CROSS COURT A front-wall shot that makes a "V" shape and lands in the opposite side of the court from which it was played, in mid-court or deeper.

CUT *See* SPIN.

DIE When a ball fails to bounce or come out because it has been hit with great touch, underspin, or has hit the nick.

DOUBLE BOAST A shot that hits the two sidewalls before hitting the front wall.

DOUBLE FAULT Two missed service attempts, after which the server loses the serve and point.

DOUBLES Squash played on a 45-foot-by-25-foot court by two teams of two players, played with a livelier ball specifically for doubles.

DOWN A call indicating that the ball hit the front wall below the TELLTALE (*q.v.*).

DOWN THE LINE Played along the alley or RAIL (*q.v.*).

DRIVE A front-wall shot hit for power; a RAIL or CROSS COURT (*q.v.*).

DROP A shot hit with great touch so that it DIES (*q.v.*) close to the front wall; literally, any shot that drops after contacting the front wall.

FAULT A missed or unacceptable serve.

FOOT FAULT A serve that is unacceptable because the server's foot was not totally inside the service box up to the point at which contact was made with the ball.

GALLERY The spectator or viewing area, and those in that area.

GAME In squash, a game goes to the first player who reaches 15 points unless the score reaches 13-all or 14-all, in which case the rules described under SET (*q.v.*) are applied, or unless the loser of the tying point declares "No SET" (*q.v.*).

GERMANTOWN BOAST *See* PHILADELPHIA BOAST.

GET A difficult but successful return.

HALF VOLLEY A shot played immediately after the ball bounces, just inches above floor level.

JUDGE The two aides to the referee of a match who handle APPEAL (*q.v.*) calls.

LENGTH Used to describe a ball hit down the line or cross court that makes its second bounce and dies near the bottom of the backwall.

LET A situation in which a point is replayed. *See* rules, page 183.

LET POINT A point awarded to a player whose opponent interferes with his potentially scoring return. *See* rules, page 183.

LOB A shot hit upward and softly on the front wall that arcs high off the front wall and comes down deep in the backcourt.

MASKED ANGLE An ANGLE (*q.v.*) shot made in the forecourt in which the body covers the shot.

MATCH A unit of tournament, or competitive play, in which three out of five games is needed to win.

NICK A shot that hits the juncture of the floor and wall, and dies. Also, the juncture itself.

NO SET *See* SET.

NOT UP A call made by a player or referee indicating that the ball was hit on (or after) the second bounce.

PHILADELPHIA BOAST A sort of boast in reverse, usually played from the front of the court, in which the ball hits high on the front wall first, near the corner, hits the near sidewall, and then sails diagonally cross court near the back of the opposite sidewall, and hopefully dies soon thereafter.

PRO A person who plays, teaches, competes, etc., for money.

PUTAWAY A winning shot. An irretrievable shot.

QUARTER CIRCLE *See* SERVICE BOX.

RAIL A shot hit close to and parallel to the sidewalls—that is, down the line or alley; a power drive hit for LENGTH (*q.v.*).

RALLY A sequence of several shots and returns during the course of a warm-up or encompassing the playing of a point.

REFEREE The person who announces, scores, calls, and arbitrates calls and appeals during match play.

REVERSE ANGLE *See* REVERSE CORNER.

REVERSE CORNER (also called reverse angle) A CORNER (*q.v.*) shot to the opposite sidewall from where the hitter is standing.

ROLL CORNER A slow, exaggerated CORNER (*q.v.*) shot that hits the sidewall well back toward the center of the court.

SERVICE BOX The quarter circular area on either side of the court from which one serves. One foot must remain within the box during service.

SERVICE LINE The line on the front wall above which the serve must hit, and the line on the floor behind which it must (if allowed to fall) make its first bounce.

SET To declare the number of points that will be played in the following situations:

During a given game, should the score reach 13-all, the loser of the tying point may elect to call:

· No set—in which case the game goes to the usual 15 points to win.

· Set 3—in which case the game goes to 16 points.

· Set 5—in which case the game goes to 18 points.

Should the score reach 14-all (without having reached 13-all), the loser of the tying point may elect to call:

· No set—15 points.

· Set 3—17 points.

SIDESPIN See SPIN.

SLICE See SPIN.

SLOW ANGLE An ANGLE (q.v.) shot that strikes the sidewall in mid- to backcourt.

SPIN The rotation of the ball in flight, which is imparted by the point on the ball contacted by the racquet, the angle of the racquet face at the time of contact, and the direction of the racquet during the swing.

Underspin (or backspin, or cut), which causes the ball to rotate backward for the direction in which it is traveling, is the most common type of spin in squash. It is basically imparted by an open-face racquet contacting the ball slightly on the underside, and the result is that the ball stays low and dies after contacting the front wall.

Sidespin or slice, which gives the ball a sideways rotation during its forward flight, is used mostly in TOUCH (q.v.) shots. It is basically imparted by contacting the ball slightly to either side and drawing the racquet across the ball in the opposite direction from the point of contact with an open-faced racquet. The result is that the ball will bounce slightly sidewise opposite from the predictable direction.

Topspin is used very little in squash, save in the hard serve. It is imparted by coming over the ball with a closed racquet face.

T The T-shaped configuration formed by the juncture of the floor service line and the center line that runs parallel to the sidewall at the rear of the court. Control of the area around the juncture of these lines is the key to advantageous court position.

TELLTALE (also called tin) The strip of metal that runs across the front wall at a height of seventeen inches that resounds loudly when hit by the ball, and below which the ball is not good.

THREE-WALL NICK See BOAST FOR NICK.

THREE-WALL SHOT See BOAST.

TIN See TELLTALE.

TOPSPIN See SPIN.

TOUCH Finesse or deftness in controlling the speed and placement of the ball, used especially in reference to nonpower shots.

TURNING See COMING AROUND.

TURNING ON THE BALL See COMING AROUND.

UNDERSPIN See SPIN.

VOLLEY A shot in which the ball is hit before it bounces.

WINNER See PUTAWAY.

Victor Niederhoffer and Stuart Goldstein